INTERNATIONAL EQUILIBRIUM

INTERNATIONAL EQUILIBRIUM

A Theoretical Essay
on the Politics and Organization
of Security

GEORGE LISKA

HARVARD UNIVERSITY PRESS
Cambridge, 1957

To Arnošt Heidrich

A Czech in the tradition of the *grands commis*
into whose unchronicled stewardship is committed
the patrimony of nations, in time of trials yet
more fully than in the briefer spells of glory.

Acknowledgments

In writing the first draft of this essay, I enjoyed the advice and encouragement of Professors Inis L. Claude, Jr., who shared generously his time and thought, Rupert Emerson, Carl J. Friedrich, and Dean McGeorge Bundy, all of Harvard University. In expanding and revising the original manuscript for publication, I was free from other responsibilities thanks to a Fellowship in Political Theory and Legal Philosophy of the Social Science Research Council. And finally, in seeing the manuscript transformed into a book, I could do little else but admire the sensitive editorship of Mrs. Carl A. Pitha of the Harvard University Press. I am grateful to them all, and attribute to none but myself the shortcomings of the work.

I wish also to record here a manifold debt for his unfailing friendship and guidance to my former chief, Ambassador Arnošt Heidrich, one-time Secretary General of the Czechoslovak Ministry for Foreign Affairs, to whom this book is dedicated.

A substantial part of Chapter 6 appeared in a somewhat different form under the title "The Pattern of Integration: Western Europe and the Atlantic Community," in Vol. VI of *Public Policy: A Yearbook of the Graduate School of Public Administration, Harvard University* (1955), edited by Carl J. Friedrich and John Kenneth Galbraith. The book also draws on ideas first put forth in the *Harvard Studies in International Affairs*, February 1954.

G. L.

September 1, 1956

CONTENTS

CONTENTS

INTERNATIONAL EQUILIBRIUM

TOWARD AN EQUILIBRIUM THEORY OF INTER-NATIONAL RELATIONS AND INSTITUTIONS

In a world in turmoil, the study of international relations is passing through a period of ferment. The somewhat fruitless contest for the crown of genuine realism between the proponents of power and the defenders of morality in international politics has spent its fury, leaving a residuum of substantial agreement underneath the lingering verbal disagreements. While it lasted, the "great debate" served its purpose. A constitutional society like the United States needs in times of stress to be periodically confronted with the harsher verities of politics. But the salutary correction of illusions must not entail the surrender of the more generous aspirations embedded in the national ethos. The will to power must not overwhelm the desire for coöperation; the latter is frequently a more effective means to legitimate ends. There are many ways — too many for the comfort of the analyst using the concept — of achieving a country's national interests; and no fewer paths for approaching the sphinx that guards the clue to a theory of international relations.

I would distinguish between a conception and a theory of international relations; the one is characterized by more or less sensitive judgment, the other by more or less rigorous analysis.

POWER AND NORM IN INTERNATIONAL RELATIONS

Any conception of international relations implies a philosophic judgment about the structure of reality and the role of power and norms in politics; it suggests the behavior most likely to be effective, just, or both, in the postulated situation. The perennial cleavage between the realists and the idealists, the Sophists and the Socratics, in Western political tradition bears on this aspect of our effort to understand and control the world around us. An observer's thought and feeling are propelled in the one or the other direction by his response to the actually predominant modes of thought and action, depending largely on the extent to which these modes are (or appear to be) fit to deal with contemporary reality. As compared with the fundamental option, the particular way of elaborating it is secondary and depends on the thinker's ability to rephrase traditional arguments and invent new ones in support of his thesis.

A mature conception should express the composite character of international reality in which diverse values and interests interact and must be reconciled, where morally defensible, in an over-all equilibrium. International relations are not made up exclusively of conflict, and coöperative behavior is not merely a matter of accidentally coinciding self-interests and interplay of power. Neither do international relations take place exclusively in terms of rights and the relative certainties of a developed social order under law. In a mixed order there is room for the dynamics of power and the normative restraints, including law; for areas of conflict, indifference, and coöperation among states; for areas of coercion and induced or spontaneous consent; for areas of anarchy and incipient constitutionalism. The struggle for power occurs in a climate of variably effective normative rules and restraints; the pursuit of national interests is frequently modified by larger purposes attainable in great part only by coöperative international action.

Like all politics concerned with the adjustment of conflicts and the legitimization of resulting arrangements, international politics is reducible to the interplay of power and norm; this interplay corresponds to the dual nature of man — both good and evil, social and egotistic — and to the ideal and material character of reality. To affirm explicitly both aspects of the human condition is to avoid overly pessimistic conclusions from a one-sided statement of the same idea, dwelling on the corruption of human nature and action by the sins of pride, selfishness, and lust for power, and distinguishing only the degree to which the corruption occurs in different realms of action.[1] This way of stating the problem harks back historically not so much to Machiavelli and Hobbes as to St. Augustine and Calvin, and disregards both Plato and the Aristotelian corrections in St. Thomas Aquinas. Analytically, it is the product of too narrow a conception of politics and too broad a conception of power. Politics is identified with a single-minded contest over practically all-inclusive power, and the coöperative and welfare features of politics and the state tend to be either ignored or explained away as a function of the power struggle. Yet it is at least as plausible to hold that competition for power and control is not only muted in the coöperative aspects of politics, but is very often subsidiary to the positive function. The latter is, of course, less prominent in international than in national politics, but is not entirely absent from it either. And, even if the stern view of politics were admitted as a striking theoretical abstraction from too complex an actual process, such an abstraction could not by itself be accepted as a valid basis for moral judgments on the totality of organized life within and among nations.

If power is pervasive, it is not all-inclusive. With that reservation one can readily agree with the prevailing interpretation of power.[2] Power can be reduced to mostly quantitative factors, but ultimately it is a psychological relationship of control based on some superior advantage on the part of the controlling subject: it ranges from physical force to the most intangible and indirect means of control. Power has different bases, forms of expression and sanctions, such as military, political, economic, and institutional. It is operative not only in coercion, but in variously induced consent and coöperation as well. The notion that power is subject to certain inherent tendencies of its own is an old one. It runs from Thucydides through Machiavelli, Hobbes, and Spinoza into our own day. Accordingly, power must either grow or decay, it will fill a vacuum, it tends to dominate and destroy weaker subjects in an intrinsically limitless expansion, and it is stopped only by an equal or superior power released in response to the original expansion — the result being conflict or deadlock in an equipoise.

There is some truth in the deterministic prejudice of most philosophers and practitioners of power; when combined with a strong sense of inescapable conflict of rights, it highlights the tragic element in international politics. But power is not the sole factor in a social situation, and its "laws" do not, therefore, have the predictability of a law of nature. They are subject to modification by sheer contingency and by the values, ideologies, and purposes of actors within a social and historical situation. As a result, the tendency to follow the "laws" of power in a particular historical and geographical setting can give rise to only so many presumptions with respect to actual behavior in interstate relations. The tendencies and the presumptions must always be taken into account, but they must not be mistaken for invariable certainties.

The systematic modifier of the presumptions implicit in the dynamics of power is the countervailing normative realm. It does so by means of the "oughts," the community-oriented rules and restraints, derived from sources other than the instrumental rationality of immediate power considerations. It affects the motives, objectives, and methods of political action, and is practically effective to the extent that the component values have been assimilated by acting individuals and especially by the policy-making élites. This applies to values both universal in character and culturally conditioned, whether or not formalized in law and organization. The fact that interdependence among nations is an important aspect of the social and material environment gives empirical support to coöperative values and tendencies. At best, these may act as a restraint on the drive for more power and may press for a larger conception of the national interest, taking into account the long-range consequences of a policy and the interests of other nations. Yet particular value systems and ideologies can have an aggravating as well as a restraining effect on the power tendencies on which they impinge; and a coöperative response is not the only possible reaction to the fact of interdependence. Analytical dualism, distinguishing power and norm, must therefore be qualified in favor of an actually operative continuum. Countervailing power can supplement and reinforce a moral or legal norm as a restraint on expansionist power, and an abstract norm can be deformed in a particular political system so as to legitimize and activate the drive for ever more power.

The role, effect, and relative "weight" of the components of power-normative international politics are not constants in historical time or place. Liberal societies are better able and more eagerly inclined — not always wisely — to transcend the coercive implications of the "laws" of power in favor of the more consensual type of relations, internationally as well as domestically. The values and ideologies of a totalitarian system stimulate rather than contain the power dynamics. Both systems err if they emphasize too much one component to the detriment of the other. For then either the "laws" of power or the laws of the normative realm assert themselves to redress the balance. In that sense there is not only a power-normative continuum, but also a corresponding equilibrium. If it is disturbed, the equilibrating mechanism must intervene *within* international reality to redress the imbalanced view *of* international reality. Too frequently the price has been war. As regards changes in time, their extent is undoubtedly limited by the fact that the hard core of international reality changes but slowly, if at all. This hard core consists of the typical responses of human nature to the ethically and ideologically neutral "laws" of power on which, to repeat, impinge changes in the moral, emotional, and ideological climate and, last but not least, material conditions within which organized social groups seek to realize their objectives. In a hierarchically organized international society, the methods, policies, and purposes of the Great Powers have a dominant influence; but the changing manner in which people at large judge the different possible ways of conducting international relations is an important, if malleable, factor.

As a result of changes in international reality, the conditions of a genuinely realistic response change too. The calculating rationality of Machiavelli, designed to fit the princely politics of Renaissance Italy, may be less pertinent in the age of mass psychological involvement than the fear- and security-centered analysis of Hobbes. And a genuine realism of today may have to modify both Machiavelli and Hobbes by the so-called utopian idealism of Wilson. This assumes that within narrow limits the direction of international relations since Machiavelli wrote has been, on balance and despite retrogressions, away from the unmitigated politics of power. Just conceivably, *Realpolitik* in the cruder sense of the term has ceased to be realistic politics. The need for popular participation in a total war impedes the flexibility required for expedient politics in time of peace; and the application of a more exacting moral, as distinguished from "moralistic," standard to behavior among states may have something to do with the difficulty of dealing with growing interdependence by conquest, unless such conquest be universal.

Traditionally, attempts at such conquest were defeated by the operation of the balance of power. More recently, large-scale war as the indispensable ultimate expedient of power politics has appeared in a new perspective. What the universal destructiveness of the nuclear weapons will come to mean for international politics is yet obscure. But it does suggest already a compensating transfer of importance from the military and crudely territorial plane to the ideological, socio-economic, and institutional realms as areas of competition and coöperation. The significance of the ideological factor, too, may have to be reëvaluated. Current fatigue with heroic living and dying for exclusive, dogmatic systems of belief almost automatically orients politics toward the more pragmatic pursuit of the maximum attainable satisfaction of socio-economic needs. The contemporary technological revolution and the failure of both the Right and the Left to consummate a genuine ideological and social revolution have produced a widespread demand for stabilization and development by eclectic methods rather than for conflict and the extermination of either side. At the same time, however, relations among nations continue to be subject to ruthless methods on a massive scale, and the undiminished force of totalitarianism and militant nationalism lessens the likelihood of significant gains from the temporary ideological détente.

Faced with so many intangibles, the realist-idealist debate has been inconclusive and theoretically sterile. It is a classic instance of the noncumulative approach to the study of politics. Apart from its subjectivism, the concepts around which it revolves are not very useful. For instance, the contemporary discussion has been cast in the categories of "power," "morality," and "national interest." The concept of power in general — and "national power" in particular — as currently propounded is much too inclusive to be a sufficiently sharp analytical tool for the dissection of international reality. Its adoption will not, therefore, serve too well the purposes of either diagnosis or therapy in matters of policy. The notion of morality is slightly too conventional to make much sense in a theoretical discussion. We have always been deeply concerned with questions of critical moral philosophy and, more recently, with values and their cultural relativity. For some time we have been turning in circles among the logical and psychological ambiguities of fact-value and value-fact problematics. The real question seems to be not so much whether and how much of morality, but rather what kind of morality we hold to be operative in the behavior of statesmen and nations. Almost any norm of conduct can now be described as a value with some moral implications, and almost no one will couch his analysis of the moral factor in terms of a universal moral law of nature. Similarly, to emphasize purpose as a counter to power does not help much if we do not say much more about what distinguishes it from mere objective, the presence of which in the formulation of policy nobody in his senses does or could deny. And, to wrap this all up in the concept of ideology, by now effectively obscured by conflicting elucidations, does not advance us much beyond a modified verbal statement, either. The questions of power and morality are of the first importance, and every student must make up his mind about them — if only because no one can avoid the use of these or equivalent terms in thinking, speaking, or writing about international relations. Yet they are not, at least at the present stage of our insight, very helpful in the development of a substantive theory.

Finally, the concept of the national interest is fraught with that emptiness and formality which have annoyed the critics of the Kantian categorical imperative. To be sure, all theoretical concepts are in some degree formal, but the question is still one of degree. Even the Kantian imperative to test one's actions (and policies?) by their fitness to be generalized into a universal law has a less ambiguous empirical reference in the likely consequences of alternative courses of action, than the criterion of the national interest. It is a truism that almost any policy can be conceived and justified as promoting short-range or long-range national interests, depending on one's appraisal of international reality. All will agree that interest is a powerful motive of all human, not the least political, action. But this is a self-evident premise rather than a conceptual basis for fruitful theorizing.

Thinking in the categories of amoral power and moral national interest may affect one's emotional, even more than one's intellectual orientation to a problem and may influence one's decisions on policy. But this is not what concerns us here, at least not primarily.

The three concepts — power, morality, and the national interest — can be criticized for their intimate association with the question of the actual and right motivation of political behavior in international relations. Most of us are interested in a causal interpretation of social phenomena, or at least in the causal implications of our analysis, although we may prefer to play it safe and speak of correlations and interactions. But while the isolation of causes is almost insuperably difficult, the attempt to identify and range dogmatically in a hierarchy of importance the motives of political behavior is doomed to failure. The different psychological schools may have their different pat answers to the question of human motivation, of which they become less certain as they grow more sophisticated. The student of politics faces the additional problem of accounting for the perhaps fundamental modification of private behavior by the contingencies and responsibilities of action in a public, or political, sphere. The distinction between the private and the public sphere cannot be safely discarded, and continues to be as important as that between rational and irrational behavior for the purposes of political psychology and ethics alike. Yet, again, the state of our present and likely future knowledge requires the greatest caution in assigning these problems a place at the center rather than at the periphery of our theoretical scheme.

All this suggests that a useful approach to a theory of international relations and institutions will have to be largely descriptive and rely primarily on observable phenomena. This does not preclude concern with causal implications and, most definitely, a normative bias. An empirical theory must obviously include the normative factors actually operative in reality. Less obviously, and perhaps not in strict logic, it may enhance its social usefulness by making explicit its own normative implications. Such a theory would not have to rely solely on descriptive generalizations from observed facts and the progressive systematization of clarified concepts and limited generalizations into an ever more inclusive body of theory. My own belief is that it cannot. The number of the states-actors is too small for that, and our aptitude to deal with infinitely complex social phenomena on the basis of unstructured observation too inadequate. It is, therefore, sooner or later helpful to take temporary leave of the facts in order to return to them reinforced with a theoretical construct or model. This is really the old question of the respective role of observation and hypothesis, of induction and deduction, in a somewhat more radical form. The logical implications of a theoretical construct can throw additional light on the reality with which it deals, and help interpret the results of individual or state activity within the total situation.

Ideally, a theory would unify the results of political attitudes and the total environment of international relations within a single concept, elastic enough to accommodate historical changes in social reality. Any concept capable of ordering diversified empirical content into formal unity and combining such unity with elasticity is almost certain to be very general and abstract. The cost will appear in a different light to the confirmed theoretician, the factualist, and the practitioner concerned with international relations. Their peculiar prejudices can be reconciled in two principal ways. The usual compromise today is for the theory to stay close to the facts and be satisfied with generalizations on a low level. Or, one can aim at a more rigorously systematic statement by way of a construct which would facilitate both the imaginative interpretation of facts and the exercise of the indispensable gift of political wisdom. Such a theory does not have to share the fatal vice of rationalistic schemes which attempt to codify reality in terms of automatically operative laws and to minimize to the vanishing point the role of the creative statesman. The science and the art of politics have their legitimate and complementary parts, and a general theory may assist but can never supersede the intuitions of the political artist.

THE OUTLINES OF A THEORY

It is no startling disclosure for the initiate to say that many of the preceding observations were directed to the thesis most strikingly developed by Hans J. Morgenthau and to the discussion about the nature of international politics which ensued in response to the realist challenge.[3] I shall suggest an alternative approach to a theory of international relations and institutions, mentioning first a few relatively recent theoretical efforts in the field of political and social science.

In his *Study of the Principles of Politics*, George Catlin places at the center of his analysis the basic element of individual will, rather than interest, and the act of control. He conceives the political process as a more or less stabilized interaction of individual and collective wills in different control relationships within a material and social environment. Catlin professes theoretical indifference to ends; yet the end of political action implicit in his analysis is individual freedom in an integrated society balancing liberty with authority. The many writings of Harold D. Lasswell, in turn, are concerned with the value and policy-oriented approach. Lasswell is interested chiefly in revolutionary changes in the shape and composition of value, symbol, and élite patterns in national and international society. Power is merely the means toward the integration of central values such as safety, well-being, and respect. Individual personality — organized in groups within a cultural and technological environment — is central, while the theoretical ideal is a model, or speculative construct, which would isolate social trends by means of a developmental and equilibrium analysis. In the elaborate structural-functional scheme of Talcott Parsons, finally, the more "static" aspect bears on the structure of legitimately expected action of individual personalities as actors in an interacting social system and culture. The more "dynamic" aspect concerns the allocation and integration of social roles and cultural values by means of suitable institutional mechanisms. All these factors are functional in the degree to which they promote the maintenance of an integrated system of action as a going concern within the given human and nonhuman environment. A major part in the integrative function falls to organized authority, which depends for compliance on the shared values and interlocking expectations of the members of a society rather than on coercive sanctions.

Merely to touch upon a related effort, David Easton has recently suggested "authoritative allocation of values as it is influenced by the distribution and use of power" to be the most fruitful organizing formula for a systematic theory of politics. And finally, Quincy Wright has attacked the problem with special reference to international relations by way of a capability and value field theory, which would make use of the measurement of social communications.[4]

Though different in many respects, Catlin, Lasswell, and Parsons converge in their general orientation and use of certain organizing categories. They all center their analyses in the human personality, or will, and in the action and interaction of individuals and groups within a social and material environment. The interaction constitutes a process which is somehow related to structure. These writers are all concerned with the distribution and integration of chosen values by means of an authoritative institutional mechanism, seeing coercive control through power as a more or less latent and sublimated technique. With varied emphasis they try to encompass the conditions of both social stability and change. They are, lastly, more concerned with a fundamental analysis than with an inquiry into the means of implementating the values postulated or implied in the analysis.

It is not at all simple and obvious how to apply to international relations the findings of these theoretical efforts. Notably concepts developed to analyze a relatively integrated society will not automatically fit a state system that is far from constituting an integrated system of action and a community; there is moreover the increasing relevance of the ideas of Thomas Hobbes, as we pass from the dynamics of primary social groups to the dynamics of armed states. Yet a series of attempts to formulate a substantive theory will show what can and what cannot be done more conclusively than an endless debate over methodology with its diminishing returns.

One possibility is a systematic equilibrium theory. The concept of equilibrium is, of course, widely used in a number of theoretical disciplines, its application in economic theory being especially suggestive. Joseph Schumpeter saw in equilibrium a tool which, ideally, might assemble into one model the causes, mechanisms, and effects of economic phenomena, provided one can postulate equilibrium as both an existing tendency and a theoretical norm against which to assess actual dynamics. Economic theory has generated or taken over from mechanics a whole typology of the equilibrium family in order to include in the concept developments that do not conform to the ideal of a self-maintaining system. It distinguishes between general and partial; unique and multiple; stable, neutral and unstable; long- and short-term; perfect and imperfect equilibrium; between equilibrium at a low and at a high level of employment, and the like. This variety is the product of theoretical difficulty and calls for caution in defining the kind of equilibrium one is prepared to defend as operative in the investigated realm.

Fairly extreme is the maximalist idea of a "static" equilibrium as a self-maintaining system of automatic compensatory reactions to disturbances, restoring the original state. If such an unfailing equilibrium operates anywhere, it is certainly not in the social realm. More realistic and at the same time "dynamic" is the view of the equilibrium mechanism as a state of relative temporary stability, uniquely or recurrently upset by factors precipitating change and replaced eventually by a new temporary equilibrium. When applied to intelligent and purposive actors, such an idea of equilibrium may be supplemented by that of equilibration or balancing as a deliberate policy. Together with the qualifications implied in the typology of equilibrium, this lessens the austere simplicity of the maximalist equilibrium concept, but saves the general idea for use in the social sciences.[5]

George Catlin — perhaps more explicitly than any other systematic theorist of society and politics — regards the equilibrium and equilibration of wills as the fundamental condition of social order and integration. In sympathy with Spencer's law of equilibration, he assumes the tendency of progressively integrated society to realize an equilibrium of wills in variously stabilized control relationships. Harold Lasswell, apart from advocating cross-reference between developmental and equilibrium analysis as the most promising method in political analysis, uses amply the idea of the balancing process with regard to problems of power and security. Talcott Parsons, too, draws on the idea of equilibrium as a state or an ordered process of change in an interdependent social system, maintained by a variety of mechanisms of social control. It seems that all three theorists would agree to treat the equilibrium of a political society in terms of the interaction of human actors in an environment, stabilized by the existence of some kind of authoritative social control with a moral, legal, and sentimental basis. None of them, to my knowledge, defines his idea of equilibrium as a norm and as actual dynamics with sufficient rigor. And the anthropologists have not fared any better in conceiving of equilibrium in terms of countervailing tensions between groups in a pluralistic society, or of compensatory rates and frequencies of interaction between individuals and groups in response to situations of stress.[6] Although such shortcomings are largely due to the nature of the subject-matter itself, they diminish the value of the imaginative equilibrium analyses by students of literate and preliterate societies for a theory aspiring to some specificity of statement.

There is, finally, the use of the equilibrium concept in the study of public administration by Chester I. Barnard and his followers, and — a path-breaking precedent for my own efforts — Carl J. Friedrich's early discussion of the balance of power within the framework of the League of Nations.[7] My chief inspiration came, however, from the idea of the economic firm in equilibrium; it helped mightily in systematizing an until then disjointed analysis.

Drawing selectively on the surveyed ideas, I shall now present the barest outline of an equilibrium theory of international organization of security and international relations in general, merely suggesting what will be refined and elaborated upon in the course of the discussion. I shall be using the concept of equilibrium in both of the accepted ways — first, as a theoretical norm or point of reference; second, as denoting an actual tendency toward changing states of temporary equilibrium in political institutions. In qualifying the tendency, I shall rely mainly on the ideas of progressive, stable, and unstable equilibrium. My central concept is that of *institutional equilibrium*, applied primarily to international organization with respect to its structure, the commitment of its members, and its functional and geographic scope.

A composite organization is in structural equilibrium if there is an over-all correspondence between the margins of restraints it imposes on members and their willingness to tolerate them; if the ratios between the influence exercised by individual members and their actual power are not too unequal; and if the respective powers of the different organs correspond to the composition of their membership. At best, the several organs should reinforce each other in a progressive equilibrium movement; at worst, their efficiency and that of the entire organization will decrease as a result of an unstable equilibrium. More important than structure is the commitment of states participating in an international organization — in our case mainly that for mutual assistance against threats to security. What matters is that the actual readiness of members to perform correspond to their formal obligations. A disequilibrium between readiness and obligations results in pressure on the commitment toward its reduction, decentralization, or evasion, which tends to be cumulative. And, lastly, an international organization is in equilibrium with respect to its functional scope when the functions and jurisdiction which it actually exercises correspond to the extent of the needs relevant to its purpose. Depending on the adequacy of the area covered by the organization, its geographic scope can be analyzed in analogous terms.

International organization is thus related to crucial features of international relations and their environment. This is least obvious in the case of structure, concerning such matters as the relation of formal equality, representation, and influence to a hierarchically ordered society of unequally powerful states. It is more readily apparent with respect to a mutual security commitment which cannot but influence the state of the military-political equilibrium, traditionally known as the balance of power. If the balance of power is a persistent feature of international politics, it is not — as Canning among others realized — a fixed and unalterable standard. It is rather a standard perpetually varying as new materials of compensation arise.[8] These derive, however, not only from political geography, but also from newly relevant spheres of reality, now especially institutional and socio-economic. It is the latter sphere which is most directly affected by the functional scope of international organization.

Individual personalities, organized social groups, economies, and cultures are all involved in the international equilibrium. The psychological balance of individuals and groups is influenced by feelings of security and insecurity; it is stabilized to the extent that routine fulfillment of expectations relieves the contest for control among subjects of more or less complementary roles, shared values, and recognized authority. Equilibrium within and between economies is promoted or inhibited by the exchange of economic goods; the inner resiliency of cultures depends largely on the efficacy of their moral and material components in meeting the needs of both stability and change.[9] If the ideal is cultural diversity within the bounds of political and economic interdependence, unilateral abuses of power will tend to aggravate cultural antagonisms and induce the threatened party to compensate for its weakness by stressing its distinctive peculiarities. In any event, the absence of mutually responsive, coöperative, or peacefully competitive communication of values and satisfaction of needs among cultural, ideological, ethnic, and economic groups is certain to be reflected in social maladjustments and to aggravate the operation of both the military-political and the institutional equilibrium.

In view of such ramifications, international organization may be treated as part of a dynamic interplay of institutional, military-political, and socio-economic factors and pressures, constituting a *multiple equilibrium*.

An analysis of international relations can shift emphases among at least three complementary standpoints. First, it may stress individual states as collective actors in the international political process, animated by a more or less unified will under the guidance of their respective élites, and pursuing a measure of security, welfare, and prestige which would exceed — whenever possible — their share as determined by their relative power. Once the balance of power among states is controlled by means of effective international organization, the distribution of security, welfare, and prestige (within the existing conditions of the military-political, socio-economic, and institutional equilibrium) ceases to be the result of conflict and competition only, or even primarily. It is then at least supplemented by an authoritative distribution of the coveted values, governed by the norms and sanctions of the organization's security commitment, functional scope, and institutional structure. Whatever the means to it, however, when individual states feel that the existing distribution of security, welfare, and prestige is the best possible one relative to their power positions, and could not be substantially improved by unilateral efforts at redistribution, the state system as such is in an ideal state of equilibrium.

This leads to the second emphasis, from the viewpoint of the state system, or developing international community, as a going concern. Here, a theory will examine and evaluate the policies of states as being "functional" or "dysfunctional," depending on whether or not they promote the objectives and conform to the rules of a system. Criteria will vary for different systems, among which most relevant for our purpose are the international hierarchy of great and small states, the balance of power, collective security, and the more advanced forms of international integration. Among matters to consider are the sanctions attached to different forms of behavior, the conditions of stability and organized change, the functional requirements and alternatives for the attainment of postulated values, and the functionality of a course of action for the entire state system or for only one of its segments in a disunited world.[10]

Such a "functional" analysis would relate the activities of states to the third standpoint of possible theoretical emphasis, the social and material environment in which states seek to maintain and improve their position individually and in combination. The main analytical components of the environment are: first, the plurality of nations with a "personality" influenced by physical and cultural factors; second, the strictly material configuration of territorial bases of states in a geopolitical pattern conditioned by the state of technology; and third, the international and supranational processes and institutions which cannot be readily subsumed under either of the two other components.

For all these viewpoints the idea of equilibrium is a convenient unifying concept. In the first place, all states seek to secure for themselves by all kinds of policies the best attainable position in the international equilibrium. Secondly, the majority of states must behave so as to promote the equilibrium of the state system as the necessary, if not the sufficient, condition of the system surviving and evolving by no other than peaceful means into higher forms of community. Thirdly, many important aspects of the environment of international relations can be interpreted in equilibrium terms. And, finally, the dual character of the equilibrium concept as a theoretical construct and a desirable policy for safeguarding humane values brings together the analytical and the normative perspectives, as well as some causal implications, of the investigated dynamics.

Faced with the occurrence of a possibly oppressive disequilibrium, this theory sees in the institutional and the multiple equilibrium a legitimate minimum objective of national and international action. It has been said that a healthy democracy balances all social forces in a contrived harmony of power.[11] International politics, too, revolves in large part around attempts — admittedly less consistent and successful — to control the oscillations of a dynamic balance. The theory here submitted holds that a workable organization on national, regional, or global scale requires that institutional, military-political, and socio-economic factors and pressures for and against stability be deliberately equilibrated. The task is complicated by the forces generated by industrialism, nationalism, and mass democracy; cabinet diplomacy can no longer be isolated from total relationships among peoples. A measure of rational adjustment is thus both harder to attain and more necessary, in order to approximate an equilibrium which would be more than an accidental deadlock of opposites.

THE PROBLEM OF INSTITUTIONALIZATION

It may be questioned whether a theory of international relations focused on the international organization of collective security is sufficiently realistic in our day. The use of the term "institution" and its derivations to refer primarily to international law and organization and their bearing on standardized patterns of behavior may appear no less formalistic. Yet it should be clear by now that the issue of the institutional equilibrium is not dealt with as one of formal law, treaty, and constitution-making. On the contrary, it is seen within the rich social and material context which determines the nature, function, and authority of all law and organization.

International law shares the requirements of all effective law yet differs from national law by the special character of its society. All living law, which really governs behavior, grows out of a mutually supporting interpenetration of more or less widely diffused individual and group convictions about right and justice on the one hand, and of a more or less centralized power structure in the society on the other. The interplay of conviction and power generates consent, which is encouraged by diverse sanctions but ultimately rests on the sense of interdependence, solidarity, and need for order on the part of the law's subjects. Social control is the chief object and function of law. It ought first to reconcile in a dynamic and socially useful way individual and group interests backed by unequal power and intensity of conviction. Second, it ought to stabilize the equilibrium of the existing power structure in society. When formal law fails to keep in touch with changing social forces, the result is a legal disequilibrium which makes the law dubiously normative and ineffective. The sanctions of an effective law can be managed by a central power that enforces obedience to the law's imperative commands; they are spontaneous when autonomous forces in society react against disturbance so as to reëstablish a social equilibrium based on reciprocity under generally recognized rules. Hence, a sociological view of law does not regard law and force as antithetical categories or coercion as the one sanction which makes and unmakes law. It modifies, combines, and supplements the one-sided emphases of analytical, philosophical, and historical jurisprudence.[12]

International law presents special problems because of the undeveloped and decentralized organization of power and consensus about right in international society. The subjects of international law are legally sovereign and psychologically ethnocentric political societies, with but a rudimentary sense of community and right, and little willingness to undertake legal obligations. Considerations of power politics are injected into the regulation of the most reciprocal functional relationships and impede the development of supranational loyalties. The result is lawless evasion if an ambitious law outstrips underlying realities, or legalized anarchy if a "realistic" decentralized law depends on the self-limitation and self-help of states for a semblance of authority. An effective international law, too, requires a supporting organization of power and consensus. Some kind of coercive sanctions, such as those of the balance of power and of collective security, are indispensable among states endowed with sovereignty and power. They are the ultimate safeguard of the law itself and its less powerful subjects. Yet collective force behind the law is not sufficient. International law must at the same time foster the noncoercive inducements to observance by promoting a generally useful adjustment of the various needs and interests operative in international society. The legal norms and commitments concerning socio-economic, cultural, and similar matters within and outside international organization are thus crucial for the development of a living international law. As such they are relevant to the central problem of international politics, the organization of security in a broad sense including peaceful change.

Hence international law and international organization are inseparable in both function and scope. Nor are their natures fundamentally different. Also international organization registers the interaction of the subjects of power and norms under the concentric pressure of interdependence. The norms are chiefly those of the law and of the shared purposes shaping the interplay of policies in the organization. Interdependence is the very factor which brings nations together for the solution of problems which cannot be solved in isolation or by conquest. And the power involved is not necessarily only the power of the member-states of the organization.

The power-politics school still tends to interpret power in terms of a clear-cut dominance-submission nexus of control between individual states. It deals with economic resources, geographic location, population, morale, ideology, and the like, as factors of national power directly or indirectly controlled by individual states. But when these factors are transmuted into relationships and processes — such as international depression, maladjustments between industrial and underdeveloped agricultural economies, cultural and ideological tensions — they transcend the effective control by the national power of any one state.

In consequence, the concept of power in international politics must be adapted to cover a control situation which is not a pure case of dominance and submission from one state to another. The relationship basic to this enlargement is the interdependence among nations in dealing with supranational phenomena which affect national policies but over which no single state can exert an effective control independently of other states. In national societies, political power is only one of the instrumentalities of authoritative social control. In a state system without recognized ordering of powers and functions, social control inheres, among other things, in the inducement to community-oriented responses arising from relations of interdependence. To some extent, these relations come to influence national policies. The direction of control assumed by the national power analysis is then partly reversed and new institutions are needed to implement the control. Some of the relational power lost to individual states rests henceforth, together with the attendant normative restraints, in the international institutions themselves. This is especially the case when such institutions are not controlled by one or a few major Powers, or if such a hierarchy is subject to constitutional checks and balances. International organization becomes then a coactive rather than merely a passive framework of international relations and a real factor in the multiple equilibrium.

To be sure, if interdependence is in a way "objective," it must be experienced "subjectively" by national policy makers in order to become fully effective. Like all organization, the international one is a system of personal interactions in organs which tend toward impersonality. On the one hand, there is an existential interplay toward some kind of equilibrium among unequally powerful members with different policies, and among the various organs themselves. On the other hand, international organization is also a system of legal norms and general principles, agreed upon as standards of conduct. The ambiguity of the subjective and the objective, the existential and the normative, and the national and the international aspects is great. For the moment, it is enough to say that international organization is ultimately a process of multilateral balancing of influence on the part of representative élites of member-states who seek to adjust conflicts so as to promote national values and policies within the framework of institutional norms and the actualities of a primitive international community.

The fact that membership in organizations with general norms influences the conduct of political decision-makers introduces the institutional principle into international relations. It may be distinguished from the geopolitical principle, which perpetuates the crucial importance of the particular facts of relative national power and political geography for the fundamental tendencies and presumptions of state behavior. The geopolitical principle connotes direct control over the territory of a weaker nation by a stronger Power. The institutional principle is marked by indirect control over the policies of fellow member-states, as growing interdependence provides new means of influence as well as coöperation. The geopolitical principle is implemented primarily by actual or threatened coercion; the institutional principle by variously induced consent. Forcible subjection of a member-state would be resisted by collective sanctions. Multilateralism tends to supersede bilateralism and enables weaker states to avoid an unequal confrontation with an adjacent imperialistic Power. It disperses rather than polarizes power relations. A voting bloc rather than a military alliance is the typical means of increasing one's weight in the institutional equilibrium, and the criterion of a nation's power is the ability to induce support in quasi-parliamentary dealings rather than the increase or decrease of territorial possessions. The balancing of influence in the institutions of collective security supplements and complicates the balancing of power. As the institutional principle prevails, international relations are institutionalized and the community of nations becomes more than an empty phrase.

Apparently, the over-all trend has been in favor of institutionalization: the voluntaristic ideas of national self-determination and popular self-government might be expected to override the geographic determinism of *Geopolitik*. Yet nationalism can aggravate territorial conflicts where nationalities intermingle and act as a ready carrier of an imperialistic drive; and self-government need not always entail constitutional self-restraint but can find expression in the *mystique* of a charismatic leader or a militant expansionist ideology. Similarly, it is necessary to qualify the relatively steady growth of international institutions, stimulated by a real need and the faith in their utility on the part of the liberal Powers victorious in the two world wars.[13] There is a world of difference between the proliferation of agencies and genuine institutionalization; the League of Nations and the United Nations experienced but occasional and brief spells of the finer achievement. The multilateral method necessitates compromise and limits the freedom of action of the greatest among states. It implies less coercive methods and promises security through reciprocity. These are attractive prospects, especially for smaller states who can hope to exert in international organization a larger individual and collective influence. A favorable institutional equilibrium may control the bad features of the balance of power. But if institutions lose touch with realities, they are a greater threat to weaker nonaggressive states than no institution at all. They give rise to expectations which fail to be met at the critical moment.

This study inquires into the anatomy of international organization and its influence on international politics. It presents international law and organization as integral part of such politics, in the belief that excessive stress on national power can be as overdone as the earlier, formalistic juridical approach. Yet the magnifying glass of analysis must not make one overlook the actual narrowness of the margin within which international institutions affect most political situations. Thus to emphasize institutional power and equilibrium as important factors in international relations is not to disregard or deny the fact, and the consequences of the fact, that states approach international organization as an instrument of their national policies in the first place. If power is not exclusively concentrated in the separate states, they still control most of it. And if interdependence is a growing force in the life of nations, their response to it is still governed largely by considerations of power and immediate interest.

In keeping with the facts and its own premises, this study follows a distinct procedure in dealing with major concepts and institutions. At one extreme of the power-normative spectrum it distinguishes the normative theory or idea of a phenomenon; at the other, the disruption of the idea which would logically ensue if competitive responses to the "laws" of power were all there is to it. In other words, the study defines first the "idealistic" and then the "realistic" interpretation, only to concentrate on the conditions that would make the concept or institution effective. Basically, the theory of effectiveness is arrived at when the normative theory is exposed but not surrendered to the drives for national power and interest. A strictly empirical inquiry will rarely if ever sustain an unqualified option in favor of the "idealistic" or the "realistic" interpretation. A supplementary view may therefore see the reality of a concept or institution as a dynamic synthesis of its normative idea, the tendencies to which it is exposed, and the more or less realized conditions of its effectiveness in actual practice. Conflict may be the relatively most pronounced feature of international politics. But with respect to its principles there are few polarities, much interpenetration, and too many circularities.

CHAPTER I

THE TRADITIONAL
BALANCE-OF-POWER
SYSTEM

The nineteenth-century system of international relations, originating in the Congress of Vienna, was based on three major principles: international hierarchy, the balance of power, and the Concert of European Powers under international law. Within this framework, states were to pursue security, welfare, and prestige in conformity with rules designed to promote the established order. Initially the aristocratic system was in fair equilibrium, but as the century wore on it failed to cope effectively with the realignment of old, and the emergence of new political, social, and moral forces. The smaller states were the pariahs of this era of Great-Power supremacy *par excellence*. Theirs was formally an unsatisfactory position; yet in practice it was not the worst of all possible worlds.

INTERNATIONAL HIERARCHY

All social and political — including international — organization displays certain uniformities. There are always the leaders and the led, the "élites" and the "masses"; and this vertical ordering rests on a horizontal equilibrium of active forces in the society. The precariously balanced power pyramid must be stabilized. This occurs with the development of a generally recognized and progressively institutionalized authority, symbolic of fundamental solidarity among members and active in the coördination of interests and distribution of values in the society. When thoroughly institutionalized, the order assumes the form of a constitutional equilibrium. Yet however much they may be stabilized, all socio-political organization and equilibrium are but temporary.

An unassimilated new factor will sooner or later precipitate change in the configuration, and a new equilibrium takes shape, attended by the regrouping of élites, the reformulation of dominant symbols, and the reorganization of authoritative institutions.

Hierarchy, equilibrium, and authoritative organization are complementary in two ways. First, all three are requisite for a stable society and, if their operation is flexible, for an evolutionary society. Second, authoritative institutions are necessary in order that a latent contradiction in the system may be contained — the contradiction between the principle of hierarchy, which implies the harmony of an accepted arrangement of power and status, and the balance or equilibrium of power, which implies a reciprocal check on competing interests and values, both within and among the various groups in a society, including the élites themselves.

The just revealed flaw in the system accounts for much in the dynamics of social organization. On the one hand, the contradiction in the constituent principles facilitates attempts to resolve it in the harmony of an equalitarian pattern, based either on individual rights and interests or on homogeneous collectivity, and supposed to be diversified only in terms of function, not of power and status. On the other hand, the structure of a hierarchical equilibrium tends to reassert itself in ever new forms, adapted to changing conditions and ideologies: it is constitutionalized and assimilates equalitarian elements in a mobile society; or else it is aggravated into an authoritarian or totalitarian form in reaction to the individualist variety of the equalitarian pattern. Rather than a linear progression toward equality, it is this oscillation between the two fundamental alternatives that constitutes the major structural aspect of the dynamics of social and political organization, in addition to fluctuation in the extent of its functional and geographic scope.

International society is familiar with the hierarchical ordering of power and status among smaller states and the Great Powers; equality appears in international law and relations as the principle of state equality; and both hierarchy and equality are implemented through more or less authoritative institutions.

A definition of what constitutes a great and a small state might rest on primary power differentials or, derivatively, on the scope of interests and forms of institutional representation. To be a

Great Power, a state must then be admitted to a Concert of Powers or occupy a permanent seat in the League of Nations or United Nations Council, have more than limited interests, and be able to assert them by means that include the threat or act of war. A state is small or is a minor Power when it possesses fewer of the active ingredients and attributes of power, and is more vulnerable to those of other nations. A modification is introduced when, as in the theory of collective security, even smaller states assume a commitment implying general interest in global peace, and the Great Powers renounce the pursuit of their interests by specified means, among them the threat of or resort to force and war. In fact, of course, a minor state is mostly a "consumer" rather than a "producer" of security under the collective system; it follows rather than initiates joint action against aggression. Even so, a minor state like Canada can be a producer, and a major Power like France can be primarily a consumer of security. One must then differentiate between states in strategically "exposed" position and "peripheral" states in areas of lower political pressures, as well as between states favorably or unfavorably disposed toward the established international order.

Such secondary distinctions make it difficult and often impossible to speak of "small states" and "Great Powers" as categories with typical foreign-policy attitudes toward more specific issues. But a general group affinity may still underlie diverse objectives and mixed alignments. All smaller states resent arbitrary supremacy of the Great Powers and desire countervailing self-assertion. And the Great Powers, however divided otherwise, are ultimately one in vindicating their individual and collective primacy when challenged. If the diverse qualifications are kept in mind, it is possible to generalize about smaller and greater Powers and their relations.

A small state is not by definition inferior in all of the physical factors of power like size of territory, population, raw-material and industrial resources. Mere size is never a satisfactory principle for classification in politics. Where some of the material factors are large, the "smallness" of a state is likely to be due to an unbalanced combination of such factors. A state can partly compensate quantitative inferiority by qualitative superiority with respect to location, organization, social cohesion, morale, and statesmanship; it can "grow" beyond its size due to inner equilibrium of the social, ethnic, and institutional structure, and the integration of available economic and other resources. Yet however important may be the qualitative modifiers, a thoroughly integrated large territory with corresponding resources is now necessary for really impressive national power and the capacity to wage war successfully. The need for a France and a Great Britain to draw on past power for prestige and on present strategic position for importance compares unfavorably with the growing present and potential power of large territorial states outside Europe.

Indirect power implicit in interdependent relationships is next in importance. A state inferior in the hierarchy of power, but strategically located in the network of interdependence, dependence, and relative independence, may wield considerable power if other states depend on its resources in peace or war. Its importance as provider of raw materials or bases for a greater Power will vary with changes in international alignments and the state of technology. A shift from a politically peripheral to an exposed position may increase the power and influence of a small state without any change in its quantitative components. It may also, however, decrease the effective freedom of action of that state, as a Great Power asserts control over the needed asset. If uranium deposits in the Soviet Union augment her power and freedom of action at the same time, deposits of the same raw material in Czechoslovakia contributed to that country's loss of political independence at the hands of the "dependent" Great Power. On the other hand, Canada increased her influence in world affairs despite or because of her new strategic importance, notably for the United States, due to the developments in air power.

What matters is the ability to withhold the desirable asset. With respect to war, the indirect relational power of a small state depends on its alliance-value for a greater state. The power to withhold the asset or the alliance and the technique of control which the Great Power is ready to employ make up the difference between an ally and a satellite. In a security system, the influence of a small state increases when its coöperation in an enforcement action is crucial because of its strategic position.

The power to vote and act in international organization, too, is real only to the extent that the small state can exercise its privileges more or less freely. A small nation's determination to use its available power independently helps, but it should be tempered by a nonprovocative recognition of superior power elsewhere and larger interdependence almost everywhere. Thus, there is a measure of "necessity" flowing from objective circumstances, but there is also a measure of "freedom" derived from a nation's will to freedom; the result is a shifting balance between the passive and the active role for a small state within the limiting geopolitical setting.

Smaller countries frequently become passive objects of international relations as strong states seek their security in the direct or indirect control of crucial geographical areas, and their needs affect the disposition of weaker societies. The United States, as much as England, France, Germany, and Russia, expanded from a relatively small nuclear area to Great-Power status and dominion, however different may have been the methods and purposes of the expansion. A Great Power's political and economic control can be asserted by frankly imperialistic annexation, or can take on the guise of an alliance, a federation, a customs union, or a close informal relation; it may be a matter of mere fact or be legalized in the form of a protectorate, a vassal state, a lease or a mandate-trusteeship. "International frontiers," "intermediate zones of fragments," or more independent "buffers" and "cordons sanitaires" mark the point of contact between great power centers engaged in conflict or compromise. Their common denominator is more or less direct and benevolent tutelage for the weaker communities. History and geography are rich in appropriate examples. The Low Countries and Korea, the Eastern as well as the Colonial Question, Panama no less than Persia, have had in their time something in common. Ambiguities frequently arise. A buffer state or zone may be an element for peace but also for war among the Powers; "balkanization" is then decried as a cause when it is merely an occasion. And the instruments of hierarchical rule, the legal-political concepts of intervention, recognition, and guarantee can be as ambiguous in content and as discretionary in application as the ordering principle itself.

All three of these concepts are related to the independence of smaller countries. Intervention is most likely to infringe upon the independence of the victim-state when it constitutes a forcible or dictatorial interference in domestic concerns. But it has also been used to create and safeguard the independence of a smaller state, for example, when the Powers intervened in the internal affairs of the Ottoman Empire. Conversely, the recognition of a state, when regarded as constitutive, establishes that state's legal status as an independent member of the international community. But effective independence could be limited by conditional recognition arbitrarily defined by the Powers, which retain the right to supervision and intervention. The successor states to the Ottoman Empire and, in a modified form, to the Habsburg Empire experienced this procedure. If intervention is most likely to infringe, and recognition to establish, the independence of a smaller state, a guarantee is meant to safeguard it. But a guarantee can imply real dependence. This is especially striking when it extends to the internal form of government, as in the case of newly independent Greece, or when it is given unilaterally by a local Great Power. It makes little difference whether dependence and limited capacity are formalized into a protectorate or whether a satellite is created merely in fact.[1]

Ambiguities of this kind are due to the impact of power on vague legal-political concepts, easily subverted into institutional reinforcements of actual inequalities. A stronger state can intervene against a weaker and not vice versa. In general, intervention may be seen as the point at which domestic and international politics intersect. In relations between unequals, actual or anticipated intervention tends to consume the domestic policy of an exposed minor state: effective self-government in vital issues wanes with the primacy of foreign-policy considerations. Nor have recognition and still less guarantee been traditionally a two-way street. The guarantor must be endowed with superior power in order to insure the observance of a guaranteed condition or treaty as the mediator and balancer between the parties.[2] Hence Switzerland, Belgium, and the Balkan states did not extend but received a guarantee. Both statesmen and lawyers believed the preservation of the balance of power to be "just grounds" for intervention; it was equally just grounds for guarantee and recognition. Canning's unilateral recognition of the new states of Latin America was justified by the need to counterbalance French occupation of the Spanish motherland. Put succinctly, intervention was meant to safeguard, recognition of new small states to readjust, and guarantee to reinforce, the balance of power; neutralization removed smaller states out of it altogether. The motto was frequently the "European interest," meaning in effect the preservation of the concert among the oligarchs. In the absence of strict juridical rules, even the Great Powers were wary of possible abuses by others. Hence, joint measures were favored as a means of reciprocal restraint: collective intervention was advocated by the Holy Alliance; Austria's intervention in Naples and France's in Spain carried out, nominally, the mandate of "Europe"; and the collective character of the guarantee of Greece, the Ionian Islands, and the Danubian Principalities was a safeguard against "exclusive protection" and "separate right of interference" by any one Power, most particularly Russia.[3] Similarly, the collective nature of the recognition of the new international status of Greece, Belgium, and the Balkan states reinforced the constitutive character of the act and precluded the acquisition of special advantages by any single recognizing Power. When the Powers acted collectively, they governed *par excellence*. Conversely, the principle of nonintervention was upheld by those who were opposed to such a government. Consistency was not great either way, and the metaphysical phrase nonintervention was used in a flexible fashion, not the least by its foremost advocates. The practice of Great Britain was highly pragmatic, nor did the United States always apply to itself the noninterventionist precepts of the Monroe Doctrine.[4]

Naturally enough, the smaller states have been more consistently opposed to Great-Power rule than the noninterventionist major states. They like to insist on the truly independent character of their origins, revolutionary or otherwise, and the merely declaratory nature of the act of recognition. When newly independent, the United States had been no different in this respect than Belgium, Czechoslovakia or, most recently, Israel. The truth lies between the two extremes: small nations mostly rise by their own efforts, but they need and desire recognition by the Great Powers before they can become effective members of the international family. Yet they frequently fear the gift of a Great

Power's guarantee lest it be a Trojan horse concealing intervention. A guarantee from a local Power is more dangerous in this respect; one from a remote Power is less reliable and may antagonize a jealous neighbor; the passive status accompanying neutralization may also be undesirable. Belgium soon wished to get rid of it, the Baltic states feared more recently nothing more than a guarantee from their Soviet neighbor, and Czechoslovakia had a pitiful experience with the promised guarantee of the Munich Powers.

The lesson is obvious: not to exercise great power unilaterally is at least as difficult as to find a basis for its collective application; but to safeguard little power is most difficult of all. Hence the passion of the smaller states for nonintervention and their compensatory overemphasis on equal sovereignty and domestic jurisdiction for all states.

Ideally, the application of state equality would compensate smaller states for inequalities of power. But the history of the doctrine is a commentary on the fact that, in seeking for a right balance between power and norm, one must neither ignore in law what is inescapable in fact nor use law to sanction the abuses of fact.

If the natural lawyers transferred the doctrine of equality to the law of nations from a fictitious state of nature, the positivists perpetuated the doctrine as the logical correlate of absolute sovereignty of states. The naturalists forgot that a "dwarf," man or state, may be generically but not otherwise the same as a "giant," and that unlike Hobbes' man in the state of nature, a small state cannot vindicate its equality by the ability to "kill" the strongest. And the positivists failed to appreciate the consequences for international organization of a consistently applied sovereign equality, entailing unanimity, equality of rights and obligations, representation and vote, and the like, despite great actual inequalities. The result has been called "a misleading deduction from unsound premises." [5] It opened a gap between the normative precept of a formal juridical doctrine and the realities of interstate relations. An unqualified application of the principle of state equality would impose a restraint on the dynamics of power differentials which would exceed by far the margin of such restraint acceptable to the more powerful states; the ratios

between power weight and nominal institutional weight of unequally powerful states would be too divergent. These are the
makings of institutional disequilibrium. The concept of the legal
equality of states could retain, therefore, its theoretical purity
only so long as the lesser states were in fact excluded from "international government."

Even then, however, international law provided safety valves
to ease the contradiction and reëstablish covertly some kind of
balance. It supplied convenient procedural rules, really available
only to the more powerful. Among them were the validity of
consent irrespective of duress as a basis of unequal obligations, the
legality of self-help, forcible measures of reprisals, and war itself.
Such procedural license went far toward voiding the content of
equal substantive rights to existence and independence for all
states. The result was the law's duplicity and complicity with
abuses.[6]

In the more recent legal writing, the disequilibrium between
fact and norm produced a kind of downward pressure on the
doctrine itself toward its reformulation in more qualified terms.
Equality before the law and equal protection of the law are retained, while the postulate of an equal capacity of rights is
rejected as an ideal not essential to the rule of law. Accordingly,
equality does not necessarily imply equal representation, voting
power, or contribution of all member-states in an international
organization. Equality of status is held to be consistent with inequality of function, and a distinction is made between juridical,
material, and moral equality. In exchange for legal fiction is of-
fered the practicable ideal of the real social equality of great and
small states dissolved, as it were, in functional coöperation. Or,
transcending the state system altogether, social justice is looked
for in the equality of individuals rather than states: equality is
sought for the Albanians, not for Albania. Such realism and
social emphases are welcome, provided they do not discard prematurely even the more guarded doctrine of state equality. To do
so would but reverse the error of extreme equalitarianism and
legalize brute facts. Instead, compromise is the essence of equilibrium.[7]

In the final analysis, however, the rise and position of lesser
political communities is never entirely the result of legal-political

concepts, Great Power combinations, geopolitical conditions, and technology. The structure of international hierarchy varies as the tides in the affairs of men promote consolidation or fragmentation, respect for smaller nations or disregard of their right to independent existence. In conditions of international anarchy, the rise and fall of nations is accelerated by competitive power politics; effective international institutions would palliate the effects of power differentials and reduce the shocks attending the ebb and flow of vital energies in nations and continents. In the course of the nineteenth century, nationalism veered from the work of consolidation to that of fragmentation of existing political organizations. The process has been affected not only by a temporary superiority of defensive over offensive weapons, but also by the prevailing liberal ideology.

Small states and communities have been praised by philosophers from Plato and Aristotle through Jean Jacques Rousseau to the liberal thinkers and statesmen of more recent times. For the philosophers of the Greek city-state, limited size of a community was the condition of good life. For the romantic antagonist of the *philosophes*, it was the prerequisite of individual freedom and the general will. Montesquieu saw in the federation of smaller states a means for reconciling the republican virtues of a small community with the external requirements of power. In later liberal thought, sympathy for the rights and aspirations of smaller nations was linked with the faith in the inherent worth of individuals and the progress of free nations toward a coöperative world order. Wilson marked the climax and fleeting consummation of this line of thought. On the other hand, small states were denied the right to existence by a host of others. The *Politics* of Treitschke strikes a different note from the *Politics* of Aristotle; it is the first which is echoed by present-day devotees of *Machtpolitik*. The case against the small state may parade ideal arguments in terms of a Hobbesian or Social Darwinian struggle, of spiritualistic or materialistic dialectic, or of the superior rights of a master race. In the final analysis, it rests on the material facts of international life and boils down to Bagehot's belief that the strongest tend to be the best. Progress is to be achieved not by coöperative interaction, but by means of the subordination or outright elimination of weaker contenders.

The fate of smaller communities is a vital clue to the character of the forces at large in any historical period. Especially the more exposed among them are so many seismographs registering in their immediate fate the tremors and convulsions of a gathering international crisis or of an international order in the process of being reshaped. A more lasting redefinition of their individual and collective status depends then to a great extent on the outcome of the more dramatic struggle of the giants. At stake are not only the formal attributes of sovereign independence and equality of smaller states. Much more essential is a degree of effective self-direction and international codetermination within the limits set by interdependence and power differentials among nations. Translated into the problem of individual freedom and self-respecting citizenship, the three basic requirements are thus not only constitutional self-government and national self-determination, but also a decent measure of international self-direction. If the latter is absent, the other two degenerate into a deceptive fiction and a dangerous fallacy. The rights of active citizenship are negated by the passive object-ness of the state governed by external forces; satellite dependence in a degenerate hierarchy of reciprocally hostile Powers is at the opposite pole from a constitutional order, which implies the freedom of moral choice.

THE BALANCE OF POWER

A counterpart to hierarchy is the balance of power. If hierarchy is a principle of social control based on unequal power and status, the balance of power is a principle designed to control power and power differentials themselves.

The recurrent interest in the theory and practice of the balance of power suggests that in some form it is a persistent tendency of the multistate system. This is easily explainable. Like power itself, the equilibrium mechanism pervades the social and natural realm. Like all politics, the balance of power reflects the fundamental duality of human nature. It is a projection writ large in the history of nations of the tension in man's disposition between good and evil, self-preservation and self-aggrandizement, coöperation and conflict, rational self-restraint and irrational megalomania. The same principle of power equilibrium and reciprocal restraints for shared liberty and justice underlies a "mixed constitution," the separation of powers, federalism, and the state system. In the continuum of domestic and international politics there are only different degrees of sublimation of the interplay of forces within institutions permeated with the values of shared community. Internationally the balance of power has lacked a well-developed communal matrix; it is instead marked by the anticipation and practice of violence among sovereign and independent subjects with differing ideas of what is just and legitimate. Nevertheless, normative implications have not been absent from the harsher branch of politics.

They are, of course, most pronounced in the normative theory, or idea, of the balance of power. It is not the product of inexperienced dreamers. Neither is it mere propaganda. Castlereagh and others before and after him spoke of a "just equilibrium" among the members of the family of nations which would prevent any one of them to impose its will on the rest. And Gentz saw the merit of the balance of power in "that the smallest as well as the greatest is secured in the possession of his [unequal] right, and that it can neither be forced from him nor encroached upon by *lawless* power." [8] Not only power itself but also the purposes for which it can or will be used must be assessed. The objective is to prevent hegemony. Preventive war with limited objectives of containment is legitimate in the face of a clear and present danger of external (though not peaceful internal) expansion. Thus, the idea of the balance of power has come to connote the interplay of power and purpose toward a just equilibrium of power and rights. So conceived, the interplay subserves the general interest in an objective state of counter- and equipoised power and its uses.

But the normative theory does not provide a complete and realistic picture. The practice of the balance of power is frequently expedient and unpredictable in the treatment of established rights. Apart from the objective aspect there is a subjective side. The former may occasionally safeguard international purposes of the rule of law and order; the latter is the manifestation of divergent national purposes and interests. It is marked by the tendency to seek competitively not international balance but national preponderance or overbalance of power, a margin of security and other desired values superior to those of other states. Fortunately, insofar as national policy-makers behave rationally,

the drive for preponderance is tempered by the sense of diminishing marginal utility of each additional increment of effective military power, in terms of both economic and political costs and advantages. There is an ideal point for each state at which such power is maximized relative to its available potential and the potential and attitudes of other states. An equilibrium occurs, and has the best chance of being stable, when all or at least the important states individually and in alliance reach such an optimum level of relative power and security that, by definition, could not be further improved in an armaments race or by a policy of territorial conquest; efforts in that direction would either overtax national resources to the point of marginal disutility of costs in other areas of national power, or provoke a more than offsetting loss in relative military power and security through political realignments and possibly preventive war against the too-ambitious Power.[9]

If the balance of power is to preserve the state system, a well-understood principle of balancing must inform the actual dynamics of the rising and falling absolute and relative power of states. It is worth while to retain the distinction: the principle of the balance of power is to defend the continued operation of the dynamics against any "unbalancer" or other source of imbalance; the dynamics, inherent as it is in the multistate system, can be substantially modified or extinguished only with the system itself. It is morally neutral and functionally unreliable; the principle is morally unreliable. An ambiguous situation results: the sanctions of the balance of power can have the normative effect of sustaining law and justice; or, the balance of power can be invoked to vindicate the most immoral methods of implementing the principle and insuring the continued operation of the morally neutral dynamics against a fatal imbalance. If the over-all objective is unimpeachable from the viewpoint of the state system as a whole, many specific measures may be fatal to one or several members and appear to be morally indefensible by more detached standards.

The ambiguities implicit in the subjective and the objective aspects of the balance of power as dynamics and as a principle of policy cannot but have adverse consequences for the idea. They warp the functioning of the balance of power as a mecha-

nism for the distribution of security and rudimentary integration of independent states under law, including most specifically the protection of the rights of weaker communities.

There are the overtones of metaphor in the terminology of writers who linked the protection of smaller states by the balance of power with its integrating and constitutional function. Such was Vattel's rapt vision of Europe as a body politic of states tied together by concern for order and freedom, and guaranteed against the domination of any one Power by the celebrated idea of the political equilibrium. Gentz saw pre-Napoleonic Europe as a confederacy of states connected by the balance of power as the constitution of the common league; throughout almost three centuries it preserved intact the political existence and rights of all independent Powers. According to a later liberal writer, the rough equilibrium established at Vienna gave to weak states a substantial sense of security.[10] In actual fact, of course, the balance of power may also oscillate at the expense of the weak. Small states disappeared *en masse* in the Peace of Westphalia; at Vienna, additional midget states were liquidated and the not-so-small Saxony was partitioned. Poland had by then set the great precedent for the technique of partition and compensations as the hallmark of the balance of power, destroying the weak in order to preserve the accord of the strong. To the detractor, the partition of Poland has demonstrated for all time the wickedness of the balance of power. To the apologist, it was a disastrous omen, an "abuse of form" and a perversion of the idea. "*Corruptio optimi pessima*." In a sober view, it stands for one possible implication of the principle.[11]

As a matter of fact, the idea of the balance of power becomes realistic only if there is a factor ensuring actual or potential preponderance on the side devoted to the protection of legitimate rights. An intangible element is a moral climate favorable to an enlarged conception of the national interest as one served by a general equilibrium, the restraint of great states, and self-discipline of smaller nations. The tangible component is the existence of a balancer.

His task is difficult. A balancer is expected to be partial to no single national subject of the balance-of-power system but to direct his own mobile weight in such a way as to ensure the

international object of an equipoise of power. He must be both at the focus of the system and outside it; otherwise he would not be free to withdraw and engage his weight in function of the system's requirements and thus manipulate the balance. An effective balancer must be both self-restrained and quick in imposing vigorous restraints on others. Only then can he frustrate and thus reduce the incentive to any one nation's quest for preponderance. A sufficiently powerful balancer of this kind might check the irrational drives and the miscalculations jeopardizing the balance of power and promote the realization of its objective norm.

For a long time, the position of the balancer was held by Great Britain. Ideally considered, Britain managed to convert the quantitative dynamics of the balance of power into a political principle of the first order. She combined with skill the respective advantages of a politically central and geographically eccentric position. Because of her vast resources, imperial sway, navy, and the London Exchange, Britain was a major factor for integration in Europe and in the world. Her position as balancer assured her a decisive influence in the Concert of the Great Powers. Still ideally, she was the unfailing protector of the rights and liberties of small nations. Yet the kaleidoscope of international politics also suggests a different image. Britain often seemed dedicated in fact to no other principle save that of the "free hand," which is logically exclusive of any other principle at all. As always, reality is to be found somewhere between the neatness of an idealized system and an equally unreal anarchy, subject to the "laws" of power and immediate interest alone.

It is significant that when Sir Eyre Crowe spoke of Great Britain as the natural champion of weaker communities, he did so in the qualifying context of her geographical position and her role of balancer in the balance of power.[12]

Geographically, the British Isles, on the ocean flank of Europe, were in the nineteenth and early twentieth century the center of a far-flung empire. Britain's interest in Europe was mostly subordinate to her imperial concerns and was primarily preventive, opposed to any one state's continental hegemony. It was limited in that it extended directly and reliably only to the continent's northwestern shores adjoining the Channel. The Low Countries were always jealously watched, the more eastern parts of the continent only when events there happened to threaten the imperial life-line and the over-all European equilibrium. Where British sea power could not reach, or be reached, effective intervention and concern declined. Even the privileged Low Countries had long been the pawn rather than the protégé. They suffered frequently from what the one-time historical adviser of the Foreign Office called the bad side of the balance of power.[13] Britain came eventually to sponsor the liberties of other nations for reasons which cannot be reduced to expediency and national security alone. But with respect to the "eastern frontiers" British policy continued to be as unpredictable as the principle on which it was based. This applied especially to communities located in the peripheral zones of conflict with other Powers, then chiefly Russia, such as the Balkan countries, Persia, Korea, and the like. These were, in all but name (unless they were it in name too), second-category countries, more exposed to the vagaries of political fortune than the actual dependencies of the British Empire.

In regard to Britain as the balancer, her aloofness and ability to withdraw from the balance were required for the necessarily elusive and flexible operations. But the insularity of British geography and character frequently turned aloofness into isolation and the capacity for disengagement into a distaste for reëngagement, beyond the allowable margin of safety both for England and for other exposed nations.

A balancer is normally concerned with established states. Yet, at the apogee of her power, Britain frequently held or was urged to hold the balance between contending principles as well. Among them were liberal nationality versus the absolute state, nonintervention versus intervention in domestic and foreign affairs. A Cobden could urge adherence to nonintervention as dogmatically as some of the later Liberals and Labourites supported the principles of collective security. In fact, the real sympathy for constitutionalism and for the liberty of smaller nations was not allowed to interfere with the requirements of a desirable power balance — although the liberal disposition of British statesmen could and did influence the choice of ways and means in applying a general principle. Despite the indisputable cleavage between the Western and the Eastern Powers, the diplomatic messages of the time and the actually shifting alignments show that ideological divisions could be scrambled rather easily by pragmatic interest. Nor did Great Britain hesitate to use liberalism and nationalism as convenient "weights" in her contentions with the reactionary Powers. Not surprisingly, the smaller states like Spain and Portugal repaid in kind. They leaned on maritime Britain without ceasing to flirt with France and other continental local or remote Powers, in order to avoid becoming the satellites of too exclusive a protector.

The result was a situation flexible enough to please a Power committed first and foremost to the avoidance of abstract commitments.[14] It may be natural for a balancer to prefer a "free hand" and a narrow scope and construction of existing commitments; but this is cold comfort to others. It is, perhaps, more than accidental that both world wars were preceded by Britain's reluctance to commit herself unequivocally and actively in time to defend a small Eastern European state.

It may be argued, of course, that the real function of the balance of power is not to preserve peace or to protect the rights of smaller states in a constitutional fashion, but rather to prevent the forcible unification of the state system. The balance of power forbids only a few concrete solutions and dictates none. It guarantees no specific *status quo* and no particular rights, except its own right to continued existence.

Wars were as frequent among the Greek city-states as they have been among the dynastic and national states in more recent times; irreparable disaster came only when the balance of power failed to operate so as to frustrate the Macedonian bid for hegemony. Real or suspected imbalance encourages aggression and war. Yet it is difficult to assess the distribution of power correctly and impossible to maintain an equipoise over a long period of time. Hence the familiar cycle of challenges, disruptions, and reconstitutions of the equilibrium, marked by a long succession of belligerents, wars, and peace settlements. In principle, all war is legal in traditional international law; even a technically aggressive war may be "just" in the theory of the balance of power if unleashed to thwart a prospective unbalancer.

Nor will the unpredictable balance of power affect weaker states in a uniform way. It can create, rescue, or destroy the independence of individual small states as an incident to the preservation of the autonomy of the state system as a whole. Small nations may be partitioned, neutralized out of the balance of power as passive buffers, or propelled into an active role. Much will depend on the state and trend of the equilibrium-preponderance dynamics at the critical point, and the manner in which the Great Powers will evaluate the requirements of the balance of power as a principle of policy. In this they will be influenced by predominant values. The small states themselves are not without responsibility. Their behavior also counts, and responsibility goes not only with power but with claim to rights as well.

The already mentioned partition of Poland can serve as an illustration. If comparable compensations were necessary to prevent the regional hegemony of Russia in Eastern Europe or war among the Eastern Powers, then the principle of the balance of power "justified" the partition. By the same standards, however, the Western Powers and notably France were "guilty," since they failed to prevent the partition in the interest of the over-all European equilibrium. As for the small state itself (if Poland would allow herself to be thus called), it became the object of the balance of power only after it had abdicated the responsibility of active statehood by indulging in internal disorders. The balance of power was allowed to take the way of least resistance in the moral vacuum of a skeptical age yet untouched by the spirit of nationalism.

In the nineteenth and early twentieth century, liberal faith in the intrinsic worth of small nations and the old idea of legitimacy with the new nationalistic content inclined the operations of the balance of power toward the preservation and creation of smaller states. Later in this century, however, the expansionism of totalitarian systems came to play havoc with the ideas of self-government and self-determination of smaller communities. The ideas were defeated or perverted whenever they failed to be supported, as frequently happened, by a favorable balance of power and the readiness of the democratic Powers to enforce an equitable settlement in case of conflict. Then, to cite but one instance, the Munich settlement added to its other sins one against the principle of the balance of power itself: the settlement was allowed to weaken further the side already weaker in effective strength, despite its greater potential countervailing power. And the victimized small state, this time Czechoslovakia, also failed to meet all of the responsibilities of independent nationhood by defending its rights with all necessary means.

Minor states are most vulnerable when there is an imbalance among the Great Powers. They are in grave danger when caught on the "wrong" side of a balance turning in favor of an antagonized local Great Power. The result tends to be an adverse "peaceful" settlement under duress, like the Munich settlement, or involvement and frequent disaster in the war among the giants. When involved in war, smaller states can follow two diametrically opposite courses. They may join the anti-hegemonic Powers and face swift defeat by the local Power in obedience to the dictates of the principle of the balance of power, their collective conscience, and ultimate self-interest. Or, they may side with the unbalancer for short-term gain or fear of immediate loss. Like many a state during the Napoleonic wars, Rumania practiced both alternatives in the two world wars. Her vacillations reflected with fair accuracy but poor timing the oscillations of the balance.

As a general rule, the smaller states should follow the interest of the balance and their own by allying themselves with the opponents of the hegemonic Great Power or Powers. In this they are frequently hampered by internal intrigue, external coercion, and discords among themselves. Yet this does not mean, as some would argue, that insecure small states as a group indulge in the willful habit of playing one Great Power off against another in a sort of *l'art pour l'art* politics of balance of power.

Partitions of small and even great states have lately become the fashion again. But the bisection of the territorial bases of vibrant national organisms is now a dangerous expedient. It produces violent reactions within the unnaturally severed body politic, straining to recover equilibrium in wholeness and unity. The inner equilibrium of the exposed smaller states situated between antagonistic power and ideological systems tends to mirror in its multiple aspects the relative impact of the larger external forces. As a result, it cannot but be uncertain and subject to fatal strains as one or the other outside pressure fails to perform the sustaining counterbalancing function. Such intermediate states are a constant challenge, a rare index of the shifting tides of the global equilibrium. Their territorial partition is but a crude method of simplifying the balancing operation. After 1945, Czechoslovakia was not partitioned, but, prematurely written off by the West, she lost her inner equilibrium and slipped entire into the Soviet scale on the inclined plane of global imbalance. Korea was partitioned and produced a war; Vietnam was cut in two as a means of ending another. And the partition of Germany, more conspicuous in the case of a big country, constitutes a standing threat to the peace of the world. The trend may continue, as moral resistance to infringements of national integrity is weakened by the habit of tinkering with political units caught in the see-saw of an unstable balance and conflicting ideologies.

More generally, it is possible to criticize the balance of power for its intrinsic uncertainty, quantitative character, and inadequacy in meeting changed international conditions.

Uncertainty marks the entire system. First, the dynamics of equilibrium in the political world is by its very nature unstable and precarious, and the ideal of an equipoise can be rarely attained and never reliably ascertained. Second, the operation of the balance of power as a principle of policy is unpredictable, the fluctuating interests, power, and determination of the major states being the great unknowns in the equation. In itself, the balance of power supplies little guidance as to the rightfulness and political wisdom of a specific arrangement this side of universal hegemony. It is a rough rule of thumb rather than a fundamental law of international polity with precise content and certain application; it has presided over deeds of farsighted statesmanship and cloaked with its prestige acts of fumbling expediency and ruthless depredation. Hazard is king mainly in areas, such as traditionally the Balkans, which are the object of indecisive contention among several Great Powers. Under intra- and extra-regional stimuli, the local petty balances among the minor states get inextricably implicated in the larger balance and "cause" open conflicts among the Powers. No wonder, then, that the unprincipled balance of power has invited at least as much condemnation as eulogy.

Imprecision and uncertainty are a grave flaw in a primarily quantitative concept. The emphasis is on "primarily," inasmuch as the balance of power has often been linked with qualitative and normative-purposive factors. According to Gentz, the essential idea is not quantitative equality of the subjects of power, but equal protection of unequal existing rights. The international community should not oppose a pacific increment of a nation's wealth and power, but only an expansionist aptitude and, it may be added, purpose of a state. Not mere power, but the use of power is of moment. Talleyrand insisted at Vienna on moral force as the condition of power equilibrium, and on the qualitative apart from quantitative evaluation of its components. John Stuart Mill saw clearly that all imperfectly balanced political systems ultimately depend on constitutional morality. To the positivistic jurist Oppenheim, on the other hand, a balance of power was the indispensable condition of the very existence of international law.[15]

All suggest, in one way or another, the familiar interaction of power and norm. It is, of course, true that the subjective, competitive drives of individual nations pursuing power preponderance might occasionally cancel each other out in a state of deadlock. But only a purpose weighing other values against immediate power advantage can raise the dynamics of equilibrium to a principle of policy in which choice offsets the hard core of necessity implicit in power. This means that the balance of power depends largely on the self-restraint of the Great Powers in order to realize its beneficial and escape its anarchic potential; the external restraints of countervailing power can only reinforce internal restraints operative within a political system.

The qualifications from purpose are important. Yet the primary importance in the balance-of-power scheme still belongs to more or less impressionistic appraisals of the quantitative and qualitative aspects of the power of different states. The ideal is prevention, rather than repression, of an onslaught on the *status quo*, and the peaceful purposes of powerful states may be even less of a reliable constant than is their power. The dangers of faulty evaluation join then defensive fears to aggressive designs in stimulating the quest for insured preponderance with attendant competitive armaments, preventive measures, and sundry expedient adjustments.

Apart from its intrinsic limitations, the quantitative and mechanistic side of the balance of power has been increasingly at variance with the subtler dynamics of expanding international reality. The short-term achievements of the policy of the balance of power may be good or bad; but the balance of power cannot in the long run defend successfully state independence against the consequences of interdependence. Furthermore, the adequacy of a strictly political and in the final analysis military concept cannot but decrease as the social and institutional factors in international relations grow in relative importance. With the passing of the economics of free trade and *laissez faire*, the inseparable unity of all these aspects became more obvious and compelling.

There is a deep-seated incongruity between the traditional balance of power and the new socio-political phenomena. Within the intricate web of the multiple interrelations, the more or less irrational psychology of nationalism, mass democracy, and doctrinaire ideologies favors rigid or erratic alignments, rather than the flexible and secret rational intelligence of the aristocratic "metaphysics of force." [16] A dictatorship may be able to control such inconsistencies, which tend to impede, especially in peacetime, the foreign policies of the democracies. While the Nazi-Soviet pact could precede and set off the war, war was necessary to offset ideological resistance in the West to a Soviet alliance. With the restoration of peace, domestic pressures were quick to undermine the Western side of the postwar balance. And the Soviet ally had to become the enemy before he could be opposed as the unbalancer. The time-lags were fatal in more than one respect.

Nor was Canning's "New World" the last to enlarge the scope of the balance. Additional complications flow from the spread of nationalism and the extension of an active balance of power first to the East — to Eastern Europe, the Near East, and Asia — and now to Africa. Many of the ethnically and otherwise plural communities lack the internal homogeneity and resources to figure as cohesive autonomous units in the balance. The withdrawal of Western colonialism, once a way out of the European political deadlock, has recreated in many parts the power vacuum which encourages imperialism to spread in the first place. These and other factors handicap emancipated societies groping for inner stability and a position of independence in the global distribution of power. They handicap a safe distribution of power at least as gravely. Young states incline to take a parochial view of their unwonted right to claim, exercise, or reject an active part in the larger equilibrium. Intangibles become crucially important in shaping attitudes among culturally diverse nations.

These are some of the reasons why the expansion of the balance-of-power concept into something like the multiple equilibrium has to be examined at least as closely as its traditional role, shortcomings, and geographic extension. The idea of the balance of power will not remain a valid principle of international politics unless it is reinterpreted to include the new factors which impinge on it from outside its traditional framework of operation.

The critical temper applied to the balance of power must govern also the appraisal of Britain's performance as the balancer. Despite great limitations, the smaller states fared reasonably well under the aegis of Britain's world power. Its liberal cast, the nature and mobility of its sea power, and the requirements of free trade served and were served by the maintenance of order and liberty. The position of Great Britain was such that she could afford to encourage rising small nations without fear of losing all control over their future. She could thus be more tolerant most of the time than less favored Powers with a more limited orbit. As the balancer, she was not perfect, but she did block the path to universal conquest in several major wars at considerable sacrifice.

Yet the weaknesses ultimately prevailed. The economics of free trade was not an unmixed blessing. If the balance of power is designed to prevent political hegemony, the equilibrium resulting from free trade tends to perpetuate the economic hegemony of the most advanced country. Protectionism becomes a matter of legitimate self-defense and disrupts economic integration and equilibrium. A merely political and conventional international organization is then inadequate. And, although Great Britain managed occasionally to fuse the balance of power and the Concert of Powers into a highly effective informal system, its unpredictability and functional as well as geographic limitations became critical as the British position and the entire order weakened under internal and external stresses.

A transient international order resting on unique circumstances and the policies and strength of a single nation may be the best we can ever get. But it can neither be aimed at purposively nor maintained over an indefinite period of time. There is then always the big question of the politics of an unregulated state system: who will eventually replace the contemporary incumbent of decisive power in the world? That is why the most sympathetic student must dwell on the shortcomings of the *Pax Britannica* if he is to define the requirements of an international organization which would recover some of the lost security and order at a time when the separation of the political and the socio-economic is illusory and the balance of military power in itself is no longer enough.

THE CONCERT OF EUROPE

So much about the intrinsic weaknesses of the balance of power. They aggravate further its latent contradiction with the principle of hierarchy, the conflict between the assumption of a harmonious ordering of unequal power and the actual need for the balancing of competitive power. The nineteenth century was fortunate enough to have an institutional mechanism for dealing with the conflict and for distributing in an authoritative fashion security, welfare, and the prestige of independence under law among the members of the state system. This was the Concert of the Powers of Europe. Like the balance of power, the Concert rested on a modicum of international consensus and the sporadic bursts of a European consciousness peculiar to the cabinet diplomacy of the period; both of them disintegrated parallel to their social foundation in the period preceding the First World War. It is time now to apply to the ups and downs of the Concert the theory of institutional equilibrium with respect to structure, central commitment, and functional and geographic scope, as outlined in the introduction.

If the Concert of the Great Powers was a classical phenomenon of the nineteenth century, it is also a recurrent tendency in international politics and organization. The prototype is revived whenever the Great Powers find themselves in a position to exercise their special responsibilities. It is, therefore, permissible to use the term "Concert" rather broadly to include the early Congresses, the Ambassadorial Conference system of the 1830's, and analogous institutions in later periods.

The structure of the Concert was determined by its character as an international directorate of the Great Powers. It would be futile even to raise the question of an equilibrium between the Great Powers and the smaller states within the institution; the exclusion of the lesser countries was practically complete. At the Congress of Vienna, which introduced the distinction between the Great and the smaller Powers, the *sous-Alliés* were expected to ratify *ex post facto* the authoritative decisions of the principal Allies. As always, the institutional representation and influence of a Power was in direct relation to its effectiveness in the military-political sphere. All states enjoyed nominal equality of status under international law; but the major Powers exercised virtually exclusive political responsibility in making decisions. This was not a unique arrangement, then or since. Even those small states directly concerned, such as Belgium or the nationalities implicated in the perennial "Eastern Question," were not represented or asked to consent to determinations by the Great Powers on subsequent occasions. They were tacitly assumed to be bound by the collective authority of the Powers over their existence and occasional conflicts. They were the wards of their guardians. The political primacy of the Great Powers could be rationalized into a legal primacy producing beneficent results; or it could be accepted reluctantly as an actual if nonlegal manifestation of superior power.[17]

In the theory of the constitutional compromise, the Great Powers were the trustees of a European community. They guaranteed respect for the liberties of unrepresented smaller states under the "public law of Europe." In the practice of an oligarchical system, the Concert tended to become the rather inept dictatorship of frequently disunited Powers under a peculiar form of the rule of law. The Concert drew on the facilities of treaties and its own quasi-legislative authority to legalize political discretion tempered by self-restraint and mutual restraint. The so-called European interest was the highest law. It meant, in effect, the promotion of agreement among the Great Powers by all possible means.

There was good reason: the first condition of an effective Concert in structural equilibrium is the inclusion of all major Powers and their support, or at least toleration, of the *status quo*. Only then is unilateral disturbance of the established order both unnecessary and unprofitable. It served the cause of the Concert to include vanquished France in the Pentarchy; Russia's distaste for the settlement imposed on her after the Crimean War was one of the reasons for its eclipse. Standing and falling with an unreliable Great-Power accord, however, the Concert could not evolve into an authoritative European government, but remained a diplomatic device for intermittent and decreasingly effective coördination of particular objectives.

Insofar as international organization depends on agreement among Great Powers, this is always the case. Also perennial is the fact that the standing of the smaller states is lowest when the Great Powers' accord runs high. The Concert system merely dramatized this fact by denying the minor states any forum for collective self-assertion. Yet, if Great-Power agreement means mutual restraint, then for a small state it is preferable to unrestrained dictation by a single more powerful neighbor. And the system's presumption in favor of established rights and their concerted modification is not always adequately replaced by the slender checks of more elaborate and equalitarian international institutions alone.

On the whole, the system tended to reinforce rather than to disguise or qualify the supremacy of the Great Powers. They alone can be effective challengers and counterweights in their own right; hence their desire to determine the conditions of equilibrium and of their accord, on which their collective authority is contingent, without external interference. Revolt of a small state against a decreed adjustment, like that of Holland against the separation of Belgium, is easily disposed of. If expedient, the Powers will resort to the division of spheres of influence, as happened repeatedly from the dissection of Poland in the eighteenth century and the Far East in the nineteenth to the percentage-wise "immediate war-time arrangements" contemplated in the Second World War for the Balkans.[18] Upon closer analysis, however, the measures most painful for smaller states are likely to result from appeasement dictated by actual or suspected disequilibrium of power and will among the Powers, rather than from accord based on equilibrium.

When, as frequently happens, there is conflict rather than accord or stable equilibrium among the Powers, the contradiction latent in the system comes into the open. The balance of power is oriented from peace to war, ceases to be at all complementary, and becomes only antithetical to the hierarchical Concert. Cross-alliances take place between major and minor states. The contention for a new equilibrium raises the influence of the more independent smaller states and depresses the collective standing of the Great-Power élite as a group. A Sardinia became thus one of the victors in the Crimean War over a Russia as a preliminary to her expansion into another, if minor, Great Power. If the situation is sufficiently fluid and a minor state dares to shoulder the attendant risks, it may even try to play the giants off against each other. The shifts of pre-nationalist Serbia between Austria and Russia illustrate the policy and its dangers. When, however, the balance is rigid and the withholding power of a smaller state nil, international conflict is likely to diminish yet further the independence and the security of a minor "ally." Basically, the activation of smaller states as a result of Great-Power contests is as much a departure from the ideal norm of the Concert as the extinction of Poland was from that of the balance of power.

To what extent was the Concert system in equilibrium as regards its structure? Ideally, it was rather close to this position at the outset of its existence. The exclusive membership of the Great Powers and the inclusion of all of them insured that the ratios of actual power and institutional influence were pretty nearly equal for all members. The high degree of discretion under a tolerant international law made the margin of attempted restraints on the dynamics of power slim and, in most cases, well within the limits which the major Powers were likely to tolerate. Consequently, important business was actually transacted within the "international organization." A considerable measure of genuine institutionalization of international politics resulted, although this occurred on a low level of integration and largely only among the major Powers. But international institutions should also enable smaller states to take a more active part in affairs and should partly offset the impact of power differentials. From this viewpoint, the exclusion of the smaller states and the merely legalizing rather than countervailing effect of traditional international law and organization were serious shortcomings. The inadequacy was aggravated and the system began to lose its initial near-equilibrium as the increasingly significant role of the smaller states, due in part to the lack of realized concert among the Powers, failed to be expressed in corresponding institutional representation and responsibility.

Similarly, the issue of equilibrium with respect to the commitment of members concerned the Great Powers only. The Concert was described as a system of rights without duties, of responsibilities without organization.[19] A counterpart of the exclusion of the smaller states from the Concert was their limited liability and the absence of a general commitment. Even the commitment of the Great Powers was largely conventional. Apart from the obligation to observe treaties and specific guarantees, most explicit was the procedural commitment to consultation before military action. Its substantive complement was the frequently affirmed engagement to act in conformity with the requirements of the balance of power. Yet the principle of the Concert did not prescribe a specific course any more than did the balance of power. Both provided only a general framework of reference facilitating negotiation and compromise. Hence the really vital commitment was merely implicit in the system: it concerned the moral obligation of the Great Powers to modify national interests by larger, European, considerations as the condition of their agreement. No one Power was to aggrandize itself territorially or otherwise without the consent of them all. The aim was to reduce the rewards and thus the incidence of unilateral ventures.

Such a commitment was flexible enough to call forth a corresponding readiness to observe it. But when the Powers had failed to devise an acceptable substitute for the idea of a general guarantee encompassing the domestic as well as the international *status quo*, commitment and readiness began to see-saw in an uneasy, mostly unstable, equilibrium toward an ever lower level. Coöperation and action against a Great Power stepping outside the charmed circle of conventionally sanctioned conduct became matters of convenience and calculation rather than of principle and obligation. The surviving measure of institutional equilibrium with respect to commitment was exposed to great strains when the post-1815 balance of power itself was disrupted by the new principle of nationality in the guise of Italian and German unification. Both Cavour and Bismarck refused to consult "Europe" and secure her approval to aggrandizements achieved through war. But the sidestepping of an institution indicates its lack of efficiency and inner equilibrium; the *Realpolitik* of the national interest, pure and simple, challenged the reality and revealed the mythical character of the European Concert.

The expanding intricacy of the Bismarckian system of checks and balances by alliance treaties henceforth constituted a new type of international organization.[20] It did away with the prerequisites of an effective Concert system by petrifying the balance of power and polarizing the Powers. As became true later of the League and the United Nations, the central organ failed to integrate and control the two great alliance systems, the precursors of "regional understandings" and "arrangements" of later years, and through this failure lost its own internal equilibrium in this respect too. Nor were the consequences different. The Congress system languished and acted only occasionally, chiefly on the Eastern and colonial questions. When the great test came in 1914, the mere idea of the Concert was not enough. In the absence of stabilizing institutional and social influences in the environment, a transient equipoise of military strength between the two camps had the untoward effect of precipitating rather than restraining hostilities. No longer governed by the old master's rational sense of measure, Germany sallied forth on the first of her daemonic drives for European and world hegemony.

In respect to its functional and geographic scope, the Concert system was in its most patent, deepening disequilibrium. Its jurisdiction did not extend to all or most of the environmental phenomena internationally revelant at the time. If the commitment was limited, the scope was undefined.

It proved impossible for the Powers to agree whether only the external affairs or also the internal conditions of the smaller communities constituted its legitimate functional scope. The deadlock of views led to the neglect of larger social and economic problems as they caught up with the narrowly political and military issues. The negative approach of systematic preventive interventionism was rejected; a consistent positive policy toward the problems raised by the industrial revolution, nationalism, and liberal constitutionalism was not evolved. This could not but intensify the strains undermining a settlement slanted against the new forces in favor of indifferently applied dynastic legitimacy, quantitative territorial balance of power, and static repose. Although gaining in momentum, the new forces were not channeled in the direction of a readjusted social equilibrium. Neither were they allowed to modify the traditional principles of international relations. Instead, they were subordinated, too often and for too long, to the requirements of the old balance of power of 1815, until they acquired sufficient backing in military power for a strategic break-through. The ultimately triumphant integral nationality was sure to bear the marks of the power struggle through which it had to pass.

In the contest for a new social equilibrium the lines were more clearly drawn between the principles than the principals. A sharp line initially separated those who favored and those who opposed liberal constitutionalism against dynastic absolutism, popular against territorial sovereignty, and a new adjustment of nationality and state through national unification or secession. But soon antagonism among the supporters and the opponents of the social and institutional *status quo* stimulated new divisions among Great Powers largely satisfied with the existing territorial settlement. This gave rise to the early nineteenth-century version of the dialectic between the balance of power and the principle of collective security, which was to have an eventful future. The "collective security" of absolute monarchs dictated consistent mutual aid and intervention against what from their viewpoint was internal aggression of the forces of change, while geopolitical considerations, chiefly related to Russian expansionism, tended to interfere.[21] Metternich opposed Russian but favored Austrian and French intervention in Southern and Western Europe. Alexander was eager to combat rebels in Sicily and Spain, but like his successors, was equally anxious to go to war against another absolute dynast, the Sultan, on behalf of the Balkan rebels.

Nor was the half-hearted champion of the new principles any more consistent. Great Britain opposed intervention against revolution in Italy and Spain, and called a New World into existence to redress the balance of the Old. But she also opposed early aid to the insurgent Greeks and herself intervened in Portugal.

When balance of power and nationality could be reconciled, a new small state was born under the auspices of the Concert, as in the case of Belgium. Otherwise, the Concert either broke up, as over Italy, Latin America, and Spain, or else came into its own only after a war had been fought out, as in the case of the Balkans. Throughout this period, ever more new small states came into being in the name of nationality and constitutionalism, whatever their later courses. A restless movement toward a new socio-political equilibrium overrode even a reluctant Concert and the ultimately neutral balance of power.

The Concert occasionally extended its jurisdiction into the internal affairs of the smaller states. But it was helpless with respect to the domestic jurisdiction of the Great Powers themselves. It was unable even to attempt a readjustment by "peaceful change" when liberal nationality rose to its supreme challenge of the *status quo* in 1848. Subsequently, Napoleon III fell victim to his failure to reconcile the principle of nationality with the European equilibrium and the French national interest. The fusion of nationalism and military power played havoc with the traditional balance of power and the idea of nationality as well. In Bismarck, nationality found an avenger with a vengeance on the Vienna settlement. A majority of the Western European countries did move on internally toward a more dynamic social equilibrium under the aegis of liberalism. But the multinational empires farther to the east underwent a reactionary drive for homogeneous national power; and the spirit of Mazzini did not preside over the marriage of Social Darwinism and *Realpolitik* that generated a new imperialist era. Neither was that spirit, however, buried under their joint weight. Wilson and others were yet to revive the principle of national self-determination and mix success with failure.

The Concert's functional scope was no more adequate to deal with the economic consequences of the industrial revolution. A progressive disintegration of the largely apolitical free-trade system found the merely political Concert unable to provide itself with a substitute economic foundation. Military-political interventionism and occasional guarantee of small states had little bearing on the economic implications of their birth. It proved impossible for the Concert to go beyond occasional palliatives

when considerations of national power and interest deflected
growing economic interdependence into the channels of competitive protectionism and colonialism.

Gradually, Europe became too small to contain peacefully
within her confines the expanding political and economic forces.
Her diminution was accentuated by the rise of new Great Powers,
the United States and Japan. The Concert of Europe, however,
failed to enlarge its effective geographic scope in response to the
global extension of the effective balance of power. A gap opened
between the institution and its supporting principle.

Thus, a sporadic and fragmentary political Concert was not in
equilibrium as to its functional scope. A merely European Concert aggravated the imbalance with respect to the geographic
scope. A small state, Serbia, supplied the outward occasion for
the final breakup, which led to the disregard of the guaranteed
neutrality of another. It is hardly in doubt that the maladjustments feeding the crisis were most acute in the two eastern empires, the Russian and the Austro-Hungarian. In the final analysis,
however, the nineteenth-century diplomatic order was the victim
of a deepening multiple disequilibrium focused in the institutional
structure, security commitment, and scope — both functional and
geographic — of the Concert system.

Those conditions which favored international order in the
period appear in retrospect as unique and temporary; the inadequacies which led to its gradual disintegration were inherent
in the organizing principles of the nation-state system itself.

The drive for preponderance on the part of individual Great
Powers tended to frustrate the idea of their equilibrium and
concert, as well as their collective authority to distribute security,
welfare, and the prestige of independence under law among the
lesser members of the international community. Isolated instances
of such authoritative distribution assumed dictatorial forms and
did not command the free assent of all, including the most directly
affected, states. Statesmen did not behave so as to consistently
promote the functioning of the system. The required self-restraint of Great Powers, self-discipline of smaller communities,
and flexibility of all, but chiefly the balancer, states were missing
on crucial occasions. Sanctions for "dysfunctional" behavior
were arbitrary and unpredictable. Exposed to the growing pres-

sure of new moral and material forces, the system failed to combine in a satisfactory manner the seemingly competitive but fundamentally complementary needs of stability and change. The resulting maladjustment in the total environment of international relations could not be contained permanently by the military equipoise between the definitively disunited Powers.

In these circumstances, then, it is not surprising that the institution of the Concert failed to master the activated contradiction between the premises of hierarchy and the competitive implications of the balance of power.

In the harsher reality of international politics, it is possible to trace features of political theory and practice which are muted, often to the vanishing point, within a more developed community. Thus Michel's "iron law," that oligarchies arise and prevail (as long as they are united against internal discords and challenges from below), certainly applies to relations between Great and small Powers. So does the main thesis of Mosca's analysis. In international relations, too, the less numerous dominant group performs most political functions and tends to monopolize power; the more numerous class is controlled by the first, in a more or less legal or arbitrary and violent manner. Also the Great Powers like to rest their directorate on a "political formula" such as the idealized concept of the balance of power, the Concert of Powers, and various precepts of international morality and law. Nor is their discretion checked by counterforce alone. There is a measure of institutionally contrived "juridical equilibrium" between the ruling class and the governed, and among the individual members of the ruling class itself; and the anticipated approval or discontent of the controlled numerical majority amounts to an additional check from below.[22]

Yet Mosca's renovation and Pareto's circulation of the élites occurs by peaceful means even less frequently in international than in national affairs. Internecine conflict among the more powerful states is the more likely vehicle of change. A group can rule effectively only when it is cohesive, the Great Powers only when they are acting in real concert. When they are not, mutual competition with the aid of the smaller states scrambles the stratification, weakens the established, and facilitates the rise of new élites. Thus, most of the time, the Great-Power élite cannot exercise authority with appropriate social responsibility because it lacks the basic prerequisite: the sense of security flowing from unchallenged status. As a result, the Great Powers will rarely practice self-restraint on themselves and honesty on the lesser members. In such a situation, discretion easily degenerates into license; less liberty for most is the price for dubious order and security controlled by the few.

A disruptive competition for power aggravates the inadequacy of the idea of hierarchy, equating responsibility with power, in a society without firm rules of conduct and a forum where the élites can be called upon to account for the trust. This is the reason why the valid and the perennial in the idea of hierarchy is so inseparably tied up with the success of authoritative institutions, in our case international, to fill these gaps.

The international organization succeeding the nineteenth-century system moved in that direction. An acute sense of past failures, dramatized by the ascendant liberal-democratic ideology set off two complementary developments. There was, first, a swing from the hierarchical to the equalitarian alternative in political organization, manifest in a more thoroughgoing application of the idea of state equality and in the pressures for a more liberal collective implementation of the legal institutions of intervention, guarantee, and recognition of new states. The second development was the quest for a functional substitute for the two other discredited principles, the balance of power and the exclusive Concert of Great Powers.

Out of these two converging tendencies grew the idea of collective security as the new principle of a democratized international organization.

CHAPTER 2

THE STRUCTURE OF
INTERNATIONAL
ORGANIZATION

In having both traditional law and organiza-
tion reinforce rather than restrain the privileges of greater power,
the Concert system violated the first law of power-normative
equilibrium. Institutions indubitably must remain in a realistic
connection with their political and territorial bases; but they
also ought to control normatively the interaction of unequally
favored states. Only when both conditions are met can there be a
reciprocal adaptation rather than legalization of discretionary
power or its futile disregard. The ideal is a political concert of the
Powers under a dynamic law, limiting arbitrary discretion without stifling the politic in a juridical strait jacket, and generaliz-
ing rights, obligations, and their administration within the framework of an international organization which would include all
states in active, and the great ones in privileged, membership.

The structural equilibrium of international organization with
respect to its members and organs concerns in the first place the
influence and prestige of states under law; but the structure of
an organization is also important in shaping the attitudes of members and their readiness to assume and honor commitments. Since
the normative theory of international organization is best stated
in the respective covenants and charters, the discussion will in-
quire chiefly into the conditions of their efficacy.

THE STRUCTURAL EQUILIBRIUM

An organization is in structural equilibrium with regard to its
members when the ratios between the national power and the institutional influence of individual member-states are not too

disparate, and when the margin of attempted restraints does not exceed the limitations on the dynamics of power which major states will in fact tolerate. Moreover, structural equilibrium of a composite organization will depend on the make-up and jurisdiction of the several organs.

The objective is a reciprocal adjustment, within the suggested ratios and margins, between the principles and purposes of the organization and the existing facts of power and geography. A realistic appraisal must take into account a variable measure of power deformation, which subverts the operation of nominally neutral norms in the direction of greater power pressure. This is as true of concepts like sovereignty, self-help, and neutrality as of the right to vote in an organization. Deformation through power is the opposite of institutionalization of power and different from the institutional expression of superior power in privileged status and function. It consists primarily of more or less concealed *de facto* control by a Great Power of the policies and institutions of a formally independent but actually dependent state. Beneath overtly preserved legal forms the efficacy of "domestic jurisdiction" and "sovereignty" is eroded; the Great Power actually controls but has no legal responsibility for the conduct of the dependent government. The link between the form and the deformed operation of an institution is the induced or enforced compliance of the weaker state.

The more an equalitarian structure will ignore and try to level out power differentials, the greater will be the actual deformation. Excessive power deformation is, therefore, as much an index of structural disequilibrium as is the evasion or disruption of an institution by leading members.

A basic requirement of structural equilibrium is that the organization include, if possible, all powerful states which can affect its purpose; the second condition is a generally acceptable role for widely different states. A compromise must modify the principle of equality of status by the inequality of function; and the principle of legal equality, demanding representation for all, by the fact of actual inequality, attaching responsibility to real rather than merely formal power. As a rule, the smaller states will emphasize equality; the Great Powers tend to favor the hierarchical principle with discretionary authority for some kind of directorate. Yet neither position is clear-cut. The more exposed minor states will be attracted by more substantial security through less equalitarian institutions with real authority. And the history of the League and the United Nations confirms that of the Concert of Europe to show that the Great Powers are no more united or consistent regarding the place of smaller states in the government of the world; they tend to develop sympathy for the claims of others as they fall out among themselves.[1]

The quest for a satisfactory compromise takes place in and through various organs. An institution is in structural equilibrium with respect to its organs when their respective powers correspond to the composition and the average national power of their membership; the jurisdiction of the several organs ought to be differentiated and integrated in such a way as to make them reinforce and supplement rather than frustrate each other.

At the turn of the century, the principle of equality was applied rather radically in the plenary body of the Hague Conferences — the extreme swing from the Concert hierarchy to equality was in keeping with the unreality of the proceedings. The equality was in any case procedural rather than substantive; its critics were incensed still further by the excessive claims of the smaller states in connection with plans for a permanent court of justice.[2] In part as a reaction to the excess, the founders of the League of Nations were at first in favor of exclusive representation of the Great Powers at least in the Council of the new organization. They settled for a compromise which improved the representation of the lesser states in comparison with the Concert, but legalized at the same time their inequality. All member-states received membership in the plenary body, the League Assembly, and the Great Powers were to occupy a privileged — i.e., permanent and majority — position in the Council. Having insisted on admission to the more exclusive body, in order to add institutionalized self-protection of their "aggregate interests" to the promised self-restraint of the greater states, the small states were assigned merely nonpermanent membership and the status of a minority.

It did not take long for the resulting measure of structural equilibrium to be upset. Nonpermanent members rose gradually from minority to majority in the Council, and at least two Great

Powers were absent from the League at all times. This greatly reduced the average national power of the Council's members and tended to decrease the organ's effective powers. Encouraged, some smaller states sought to transform their nonpermanent into a permanent seat so as to rise institutionally to Great-Power status, while the divorce between real and formal power in the Council encouraged the disgruntled Great Powers to transact much of their most important business outside the institutions of the League, thus "putting Geneva into the framework of Locarno" rather than vice versa.[3] To make things worse, the respective jurisdictions of the Council and the Assembly remained largely undefined, and the two organs failed to interact so as to reinforce each other. The idea of checks and balances between the Council and the Assembly was explicitly rejected in Paris, but the entire organization was safely kept in check by the principle of unanimity and mere recommendations in all its organs. For the smaller states, their formal "veto" implicit in the requirement of unanimity, however modified in practice, was an additional and important weight in the scales of their institutional influence.

Some have criticized this arrangement as too equalitarian. Yet the adverse effects of too much small-state representation and influence upon the leadership and initiative of the Great Powers can be exaggerated. The tacit and false assumption of such criticism is that an organ or organization consisting exclusively of Great Powers is by definition more efficient. Moreover, the presence and influence of minor states in an organ like the League Council is the consequence rather than the cause of the failure of the international élite to lead the community.

Still, the structure of the United Nations displays a determined weighting of the position of the Great Powers in the Security Council. Theirs is a permanent membership and, despite the nominal majority of the nonpermanent members, the henceforth exclusive veto gave each individual Great Power a preventive majority in most, if not all, substantive questions. There are thus really three political organs in the United Nations, each having successively fewer members with greater average national power and larger powers: the General Assembly composed of all member-states, the Security Council with eleven members, and the nucleus of the Council's five permanent members. The principal constitutional restraint on this last group's vast discretionary powers was meant to be the obligation to act in accordance with the purposes and principles of the organization, supported by a "proper balance" between the strictly differentiated competence of the General Assembly and Security Council. If the smaller organ was endowed with strong executive authority, primary responsibility for peace and security, and powers to decide and act on behalf of other states, the plenary Assembly was vested with extensive if subsidiary powers of debate and recommendation. Mutual integration of the two organs was to consist chiefly in the interpenetration of membership and the authority of the Assembly to debate and review the reports of the Council. But the Security Council was meant to be largely independent of an Assembly which would constitute not too strong a counterweight.[4]

A considerable number of the smaller states continued at San Francisco their efforts from the League period to strengthen the plenary body. They wanted the General Assembly to be a co-ordinate organ with powers of "concurrent action" or at least "supervision" and "review" of Security-Council decisions. The Great Powers, supported by some of the more exposed smaller states, defeated in the name of an effective organization the drive for a stronger Assembly, for more nonpermanent members in the smaller organ as a means to "a more real balance within the Security Council," and for greater emphasis on international law. It seemed as if the minor states found more solace than real compensation in pushing through a constitutional theory, interpreting the more powerful and exclusive organ as a mere "agent" of the Assembly in which "originally reside" all powers of the organization. A parliamentary supremacy for the Assembly had been opposed by the Great Powers; it was at variance with the doctrine of the separation of powers, applied to the structure of the United Nations by the American delegation; and it was thwarted in practice by the refusal of the Security Council to act as the executive of the plenary body. Yet the theory laid the groundwork for the subsequent revision of the balance of relative powers between the two organs as the General Assembly moved from a supplementary and subordinate to a substitutive position with regard to the Security Council.[5]

If all these matters concern primarily the institutional equilibrium between the Great Powers and the smaller states within the United Nations, the issue of the veto bears in addition on such a balance among the Great Powers themselves.

A measure of concert among the Great Powers is a necessary condition of effective international organization, nor can its absence be fully compensated for. Yet agreement among the Powers is rarely spontaneous: the so-called agreement does and can mean in many instances no more than adjustable disagreement, resolved in compromise as an alternative to conflict. An essential inducement to such an agreement is a balance of power stabilized by a measure of self-restraint on the part of the Powers. This incentive can be merely reinforced by constitutional devices which would set up an institutional equilibrium among the Powers and counterbalance the large areas left to political discretion.

Before it became an obstacle to action, the requirement of unanimity of the Security Council's permanent members on substantive issues, the so-called veto power, had been meant to inspire Great-Power coöperation. The Yalta formula was to create "a kind of equilibrium between majority power on the one hand, and veto power on the other." The minority Great Power or Powers received at least preventive institutional influence and the restraints on any Great Power were reduced. This promised to keep both the conceded influence and the attempted restraints well within the requisite ratios and margin with respect to the claims and the likely tolerance of actual power. If this were the justification of the right to unanimity, it was hoped that the implied "duty to unanimity" would be stimulated by an arrangement making the Great Powers effective only when acting in unison. In a way, the veto power can be seen as an institutional balancer preventing the hegemony of the majority and the impotence of the minority Great Power or Powers in the organization.[6]

Anxiety over the consequences of inaction takes the place of drama once the veto power is seen from the angle of the minor states. It compensates for the minority position of the Great

Powers as a group in the most powerful organ, and is in turn counterbalanced by the collective veto theoretically available to the nonpermanent members which, if exercised, would condemn the Great Powers to "collective impotence." Yet the arrangement does increase considerably, though not without bounds, the institutional weight of the Great Powers relative to the smaller states, divested of their individual veto of the League times both in the Security Council and in the majoritarian General Assembly. Headed by the more tried ones among them, the smaller states acquiesced ultimately in the prerogative of the major Powers with the proviso that it would be exercised with self-restraint and as a trust under the principles of the Charter. They continue to prefer the restoration of Great-Power agreement to the abolition of the veto power even after the experience with the Soviet practice. Such agreement involves a measure of mutual restraint, more substantial security, and is preferable to the protection by one Great Power against others.[7]

Moreover, the Great Powers would not accept in any event a serious curtailment of their supremacy; the veto merely expresses the fact that a Great Power has a larger stake (and say) in most matters and itself cannot be constrained without a major war which would disrupt, or at least profoundly affect, the organization. If the veto protects the sovereignty of the major states, provisions concerning the duty to carry out the decisions of the Security Council would extend it while limiting that of the lesser members. Under an implemented Charter only the Great Powers would remain, more or less, in a state of nature; the smaller states would have paid the price of a limited but effective international government.

On the face of it, the original structure of organs and powers provided for by the Charter was realistic: the drafters introduced the necessary safeguards but adjusted both restraints and institutional powers to the conditions of actual power among major and minor states.

THE STRUCTURAL DYNAMICS

The structural equilibrium of both organs and members, however, is no less dynamic than the total powers and effectiveness of the organization as a whole; constitutional blueprints are modified, or their implementation prevented, by unforeseen events in the course of actual practice.

In theory, a dynamic structural equilibrium can be progressive, stable, or unstable. It is progressive when the several organs reinforce each other in such a way that an increase in the powers of one organ sets off a countervailing increase in the powers of another organ, resulting in greater sum of powers for the entire organization. This might be called the internationalist ideal with regard to international organization; an ideal which has, however, been hitherto realized only nationally, e.g., when the expansion of the American federal government was stimulated by competition between the executive and the legislative branches at the expense of the states. An equilibrium is still stable, though no longer progressive, when the decrease in the effective powers of one organ produces an offsetting increase in the powers of another, returning the total powers of the organization nearer the original position. In an unstable equilibrium, finally, a shift in the distribution of powers among organs initiates a cumulative decline in the powers of the organization as a whole.

While the stable-equilibrium mechanism may be applied to the United Nations, the organization now displays also the signs of an unstable equilibrium, characteristic of the sliding decline of the over-all powers of the League. The unifying feature of the structural dynamics in the two organizations is the shift of the point of gravity from the Council to the Assembly, increasing derivatively the relative institutional weight of the more ambitious small states after the Great Powers had failed to agree and lead in the Council.[8] An unstable equilibrium is fatal when the apparently gaining organ and members are the weaker ones with less effective powers and average national power; responsibility is then divorced from power and the victims of aggression are not saved.

In the League, the increase in the relative competence of the Assembly — manifest in the Sino-Japanese and the Chaco conflicts and accelerated during the Ethiopian crisis — was paralleled by a gradual decline in the powers and effectiveness of the Council and the organization as a whole. The discomfiture of the Assembly after the Ethiopian fiasco generalized and deepened the downward movement.

In the face of deadlock in the veto-ridden Security Council, the idea of a concert of Powers degenerated within the United Nations, too. The permanent members of the Council managed to agree on joint measures only occasionally, when and as long as they happened to be neutral, uncommitted, or their policies ambivalent with respect to specific issues such as Kashmir, Palestine, or Indonesia. The resulting deflection of jurisdiction to the General Assembly started with the cases of Franco Spain and Greece, gained momentum with the "Little Assembly" scheme, and culminated in the passage of the Uniting for Peace Resolution in 1950; it has of late reduced the relative stature and autonomy of the specialized councils and agencies as well. The Security Council, except for fitful bursts of mostly controversial activity, has receded into relative obscurity, the authority of the now preponderant General Assembly has not been meaningfully strengthened in the long run, and the prestige of the organization itself has declined. Yet certain features did suggest the operation of a stable equilibrium.

The Uniting for Peace Resolution extended the competence of the General Assembly and its responsibility for international security in order to counteract the danger that paralysis in the Security Council would reduce to zero the organ's effective powers in a moment of crisis; the shift filled a jurisdictional vacuum and restored to some extent the total security powers of the organization. The United States initiated the counterbalancing move so that it might be able to employ its resources and those of like-minded states under the auspices of the General Assembly in the case of a future aggression. Therein lies the chief difference from the League pattern, but also a major weakness of the arrangement.

In the first place, the Resolution formalized the failure of the idea of a Great-Power concert embodied in the Charter. One of the Great Powers called the smaller states of the Assembly to greater institutional power and responsibility so as to redress the balance upset in the Security Council. Many of the smaller states coöperated with the move. But, as in the case of Red Chinese aggression in Korea, they are unlikely to use their new institutional power to authorize enforcement if this means provoking the possible reprisals of actual military power. And the United States itself can be expected to support the new arrangement only when it controls the required majority in the Assembly and is disposed to act against a particular case of aggression. Besides, the General Assembly can merely recommend, so that the newly distributed total powers of the United Nations remain far short of those under a really implemented Charter. The circumvention of the veto power altered radically the original institutional equilibrium to the detriment of the minority Great Power. This was certain to antagonize the Power aimed at, encourage it further to transact important business outside the organization and, in the view of some, reduce the usefulness of the United Nations as an agency of conciliation without materially increasing its stature as an agency of enforcement.

Another dynamic factor in the structural equilibrium are the alignments of member-states as they develop within a functioning organization. Great Powers wish for a more or less voluntary voting support by smaller states, which can amount to practically automatic majority for a favored Power; the smaller states on their part like to combine into independent voting blocs. Both types of groupings are brought together by affinities of various kinds, such as geographic location, security concerns, ideology, cultural and historical kinship, and the desire to control an issue or the organization as a whole. They display different degrees of solidarity and fixity. France was frequently able to count on an automatic majority in the League, the United States is experiencing the weakening of a similar position in the United Nations. The Little Entente states constituted a voting bloc in the League Assembly, and the General Assembly saw the emergence of Latin American, Arab and Arab-Asian, Soviet, NATO, Scandinavian, and British Commonwealth blocs.[9]

Unless completely dominated by a Great Power, a voting bloc cannot but strengthen the position of its members in the parliamentary game of balancing and bartering influence in multilateral diplomacy. Today, the combination of any two important blocs can exercise a collective veto over the two-thirds majority requirement of the General Assembly; the Latin Americans have a strong bargaining position with regard to the United States as an indispensable nucleus for a friendly majority; and the expanding Asian-African bloc is even more independent, unpredictable, and thus influential. The cohesion of the blocs was always great on procedural and notably electoral issues; it has been growing on substantive issues, such as colonialism, as well. Fixed blocs and majorities are certain to reduce the desirable flexibility and realism of the structural equilibrium. They distort the requisite ratios between power and influence by increasing disproportionately the influence of one Great Power supported by a host of weak states or of a mass of largely powerless minor states. This is not, objectively considered, too good for the organization. A gap or imbalance between institutional and actual power entails dangers, notably for the weaker states, which can be increased by their irresponsible and unduly pretentious behavior with regard to conflicts among the Great Powers.

Having quite a special interest in international organization, the smaller states like to visualize themselves as a qualitative and moral factor in world affairs. They stress normative principle against power and excessive political discretion; objectivity, independence, and good faith against opportunism and satellitism. They wish to shape the structural equilibrium so as to maximize their influence and compensate for their weakness. The less involved small states may even try as mediators and uncommitted voters to "hold the balance" among the Great Powers within the organization so as to escape absorption in the military-political balance outside it. In theory at least, many of them favor the expansion of the organization's functions and jurisdiction.[10]

In fact, however, the small states frequently obstruct such expansion when the price is less national sovereignty and more international commitment. They oppose extensive authority for the Great Powers, but make them responsible for the results of defaulted leadership. Lesser members have often provided excellent individual leaders for international organization, but have also made a nuisance of themselves by interfering in matters beyond their purview. They do not always realize that mediation between major Powers will be successful only when those Powers desire it as a face-saving avenue to compromise. The lesser states were not immune to abuse of their veto in the League and are thus in no good position to be critical of the Great-Power veto in the United Nations. Their emphasis on principle is in their best self-interest. For states which are light on the scales of power, realism lies in a show of idealism. But actually they fail to act on principle as often as the Great Powers, and thus also fail to exploit to the maximum the potential of international organization for strengthening their position in world affairs. Their great excuse is that in most instances the area of their freedom and choice is smaller than that of the major states.

It would seem that the Great Powers have no comparable interest in international organization. They may fancy themselves free to use, advance, or obstruct its operations as their momentary interests dictate. Yet, in fact, even a Great Power like the Soviet Union has remained within an organization where it is in almost permanent minority and wields relatively little positive influence — the mightiest find it worth while to contend for, or at least frustrate, the "power" of international organization.

There is one point of agreement among Great Powers most divided on concrete issues: they are united in wishing to perpetuate and if possible enlarge their actual power by institutional means. They distrust, however, the rigidity and the limitation on freedom of action implicit in normative rules laid down in advance, and resent the interference of smaller states in matters of high policy. They wish that the powers to be exercised in the organization were permissive rather than mandatory so as to strengthen their hand but keep it free at the same time. They expect the organization to be active or passive, an impartial mediator or active partisan, according to their changing needs. When they are in accord, they favor a structural arrangement which would mirror accurately the disposition of relative weight in the balance of power. When they are divided, the majority Powers seek to reshape the original structure in favor of the smaller states through whom they may hope to control the organization, while the minority Power or Powers tend to insist on the privileges of the more hierarchical structure. Once the influence of any Great Power in the organization wanes, so does its positive interest in promoting the institution's standing and authority.

The pattern is clearer in the United Nations, but its elements were present in the League, too. When divided Great Powers desire a concrete settlement or compromise, they are likely to pursue it outside rather than through the facilities of the organization

— irrespective of whether such a procedure is or is not provided for and sanctioned by the organization's constitution. This is especially the case when one or more Great Powers are not its members. Locarno bid fair to supersede Geneva in the 1920's, and Geneva to take place of the United Nations in the 1950's. Weimar Germany and Red China were still outside of the world body, and all Powers wished for privacy from interference.

Such problems go deeper than to points of prestige and procedure. They suggest a relationship between an organization's structure and its fate.

THE DILEMMA OF STRUCTURE

An evaluation must neither belittle nor overestimate the importance and possible effect of a structural arrangement. A good structure should mitigate the inequalities and help institutionalize the more drastic uses of power. Any attempt, however, to counterbalance actual power by institutional checks beyond an ideal equilibrium point is futile and dangerous; the impact will in any event be limited by the power deformation of too far-reaching restraints.

An institutional arrangement should not try either to repeal or merely to legalize the natural law of Great-Power ascendancy, but should constitutionalize it. The important question is whether the Powers will exercise their controlling influence in world affairs within or outside of restraining institutions. As the integrative process advances to institutions with more authority, emphasis is transferred from formal equality of juridical status to inequality of function; the "ruling class" of the organized international community comes to exercise its supremacy within a general organization under law rather than merely in fact or within particular and exclusive institutions. More international "democracy" will mean less integration. The password to ordered international relations is, therefore, not international democracy overnight but progression toward constitutionalism, conceived as the protection of legitimate rights and restraint on unruly power from the interplay of the institutional, military-political, and social factors in international relations.

Whatever one may think of its initial equilibrium with respect to its members and organs, the League deteriorated as several

Great Powers failed to join, left, or lost interest in the organization. In the resulting vacuum one or two of the remaining Great Powers, supported by like-minded smaller states, could dominate increasingly powerless organs. Relatively speaking, Europe was as overrepresented in the League as it has been underrepresented in the United Nations. The virtue of the less elaborate structure of the League was its flexibility. It did not stake so much on an elusive agreement among Great Powers. In the United Nations, as originally contemplated, the power and influence of the Great Powers were to be exercised in the Security Council within the bounds of broad principles and the general interest. The smaller states accepted their subordinate position in return for the promise of security under law; they kept at least in constitutional theory their collective veto in the Council and their numerical superiority and equal vote in a General Assembly endowed with subsidiary but still important powers. The privileged position of the major states entailed more realistic power-influence ratios and margins of attempted restraints on power than the League's bent toward equalitarianism, legalism, and automatism. Yet the hard core of the elaborate structure hinged on the frail premise of Great-Power agreement. With its collapse went the Charter's full implementation and the organization itself was jeopardized.

We are touching here on the perhaps crucial problem of international organization. Coöperative adjustment of disagreements among the Great Powers is indisputably the most important single prerequisite of a really effective organization. Such "accord" is, however, neither easy to materialize nor likely to endure. It is preposterous to suspect the Western statesmen responsible for the Charter of the naïveté to have thought otherwise; their error, if any, was to extend to the organization of powers in the United Nations their single-minded approach to the conduct of the war and the postwar settlement. They failed to reinsure themselves sufficiently against bad faith and failure. By aiming high, they risked correspondingly much. The gamble with regard to the United Nations was to centralize it to a point that required a corresponding concentration of powers in the hands of the Great Powers. It took a controversial interpretation and adaptation of the Charter later on to escape the bad side of the original alternative: international government by the major

Powers, induced to union by their very immunity and virtual omnicompetence, or international anarchy with no central authority at all. In a way, the unrealism of the Charter is in its attempt to be too realistic. The pendulum again swung too far the other way.

After the original structure of the United Nations had been undermined by the cleavage placing the Great Powers into rigid majority and minority positions, the veto became an even more vital feature of the structural equilibrium than was initially assumed. If the presence of all Great Powers in a world organization is the minimum condition of its global character, structural equilibrium, and efficiency, the veto may have saved the United Nations from one kind of disequilibrium fatal to the League. Even as it is, the League's successor, too, no longer includes all effective Powers of the day. On the other hand, the abuse of the veto power by the Soviet Union — chiefly, if not exclusively; and on a large scale, if not as outrageously as commonly believed — has been a source of frustration for the central organ of the United Nations and the majority of the Great Powers therein.

This suggests a dilemma for international organization. To be really effective it must be centralized; centralization involves more individual and collective powers for the big nations; yet these powers will tend to cancel themselves out as the latent conflict between the principles of hierarchy and equilibrium of power is activated by conflict of political objectives among the major states. This will hit hardest the more authoritative organ. Thus, in actual operation, the requirements of structural equilibrium with respect to individual members may easily frustrate the equilibrium of the really exercisable powers of the more exclusive Council and the more representative Assembly. There is one way out of the deadlock in the authoritative organ: regional and jurisdictional decentralization. Impaled on the horns of the dilemma, the majority in the United Nations sought (with no assured lasting success) a new structural equilibrium and greater actual effectiveness on a lower level of jurisdictional centralization, in addition to a concurrent process of regionalization.

To be sure, structural arrangements, formal powers, and institutional balancing in themselves mean little without an adequate security commitment and functional and geographic scope for the organization, which would counteract military-political and so-cio-economic disequilibria and mold conditions in all relevant spheres of international relations. The vital problem of scope will be elaborated upon in due course. At this point, the discussion of the structural equilibrium gives way to the analysis of institutional equilibrium with respect to collective-security commitment.

CHAPTER 3

THE COLLECTIVE-SECURITY COMMITMENT

It seemed for a while that the era of the balance of power was superseded by the era of collective security. Yet the stubborn continuity of international politics lurked beneath an apparently revolutionary change. The need for a link between the old and the new principle is disclosed the moment one inquires into the conditions of an effective system of collective security. Such a link can lessen some but not all of the shortcomings of collective security; among them is the issue of peaceful change, which highlights the problem of a judicious balance between stability and change in international relations.

THE THEORY OF COLLECTIVE SECURITY

It is a moot point whether the Concert system was or should have been recognized by international law. There is, however, no doubt that the traditional law sanctioned unilateral exercise of power in war, forcible self-help, reprisals, and duress in the conclusion of treaties; and the exercise of the right of intervention, recognition, and guarantee by the Great Powers, too, emphasized rather than checked power differentials. As applied, these concepts were the legal instruments of the policy of the balance of power and Great-Power supremacy; when redefined, they became the seminal concepts of collective security.

Henceforth, the norm is nonintervention or collective intervention in the affairs of other states, general reciprocal guarantee, and joint recognition of new states, implemented by all members of the international community under definite rules and procedures. The "collective measures" against a threat to the peace in accordance with the principles of the United Nations Charter carry on the spirit of the League Covenant. Collective intervention, overriding domestic jurisdiction in the case of enforcement, is now the sole lawful exception to the general prohibition of forcible intervention. And there is an incipient trend toward collective recognition expressing the interest of the entire international community in the rise of new states; once they met well-defined criteria, they would have a right and the other states a duty to recognition.[1] In one way or another, the League and the United Nations were concerned in the rise to international status of Iraq, Israel, the Republic of Korea, and Libya, among others. Nonetheless, collective recognition is still largely *lex ferenda*. Yet a generalized mutual guarantee, undertaken by all states under conditions defined in advance, has been *lex lata* since the adoption of the Covenant. It represented the high-water mark of the rise of smaller states to responsibility in world affairs.

There is, however, a reverse side to the progress. Thus the precept of nonintervention is liable to give rise to an interregnum of anarchy when unilateral self-help has been repudiated and reliable collective intervention is not yet practiced against abuses of independence that hide behind the taboo of domestic jurisdiction.* This may weaken the none too effective sanctions of a decentralized legal order and certainly has encouraged the more insidious forms of intervention which, by avoiding the illegal use of overt force, deprive the victim of any juridical recourse whatever. The gunboat has given way to the fifth column of a national or ideological minority controlled by a kindred Great Power, and the victim-state is all the worse for the change. Hence, protection against subtle forms of "internal aggression" is as imperative as safeguards against overt international aggression; and substitutes for unilateral Great-Power intervention as a police factor are no less necessary than substitutes for war as an instrument of change. Furthermore, without the backing of superior power, nonintervention as national policy or international precept is as futile as was the so-called Stimson Doctrine of nonrecognition of forcible conquest. The generalization of guarantee, too, does not constitute a genuine advance unless it is matched by the ability and willingness of states to observe the new commit-

---

* Witness the perplexities attending the Anglo-French intervention in the Middle East in reply to a series of provocative acts indulged in by Egypt's President Nasser.

ment. And, finally, another gap opens all too easily, as evidenced by the self-creation of Israel, between the ideal norm of international establishment and recognition, and the unilateral practice in an atmosphere of violence.

The international organization of security following World War I was a reaction to changes progressively wrought within and around the old central structure. It was basically a response to the disintegration of the Concert system, left behind by the changing conditions and dimensions of international relations; the reaction was aggravated by the disparity between the traditional principles of European organization and the new moral, and in part moralistic, outlook, made sensitive by the experience of the war and the retarded transference of democratic and liberal ideas into the conduct of foreign affairs. The insufficiency of the old system called for a substantial adjustment to altered conditions within the persistent realities of international life; the moral reaction, however, went beyond mere revision to an indiscriminate rejection of the sound and the perennial along with the obsolete and the temporary. Under the combined impetus of moral and very practical considerations on the part of the victorious but weakened Powers, the pendulum swung well beyond a realistic power-normative balance toward a radical attempt to transcend power through an organization designed to embody the norms of an overtaxed international law.

Rather than an adaptation and synthesis, the first result was a contradiction. Phrases like "balance of power," "Great-Power Concert," and "imperialism" were repudiated, while the corresponding facts persisted unintegrated and, as it were, illegally within the new system. They could not but distort its operations. A discrepancy arose between reality and naïve thought, between the measure of international reform deemed feasible and that which was actually possible.

In terms of the earlier discussion of the balance of power, the principle of collective security was designed to moralize the morally neutral and unreliable features of the older principle, and to systematize in the form of law its conventional normative aspects. Competitive balancing of military-political power was to be sublimated into the weighing of rights in peaceful settlements; a general guarantee was to implement the interdependence of states irrespective of their geographical location. Where the balance of power proscribed imbalance and directed its fundamental sanctions against the suspected unbalancer, the law of collective security outlawed aggression and prescribed specific sanctions against the objectively identified aggressor. The declared object of the new system was to preserve the territorial integrity and political independence of individual states; concern with the distribution of power and security, equated with established rights, was merely implied. The mutually tolerant association among the balance of power, war, and international law ceased to be legitimate. A collective order is antithetical to concepts like self-help, self-judgment, and unilateral reprisals; resort to war and force became progressively illegal except for self-defense and the implementation of joint sanctions, constituting a *bellum justum* against the crime of aggression.[2] A reciprocal general guarantee among fully sovereign states was to ensure the maintenance of a just peace, rather than a just equilibrium. Thus, a new doctrine of aggression combined with the revived doctrine of the just war to modify the principle of the balance of power.[3]

Superimposing the idea of international community on the nation-state system, a fairly systematic doctrine, the normative theory of collective security, evolved out of the reaction to traditional principles. It based its major promise to the states on a major premise about peace, war, and the international community. The promise of spontaneous or directed mutual assistance against aggression was derived from the premise of the indivisibility of peace in an interdependent world. From this relation between promise and premise stemmed the expectation of a reliable connection between promise and performance. A war of aggression was considered unlikely among nationally self-determined democratic states. If it should occur, economic interdependence would lend compelling force to automatic sanctions. Military coercion was thus but a hypothetical last resort in the background. War, though still possible, was considered to be controllable, and general disarmament would further reduce the likelihood of conflict. Even though the defensive use of force was not abdicated, the moral force of public opinion was chiefly relied upon. Peaceful settlement was to be the substitute for war.

The shift was from the supremacy of power to the rule of law, from a competitive to a coöperative international order, from coercion typical of imperialism to consent characteristic of federative organization. Collective security rested on the good faith of the member-states and the impartiality of the system. Since a general system is best suited to serve the common good of peace, particular arrangements and alliances would be largely superfluous. In the event that dissatisfaction with the *status quo* could not be met within existing treaties by methods of peaceful settlement, justified claims for revision might still be dealt with. Appropriate provisions and the evolutionary character of the system would facilitate an equitable adjustment of conflicting requirements of stability and change. Another apparent incompatibility between national sovereignty guided by the Reason of State and international obligation with respect to war was declared resolved by means of "self-constraint." [4]

Thus, collective security seemed well designed to fulfill its two basic functions: first, to prevent or at worst repress by joint action in accordance with an advance commitment any aggression against the legal and political order; second, to encourage the peaceful adjustment of demands for change by creating a sense of security among nonaggressive states. As for the smaller ones, their position seemed to be guaranteed by equal representation, active participation, and extensive safeguards. Collective security could be confidently expected to rescue weak states if at all possible and never to destroy them as the balance of power had done on more than one occasion.

If the idealized definition of collective security, however, is submitted to a realistic examination emphasizing the competitive tendencies of power, the result is fairly damaging. The new principle is torn to pieces in the tension between the antithetical extremes of "Wilsonism" and "Hobbism." [5]

A self-consciously realistic critique magnifies the subjective, relative, and competitive character of security and welfare to a point which minimizes the interdependence of states for achieving these values. It represents the division of states into territorially satisfied and dissatisfied, *status quo* and *anti-status quo* nations as absolute and inevitable; and it contrasts the altruistic motivation allegedly requisite for effective security with the precarious state of international morality, public opinion, and observance of law. If in addition the ethics of behavior in affairs of state are defined in terms of self-interest and self-assertion rather than self-sacrifice, a devastating syllogism suggests itself easily. Participation in collective security frequently requires immediate self-sacrifice; states are motivated by self-interest and self-assertion; hence there can be no collective security. Nor is it less easy to ridicule the premise of an automatic or ultimate harmony of interests presumably underlying collective security.

It is possible to weaken these points. Collective security does not presuppose universal harmony: to provide for peaceful settlement of disputes and for collective enforcement is to admit the need for harmonizing national policies by deliberate efforts. Its real assumption is the possibility of expanding gradually the areas of community of interests, security, and welfare so as to contain and reduce the coexisting areas of conflict.

As already noted, states pursue not only immediate security, but also welfare and institutional influence as a form of prestige; they seek not power per se but a measure of security, welfare, and prestige exceeding, whenever possible, their "due" as determined by relative national power. To treat power as merely a means to other values is to mute the quest for an ever larger share of an apparently fixed quantity, equating the gain of one with the equivalent loss of others. Such an outlook is, of course, self-defeating: in mercantilistic trade policy, if the quest for a favorable monetary balance impoverishes the customer countries and transforms them into low-cost competitors; in "mercantilistic" security policy, if a limitless quest for a favorable margin of power is pressed so far as to impoverish the power-seeker himself and array against him a more powerful alliance of henceforth competing Powers. But, to make real sense and to do more than translate competition for power into a still aggravated contest for equally scarce values, the more liberal view must assume one thing: that there are policies qualitatively different from mere maximizing of relative national power which can generate and help distribute an increased supply of security, welfare, and prestige for all. Support for collective security — and for any kind of international and supranational institutions — implies faith in nothing more than their ability to be a means to that end. Interdependence is believed to provide a realistic foundation for an enlarged conception of the national interest that will induce ever more nations to coöperate in the undertaking.

And, it may be argued in counterattack, the realists' all-inclusive conception of national power and their exclusive interpretation of the national interest make any coöperative scheme appear utopian. It is easy for a viewpoint which focuses only the power struggle to avoid the naïveté of mechanical harmony; but it must postulate an equally mechanical coincidence of interests in order to escape the nightmare of incessant conflict.

On the other hand, the realistic critique is not alone in questioning, apart from the practicability, the extreme implications of collective security as an absolutist, legalistic, and static system. It is altogether possible that the drive for absolute security may become an obsession, and peace be seen as a purely formal state signifying only the absence of war; this may obscure the plurality of legitimate values and the many ways of attaining any one of them. Moreover, an a priori legal system may reject the use of force totally only to expand it into a total war by all when challenged.

If the traditional philosophy attends primarily to the consequences of a war for the balance of power, the ideology of collective security is preoccupied with the origins and the responsibility for a breach of peace. Consequently, preventive war against an obviously expansionist and provocative Power is as much anathema as an aggressive war of expansion. The blessing can be a mixed one. A government bent on subverting the established order, as for instance Nazi Germany in the thirties, will avail itself of the privileged sanctuary of the collective-security system in order to prepare for its destruction. Poland had suggested in vain a preventive action against Hitler before she tried to make her private peace with him by means of a bilateral pact of non-aggression; and Ethiopia had to desist from timely preventive measures against Italian troop concentrations in order not to become technically the aggressor.[6]* Once aggression has been committed, however, collective security seems to be a perfect medium for spreading the conflict. The balance of power with

---

* Most recently, Israel has put herself very nearly in such a position when resorting to fairly legitimate self-defense against actual and threatened harassment by another dictator.

the aid of neutrality is supposed to promote localization of strife; under collective security, the premise of the indivisibility of peace implies general mobilization of all members against the aggressors, making a limited war possible only against minor states. The problem is real, especially in a world divided into antagonistic power blocs. But, under whatever principle, a localization of conflict among unequally powerful states is likely to mean the abandonment of the weaker to the mercies of the stronger Power. This was the idea when Imperial Germany sought to localize the Austro-Serbian clash in 1914 and when Mussolini boasted of having localized the Ethiopian war. On the other hand, the Korean experience suggests that a fairly effective collective action can keep the scope and the objectives of a conflict within limits, despite direct or indirect involvement of several Great Powers.

In the final analysis, the distaste for collective enforcement would seem to stem from the more general view that the coercion of whole nations is impracticable, impolitic, and inhuman.[7]

Apart from its absolutism, the legalism of collective security is most flagrantly open to criticism with respect to the problem of peaceful change. The issue is one of a right balance between security and justice, stability and change. A system which outlaws force and war without providing adequate alternative methods of legitimate change may be charged with substituting its own moral ambiguities for those of the balance of power. It is then questioned as static and negative, and attacked in the name of a desirable and in the long run irresistible dynamism of life itself. And indeed, the attempt to abolish politics in a system of legal rights and automatic commitments is likely to aggravate the contrary power drives under the impetus of one more form of power-normative disequilibrium. The interwar experience in Europe may, in fact, be simplified into a contest between opposing conceptions of stability and change on the part of the revisionist and the anti-revisionist states. Today, the problem survives chiefly in the colonial issue and its impact on the requirements of collective security.[8]

The gap between collective security and change is not unbridgeable, even in law. It is, however, only widened by a formalistic notion of peaceful settlement and a territorial view of peaceful change. Both approaches are static: one in seeking a frozen *status quo*, the other in attempting to move from one fixed territorial frontier to another. Peaceful settlement by arbitration or adjudication is inadequate unless judicial discretion is sufficiently authoritative and dynamic to reconcile rights with interests. In fact, the more powerful states are especially unwilling to submit their really vital interests to compulsory adjudication within the framework of established rights. Methods of change by international legislation have been no more adequate, although the United Nations has won a few credits in dealing with the former Italian colonies and Palestine. Change by means of traditional diplomacy has resulted in most cases from some kind of pressure or coercion. If methods of effecting change are not satisfactory, demands for change in the name of sovereign independence, ethnic unity, economic self-sufficiency, population pressure, or national prestige are often exaggerated. They frequently hide the lust for territorial expansion and domination under a respectable phrase. A deeper and more constructive approach to this issue, yet to be discussed, is needed.[9]

Thus, collective security and the study of it have been caught between the extremes of legalistic idealism and power-political realism. Like the balance of power, collective security has been criticized for its inability to make ideal and fact coincide. Some idealists saw only the less attractive manifestations of the balance of power and substituted collective security for the discredited principle of a less enlightened period. Many realists condemn collective security by contrasting its actual achievement with an impossible ideal or with the mirage of an idealized balance of power. They reject collective security as unworkable and as dangerous if it should happen to work.

It is worth while to try to mediate between the opposing views and seemingly opposite principles by examining the realistic conditions necessary to the ideal's approximation.

COLLECTIVE SECURITY AND THE BALANCE OF POWER

It is possible to list the prerequisites of an effective collective security almost *ad infinitum*.[10] Some of them are essential; and among them is an extensive conception of the national interest on the part of nonaggressive states and a determined initiative to collective action on the part of at least some of the Great Powers.*

With the political requirements merges a set of conditions bearing on the concept of equilibrium. They include a relatively diffuse distribution of power among individual states capable of coalescing into an at best overwhelming preponderance of power against the aggressor; an over-all institutional equilibrium of international organization, most particularly with regard to a mutual commitment against aggression; and a high degree of socio-economic interdependence and equilibrium constituting a check on unilateral ventures and a welfare foundation of security.

Although the relationship between collective security and the balance of power is relatively recent, it has a chequered history. Woodrow Wilson did not, as some latter-day exponents of "Wilsonism" suggest, ignore the place of power in international life. But he contributed to the confusion by sweeping attacks on the "balance of power," failing to distinguish between aspects unnecessary to his vision and aspects which he himself emphasized as the vision's necessary underpinning. The "old order" of the balance of power was to be supplanted by the "reign of law" under a League of Nations. Collective security as a principle complementary to that of national self-determination was opposed to the "great game, now forever discredited, of the balance of power" as the symbol of territorial dealings in dynastic relations. The balance of power stood condemned as "having always produced only *aggression and selfishness and war.*'" The "idea of the Great Powers" was included in the repudiation. Yet only the "unstable equilibrium of competitive interests" as the breeder of wars and destroyer of weaker states was really rejected in favor of "elasticity and security . . . under a League of Nations." Within the League, the "new balance of power" was to be "steady" and consist not of "one powerful group of nations set off against another, but a single overwhelming, powerful group of nations who shall be the trustee of the peace of the world." The requirement would be eased by the immediate disarmament of the defeated, and progressive reduction of the armaments of all Powers.[11]

The debate was not confined to the American President

---

* The distinction throughout is between *currently*, not *intrinsically*, aggressive and nonaggressive states.

Georges Clemenceau, the realistic leader of victorious but weakened France, eulogized the balance of power in opposition to the new ideas. An idealistic British Prime Minister, Ramsay MacDonald, considered the policy of support for the League of Nations as "exactly opposite" to that of the balance of power. It was left to the statesman of a small exposed state to hope for a favorable mutual reinforcement of the two. For Eduard Beneš the dominant need of the postwar era was a balance of power which would sustain the principles of the League. Otherwise, the League would fail and yield to blocs and coalitions.[12]

Throughout the debate the sobering insight of statesmanship was required to reveal the true nature of the interplay between the balance of power and collective security, obscured on the plane of doctrinaire ideology. A formal statement of the relationship will draw on the distinction between the dynamics and the principle of the balance of power, established in the discussion of the latter. Accordingly, the requisite preponderance of power on the part of the sanctionist Powers will result when the ideologically neutral equilibrium dynamics responds to the principle of collective security, specified in the general commitment, and enough powerful nations join in collective action against aggression. The preceding section described how the principle of collective security modified the principle of the balance of power; it remains now to add that the new principle must include and control the dynamics of power equilibrium in order to be effective. There is no mutual exclusiveness but there is need for a synthesis. The pattern reminds one of Hegelian dialectic: the balance of power is both negated by the idea of collective security and included in an effective security system as a devalued instrumental component.

It might seem that the requirement of a decisive preponderance of power on the side of the defenders of the *status quo* against aggression is not only a modification of the principle of the balance of power, but is also contrary to the flexibility of the equilibrium dynamics. The requisite preponderance is, however, not a fixed situation. It results when the ideology of collective security elicits joint opposition of states to concrete aggression. What really matters is potential preponderance of power in defense of the established order, actualized in response to the mutual-assistance commitment. Flexibility is implied in the theoretical impartiality of the collective system, directed against any and all aggression anywhere. From another viewpoint, even a fixed preponderance is justified as long as it is not available for the overthrow of the *status quo* by aggression and conquest. Inasmuch as both are outlawed under the system, such a preponderance would, in theory, immediately dissolve if one or more states attempted to misuse it to such an end. It is thus possible to speak not only of potential but also of conditional preponderance as the condition of effective collective security.

Once the balance of power does not sustain collective security, it tends to inhibit or altogether destroy it. Ideally, potential or conditional preponderance should be the ready if indispensable instrument of collective enforcement. In fact, however, the balance of power tends to interfere with the collective system as a directive principle in proportion to the latter's imperfections. In the case of Ethiopia, the desire to preserve the balance of power in Europe against Germany as the chief potential unbalancer weakened the will to employ the existing preponderance against Italy, the actual aggressor in the Mediterranean but possible ally in Europe. The situation becomes bizarre when the principle of the balance of power is revived by one *status quo* Power against another in order to contain a real or imagined preponderance brought about in the name of collective security. Such was the three-cornered contest involving Great Britain, France, and Germany in the interwar period. By withdrawing, the United States invalidated the original presumption of assured preponderance on the side of the Versailles Powers; France reacted by seeking a less certain and therefore more rigid preponderance on a smaller scale; and this in turn provoked the British to counterbalance France by Germany. The result was balance-of-power politics within and outside both the League as an institution and collective security as an ideology.

When a general system is weakened, regionalized collective security may itself become an instrumentality of the global balance of power. This tends to be the situation today. The circle is then both complete and vicious, leading the expositor to the thought that the statement of the problem from the angle of the balance of power, if not overly helpful, would at least be simpler:

the ideology of collective security either impedes the operation of the balance of power and is then disregarded, or subserves it and is used as a convenient instrument.

Conversely, however, there is a sense in which effective collective security can be a means for nonaggressive states to overcome the limits of the balancing process. It will be remembered that, according to the principle of diminishing marginal utility of increasing politico-economic costs and decreasing advantages of progressively piled-up national or allied effective military power, there is ideally a point of greatest possible relative power and security in the balancing process. Yet nonaggressive states can increase their joint power and security beyond such a point by substituting for the traditional method a generalized collective-security commitment; apart from lessening the economic burdens of separate national armaments, an effective commitment of the kind would give rise to a potential preponderance of power without of itself provoking a counter-alliance or other preventive measures of the usual sort.

In any event, to the extent that the law and ideology of collective security are in themselves unable to govern the balance of power, additional means of control become important: international integration and international regulation of national armaments. The first approach would institutionalize the power equilibrium by means of advance coördination of the military and economic resources of member-states designed to sustain the mutual-security commitment; the second approach, which may but need not deëmphasize the security commitment, would at least stabilize the balance of relative power on a lower level of expenditure and tension by reducing and supervising properly adjusted armaments of the Powers. Both of these complementary and far from easily realizable methods may be necessary; they are not sufficient.

In a really effective collective system, the balance of power would be only one component of the requisite larger equilibrium. The long-range foundations of security are woven of interrelated military-political, socio-economic, and institutional threads. A favorable military-political balance may prevent or repress aggression and check expansionist responses to economic interdependence. A socio-economic equilibrium lessens the strains and incentives to conflict, and the complexity of social and economic relations in the modern world makes a victory almost as onerous as defeat. This may constitute as great a deterrent to war as fear of rival national power. And finally, the institutional equilibrium is also important because it is intimately related to the military-political and socio-economic equilibrium by way of the equally interrelated structure, security commitment, and functional scope of international organization. All this suggests that long-range security is inseparable from welfare and the satisfaction of national prestige under law, and that these rest on the existence of a multiple equilibrium in the world. This fact is reflected in the attempts to combine military-political integration and a coöperative approach to long-range socio-economic problems in a concentric attack on the problem of war and peace through international organization, beginning with the League of Nations.

The trend is important since an integrative approach in multiple-equilibrium terms might mitigate the conflict between collective security and peaceful change. If Articles 19 of the League Covenant and 14 of the United Nations Charter proved inoperative, a deeper approach is contemplated in Chapters IX and X of the Charter and schemes for the European Coal and Steel Community or the Jordan River Valley development in the Near East. Especially where territorial disputes divide neighbors, different areas and levels of functional and institutional integration may be the only substitute for repressed claims or war.

Peaceful change of a coöperative character depends, of course, on the disposition to mutual compromise under the pressure of common interests. In any event, the security of the parties to constructive peaceful change must be dealt with concurrently. This means that in most cases the new equilibrium to be established will require simultaneous institutional, socio-economic, and military-political adjustments. Where this can be done, requirements of collective security and peaceful change, instead of being in conflict, can be dovetailed both materially and organizationally. A European Community might be the framework of mutual and external security as well as of peaceful change without upsetting the internal balance and being subverted into a vehicle of "peaceful" conquest by the stronger party or parties. If an equilibrated adjustment cannot be achieved because the potential integration area straddles two or more antagonistic security areas, then the likelihood of deadlock between collective security and peaceful change remains. Yet the real culprit is then the sovereign multi-state system itself.

THE COLLECTIVE-SECURITY COMMITMENT

If the principle of collective security is to be brought to bear on the dynamics of the balance of power so as to muster a preponderance of lawful power on the side of the defenders of the *status quo*, international organization must be in equilibrium with respect to a high level of security commitment. Only then can the general norms of the system contain anarchic power and counteract the tendencies inherent in unequal power and particular geographical location of individual states.

A collective-security commitment can be on different levels. It is lowest in the case of neutrality. It is possible to argue that neutrality was superseded by the principle of collective security as obsolete ideologically, morally, and materially. Ideologically, it is incompatible with the idea of a universal obligation. Partiality becomes a duty. When interdependent nations engage in contests over the fundamental questions of man's destiny, neutrality acquires the odium of an immoral and antisocial status. In addition, it is legally precarious. The supposedly "neutral" law of neutrality tends to be deformed in the pragmatic adjustment of belligerent and neutral claims in favor of the always more active and often greater power of the belligerent. Only materially strong neutrals can assert and maintain their status. Weaker states, except for the most favorably situated, must endure the arbitrary will of the belligerents individually and can rarely unite to enforce their rights collectively. Finally, the strategic requirements of modern warfare have rendered neutrality difficult to observe and in most cases impossible to maintain. Where Belgium has become the symbol of the violation of neutrality as a rule, Ireland, Switzerland, and Sweden illustrate dubious exceptions. Yet neutrality continues to be the refuge of states protected by others. As long as there are nations ready to rise against the ultimate consequences of large-scale aggression, the "indivisibility of peace" can be treated as a slogan of disreputable origin and questionable empirical foundation.[13]

On the other hand, the collective-security commitment can be on a high level. Its object then is for the obligated states to desist from, and collectively resist, all use of force except in support of the law. The scope of such a commitment has to be inclusive and obligate all states against any aggression anywhere; it does not differentiate or specify the aggressor, victim, or the geographical area to which it extends. It is universal, abstract, and general. Its prohibitory part is applicable to nonmembers as well as to members of the organization. Military, economic, legal, and diplomatic sanctions and forms of mutual assistance constitute the substantive content of a high-level guarantee. As regards procedure, such a commitment will provide for some kind of centralized verification or determination of the *casus foederis* and coördination of collective action. The level of the commitment, whether it be automatic or subject to political determination in each particular case, falls with the rising level of arbitrary discretion of individual member-states. Finally, a high-level commitment would make mandatory the peaceful settlement of disputes, preferably in judicial or arbitral proceedings. It would bar all aggrandizement at the expense of other states unless the curtailed state agreed to it in a procedure of peaceful change.

In all this the collective-security commitment goes far beyond the conventional rules of the balance of power. If observed by most states, anxious to maximize their security beyond the limits set to profitable balancing of national military power by the principle of diminishing marginal utility, it would either not have to be invoked at all or would ensure adequate preponderance of resources for the repression of aggression. The "if" is, however, a big one. It adds to the requirement of a high level that of an equilibrium level of commitment.

An organization is initially in equilibrium with respect to the collective-security commitment (or, in other words, there is an equilibrium level of commitment) when the obligations correspond to the anticipated ability and readiness of states to perform, i.e., desist from, and collectively resist, all use of force. This is likely to occur only if, first, the margins of attempted restraints, implicit in the commitment to nonaggression and peaceful settlement of disputes, do not exceed the limitations which powerful states are likely to tolerate. Other things being equal, the less opportunity there is for peaceful change, the smaller will be the safe and equitable margin. Yet if the ethics and the equilibrium of collective-security commitment are jointly at stake in a proper adjustment between repression and change, they tend to diverge when it comes to attempted restraints on Great Powers as distinct from smaller states. The Covenant was meant to eliminate only the resort to war, the Charter any threat or use of force; but both organizations failed to implement adequate substitute methods for change. The net margin of attempted restraints was correspondingly great. The Covenant contemplated collective security against great and small states alike; the Charter's veto power and the small size of the national contingents to be made available for enforcement purposes implied a zero margin of attempted restraints on the Great Powers and their protégés, and a disproportionately great margin with regard to others. This may be a realistic adjustment, but it certainly restricted collective security to a very limited range of cases.

Second, commitment to mutual assistance should stay within the margin by which notably the leading members can be expected to extend their conception of the national interest in response to the awareness of interdependence. The question is how much the determination of collective intervention against aggression may limit national autonomy and prejudge complex political reality. One estimate underlies an abstract commitment to automatic findings based on advance definition of aggression; another the provision for political determination of each particular *casus foederis* within the broad framework of juridical principle. Automatism strives to substitute reflexes for statesmanship and can lead to politically absurd situations; political discretion tends to degenerate into opportunistic license. Automatism constitutes a greater demand on all; discretion a lesser one on those who make the determination. While the League had leaned toward an automatic commitment, the United Nations chose first the legislative discretion of the Great Powers.[14]

Insofar as they seek rationally to maximize their security, states will accept greater or lesser margins of commitment to nonaggression and mutual assistance depending, among other things, on their calculation of anticipated costs and advantages from the commitment.

To strain further the marginal-utility idea, the equilibrium point is reached when rising marginal and total costs and diminishing marginal and total advantages from additional "units" of a progressively raised and generalized commitment — augmenting risks of involvement in remote conflicts and lessening the certainty of performance by other states in conflicts closer to home — cancel themselves out; and when the ratios between anticipated contributions and advantages, including share in the decisions about the use of joint resources, are approximately equal for all members. Consequently, if a high-level commitment is to be accepted and implemented, states have to rate sufficiently high the resulting advantages to offset the likely costs. It goes without saying that the ratios to be equalized are difficult to compute and to contrive in view of the data involved, the general character of the collective-security commitment, and the disparate particular conditions of individual members as regards their national power, security potential, and security location.

The question of a fair share in the midst of diversity falls into at least three categories. First comes the difference in power and resources among great and small states. This concerns the ability of a country to meet its obligations or, in other words, its collective-security potential. A share will be "fair" if states bear an approximately equal relative burden from resources exceeding the necessary minimum for self-defense. The second group of differences concerns the security location and readiness to perform. Here the major distinction is between exposed states as the likely "consumers" of collective security, and politically peripheral states as the more likely "producers" of security for others. The final distinction is between actual victims and the sanctionist states. Any attempt to evolve equitable ratios from such divergencies in resources and risks seems incompatible with a reasonably general commitment. But a realistic calculation is less hopeless. It must include, on the side of "idealism," ultimate interdependence and indivisibility of security. On the side of "realism," it must take into account the fact that even under a nominally general commitment, actual contributions will be affected by the power and the location of the various states. The attacked state will derive the greatest advantage, but also its stake and sacrifice will be total. And the most peripheral state may consider it wise to make a limited contribution to enforcement in order to insure itself against the consequences of unpunished aggression and to gain the premium of legitimate influence over the direction and settlement of the case.

The two world organizations adopted a different approach to the problem. The League relied, on the whole, on a formally undifferentiated and decentralized commitment. The small as well as the major Powers were both to give and to receive a general guarantee. Theirs was to be equal obligation and self-determination. The Covenant contemplated security by, against, and for all member-states alike. In contrast, the United Nations Charter implied a differentiated commitment to collective security by Great Powers, against aggression by small and ex-enemy states, for all the world. The permanent members of the Security Council were to have the really "primary" responsibility for the maintenance of security. Their superior power and, supposedly, superior interest in peace and security were to be expressed in greater contribution of armed forces, decisive authority in the Security Council, and exclusive membership in the Military Staff Committee. The contribution of the minor states was to be initially less important and rise only with the growth of their "collective capabilities." [15] A total input on the part of directly involved states is implied in the provision for individual and collective self-defense. Both constitutional documents discounted but neither of them ignored differences in the security location of individual member-states. The League Covenant allowed for regional understandings to reinforce the general commitment in a reluctant deviation from a purely universal undertaking. The Charter balanced deliberately the general commitment with provisions for supplementary arrangements among states more intimately concerned. Neither organization differentiated between the victim and the sanctionist states.

Thus, the provisions of the Covenant were more equalitarian also with regard to the security commitment. The Charter made institutionally explicit the implications of any system of security among unequal states, including the alleged political and material impossibility to apply collective security to a Great Power. On the whole the Covenant established a decentralized commitment on a fairly high level, limited chiefly in the kind of sanctions likely to be applied. The Charter contemplated a differentiated commitment, centralized on a high level with respect to only a limited range of cases. The question is whether the League ever was and the United Nations has been or is likely to be in equilibrium with respect to their particular kind of security commitment.

The quest for an equilibrium level of security commitment which would correspond to the actual (as distinct from the initially anticipated) ability and readiness of states to perform, constitutes the central dynamics of international organization of collective security. The problem is to keep as small as possible the ever-threatening gap between the promise of the commitment and the actual response of member-nations or, in other words, between the principle of collective security and the dynamics of the balance of power. Only to the extent that this occurs will the organization be in equilibrium at any particular time.

As to the conditions for narowing the gap, these are primarily political and only secondarily organizational. This is especially true of a spontaneous *ad hoc* system of collective security. In such a system the resources of individual members are expected to be mobilized in response to the law of collective security only when aggression had already occurred; the abstract normative precepts alone are to span the distance between the internationalist factor of mutual dependence and the nationalistic postulate of sovereign self-dependence amid conflicts implicit in the state system itself. Much depends then on the major members of the international community, their willingness and ability to compose extensively conceived national interests and to exert the necessary initiative toward action against aggression. If all the Great Powers were disposed to support collective security and refrain from aggression, they would ensure a reliable, if conditional, preponderance on the side of the *status quo*. This was the stillborn premise of the Charter. A second-best alternative is determined and reasonably consistent initiative toward collective action on the part of one or more Great Powers opposed to violent change. This was the tacit premise of the Covenant and became that of the restructured United Nations.

The frailty inherent in an *ad hoc* system has encouraged experimentation with the integrational type of collective security. Ad-

vance international coördination of military and economic resources is expected to shape material conditions into greater
conformity with the commitment and close the gap more reliably.
A sufficiently authoritative international organization with armed
forces at its disposal would be raised to a position not unlike
that of a balancer, capable of ensuring the requisite preponderance to the side entitled to assistance under the law. When the
French had tried to have the basic idea applied to the League,
they were dismissed as proponents of "international militarism." [16]
And when the founders of the United Nations adopted integrational collective security in less favorable circumstances, their
scheme failed subsequently to be implemented by agreements ear-
marking national contingents and facilities for use by the organization. In order to work, integrational collective security on a
global scale would probably necessitate far-reaching surrender of
sovereignty on the part of all, at least partly disarmed states.
Otherwise it would be difficult to secure sufficient collective resources and their impartial application. Abuse would be always
a possibility, paralysis a likelihood. If spontaneous *ad hoc* collective security is unreliable, the integrational type might easily
prove to be too inflexible. Yet if integration avoided the pitfalls
of rigidity, it might help contain the fluctuations of the collective-
security commitment, manifest in both the League and the United
Nations.

Both organizations had to adjust the margins and ratios of the
initial obligation to unfolding concrete circumstances and attitudes. One manifestation of disequilibrium is aggression in violation of the commitment. It may be stimulated, though hardly
ever caused, by a discrepancy between the margin of attempted
restraints and the substitute provisions for change. A more relevant evidence of disequilibrium is progressive reduction of the
commitment on the part of states that should oppose aggression.
The level of the original commitment under both the Covenant
and the Charter proved to be higher than the level of actual
readiness of member-states to observe it and to perform. This
produced a downward pressure on the level of the commitment
toward its decentralization and differentiation. Both developments may be procedural, substantive, and geographical, i.e., they
may bear on the method, the kind, and the territorial scope of

the commitment and the sanctions to be applied. Formal adjustments may merely sanction intended or actual evasion of the more exacting commitment. The big issue for both organizations was to stabilize an equilibrium commitment on a level sufficiently high to realize the essential purposes of collective security. Gaps between promise and performance always threaten; the question is whether they are narrowed by an increase in the ability and willingness of members to perform or else by a reduction of the commitment itself.

In the League, the commitment was progressively decentralized and differentiated in all respects. The discrepancy between the premises of the original obligation and the reality of a League without the United States gave momentum to the second thoughts of the less exposed countries on the extent of their obligation.

A strict construction of the Covenant, implicit in the early interpretative resolutions and proposed amendments, registered the downward pressure on the commitment. Spearheaded by the Scandinavian countries and Canada, the peripheral security-producing states desired to redress the alleged "inequality between risks and benefits" (i.e., difference in marginal utility), accruing from a too demanding collective-security commitment to states in a "fireproof" and those in an "inflammable" geopolitical location. They sought further to decentralize the commitment by stressing discretionary determination by individual member-states at the expense of the automatism of the original obligation. Military sanctions were deëmphasized to the vanishing point. The central provisions of the Covenant were to be less coercive with respect to the aggressor and less compulsory for the rest. They became "vague as regards their principle and fortuitous as regards their application." Certainty, the prize of automatism, was lost before it had been secured; the outcome of sanctions became as unpredictable as their initiation.[17]

A decentralized law enforcement was paralleled by geographical decentralization of the general commitment into particular alliances and arrangements. The Draft Treaty of Mutual Assistance pointed the way toward a regionalized application of sanctions. The Geneva Protocol contemplated concessions to territorial location; its rejection engendered in its wake the re-

gional Pact of Locarno; and the latter established definitively the
trend toward "regional understandings" nominally related to the
Covenant. Moreover, a *de facto* differentiated as well as formally
decentralized general commitment was to reflect, rather than
counteract, the diversified geographical and political position of
individual states. A dual standard regarding states within and
those outside the "practical" extent of the guarantee was taken
for granted. According to some, only the Great Powers were to
be the guarantors and the smaller states were to be relieved of
the duty to all, or at least to military, sanctions. They were to be
returned to their passive position of the Concert period.[18]

An attempt by the consumer states in the League to stem the
tide produced an abortive stable equilibrium movement. The
Geneva Protocol was to revitalize the commitment by reëmpha-
sizing automatism, centralized verification of aggression, and
coercive sanctions. By thus counteracting the decreasing readiness of member-states to honor the Covenant, the Protocol was
to restore the originally contemplated level of over-all effectiveness. In order to bring together the negative and the positive
approaches to security — and win the support of all proponents
of Disarmament, Arbitration, Security, in any possible sequence
and variation — the new commitment was to combine automatic
coercive sanctions with compulsory arbitration and reduction of
armaments. In the final analysis, the Protocol would have resolved
the problem of power contests by dissolving them, as it were,
into legal relationships among partially disarmed states.

Yet the carefully assorted inducement to the restoration of a
high level of commitment proved to be too weak. Instead of re-
versing the trend, the Protocol was rejected and its failure set
the stage for the eventual self-assertion of an unstable equilibrium
movement with regard to the commitment, matching the same
process in the League's structure. Lessened readiness to perform
released pressures for ever lower commitment, which in turn
further depressed the willingness and ability of member-states
to meet their obligations. The down-scaling of the commitment
was in part responsible for, and was accelerated by, the nonap-
plication of the Covenant against Japan and the merely half-
hearted sanctions against Italy. In the post-Ethiopian nadir of the
League, the quest for a revised equilibrium became hopeless. It

centered around the increasingly unreal choice between a coercive and a universal League. The "compulsory sanctionists" sought to maintain and even enlarge the coercive character of a League composed only of states opposed to aggression. In their opinion, advance assurances and automatism were necessary to safeguard the autonomy and freedom from fear of reprisals of the smaller sanctionist states. The "optional sanctionists," on the other hand, advocated more or less far-reaching emasculation of the organization into an inoffensive forum of conciliation with the revisionist countries. They dwelt on the dangers and the reluctance of smaller states to be "dragged into conflicts between the Great Powers" by the deceptive guarantees of a fictitious system of mutual obligations.[19]

No formal change was made in the Covenant, but the damaging psychological and political impact of the debate proved fatal. The gap persisting between the gradually reduced promise and the actual performance was more detrimental to the League than all the technical "gaps" in the Covenant taken together.

It fell to the United Nations to reproduce the League pattern of reduction and decentralization of the collective-security commitment in a somewhat modified form. An ambivalent pressure on the security commitment resulted from the unwillingness or inability of the Great Powers to honor their yet more fundamental commitment to self-restraint and coöperation. The political and procedural deadlock had four major consequences. First, the Charter was not implemented. This in itself kept the security commitment down to mere recommendations by the Security Council in lieu of decisions and enforcement by means of military facilities controlled by the Council. Second, the combination of an excessive use of the veto and of aggressive tendencies on the part of the Soviet bloc reduced to zero the level of the actually practicable commitment in the vital cases. When that commitment was found to be yet lower than the none too high level of readiness of the majority to act collectively against aggression, this new type of disequilibrium set off, after the narrow escape in the case of North Korean aggression, an upward pressure on the level of practicable commitment, so as to make possible some, however decentralized, collective action.

The product of this pressure, and the third consequence of the deadlock, was the Uniting for Peace Resolution equipping the General Assembly with larger security functions. On the one hand, the adjustment undifferentiated the commitment by making it applicable to Great Powers and their protégés. On the other hand, the new decentralized commitment, while broader in the scope of its application, is "lower" than that originally contemplated by the Charter. Having no integrated resources at its disposal, the United Nations can act only as a watered-down institutional balancer: the organization can strengthen the states opposing aggression by sanctioning their intervention in the first place, and then restrain the sanctionist side from doing more than to restore the originally disturbed equilibrium. Implicit in the change is a revision of the original margins. At least some restraint has been put on the Great Powers, and the restraint on other states, subject now to mere recommendations without binding force, has been lessened. Similarly revised have been the ratios of contribution, advantage, and decision-making authority. In return for the additional protection against major states, the smaller member-states are henceforth to take an active part both in the recommendations of the General Assembly and in the enforcement. The emphasis in the theory of effectiveness of the United Nations as an agency of collective security has shifted from Great-Power accord to participation by as many smaller countries as possible.

The question whether the revision will be upheld as a stable equilibrium movement or whether the unstable equilibrium pattern of the League is only being reënacted must wait for a conclusive answer. It depends on the response of the leading non-aggressive Great Powers and smaller states to other possible cases of aggression. The signs, such as the hesitant reaction to Red Chinese aggression in Korea and to attempts of the Collective Measures Committee to be at least a pale reflection of an effective Military Staff Committee in the revised scheme, have not been very encouraging. And the outlook for a reliable two-thirds majority in the General Assembly willing to back determined action is especially dim since the admission *en masse* of new, largely neutralist or Soviet-controlled members has inordinately increased the influence of weak states hostile to military collective security in general and to enforcement under Western leadership in particular.*

As the fourth consequence of the collapse of the original premise, the geographic decentralization of the commitment is yet more pronounced within the United Nations than under the League. Hopes for effective national and collective security on the basis of advance integration and planning have been transferred to competitive regional systems. In the view of many, the United Nations has become a mere legitimizing framework for more reliable security arrangements, and should reserve the potential of a universal organization for noncoercive, conciliatory functions.

Thus the parallels between the League and the United Nations are striking and the differences not too promising.

Behind the dynamics of a collective system are the attitudes of individual states and their representatives in the organization. A major conditioning factor in the formation of such attitudes is, to repeat, the tension between a general abstract principle and concrete particularistic tendencies and interests. Nations are not only members of a juridical system, but are also historic organisms with special concerns and special conceptions of security as of other things. Not only is there the difference between internationally conservative and revisionist states, but also the conservatives differ among themselves on questions of method if not objective.

The League was opposed in principle by the self-styled dynamic states as a static device for freezing an unjust *status quo*. Their objective was revision, their leader at first Italy and later Nazi Germany. Great Britain and France started out from the identical purpose of containing Germany and arrived at divergent approaches to the problem of security. The politic British preferred a flexible equilibrium sustaining an order changeable by peaceful means. The French worked for a juridically sanctioned preponderance of military power behind the carefully but pre-

---

* In this respect little has been proved or disproved by the General Assembly's recent prompt call for a cease-fire in the Middle East, and little comfort can be derived from the ultimate compliance of the Israeli and the Anglo-French — under threat from an *ad hoc* champion of collective enforcement engaging simultaneously in unchecked aggression in Hungary.

cariously poised territorial settlement. The British emphasis on pragmatic adjustment clashed with the French desire for compulsory arbitration of established rights. And where the British stressed "negative" security against war by means of particular arrangements, disarmament, and conciliation, the French insisted on "positive" security in, as well as against, a war by means of coercive military measures.[20]

In their over-all conception, the British saw in the League — as they do today in the United Nations — an informal consultative framework and an enlarged replica of the Concert of Europe. They opposed the accumulation of formal obligations which would transform the League members from "living nations" into "dead states." They emphasized instead political agreement among the Great Powers and, when still necessary, their *ad hoc* initiative toward concrete collective action backed by an aroused public opinion. After the defection of the other major English-speaking nation, the British were not averse to the progressive weakening of the coercive heart of the Covenant in favor of a conciliatory, universal League. They toyed with the idea of reducing the margins of attempted repression of the vanquished states by means of limited reconstruction and revision. The main cost would have been borne by the second-class eastern frontiers of Europe; the incidental advantage would have been a check on the suspected French drive for hegemony on the continent. However, there was real leadership for nothing and drift in almost everything. The British stand radicalized French attitudes in the first phase, and aggravated their reunited futilities vis-à-vis the Facist Powers in the second.[21]

The French position was more consistent in its objective but suffered from an imbalance between objective and means, commitment and power. France strove to exhaust all the potentialities of a general system as a means to the limited practical objective of containing a single nation. She extended her general and particular commitments far beyond her ability and willingness to back them by national power. Throughout, France vacillated between the institutional approach of abstract collective security and the traditional methods of bilateral guarantees, first from the Anglo-Saxon Powers and then with the Eastern European nations. She tried to combine both approaches and failed.

One reason was her inability to reconcile the requirements of the power balance and of the institutional equilibrium. Locarno, by bringing Germany into the League, was to square the circle only to demonstrate its viciousness. As the protector of small states, Great Britain focused her balance of power politics on the Low Countries. France, in the pursuit of an *équilibre continental*, became the natural leader of the exposed successor states of Eastern Europe. They were to serve as "counterweights to German power" and be in turn protected against that power aimed through them indirectly at France.[22] The League, apart from being itself a grand alliance against Germany, was to be the legitimizing framework for this privileged system of alliances. But the complex design was destroyed as a result of political and psychological failures. The incongruity between a general organization and a particular function (not unknown to the successor of the League), came into the open when effective sanctions were to be applied against Italy. And the gap between commitment and power was revealed when France allowed herself to be separated from her small allies: the remilitarization of the Rhineland added a solid physical barrier to the legal curtain of the Locarno Pact and the psychological fixation of the Maginot Line. In no time, France fell from leadership into dependence and from dependence into defeat. Unlike Great Britain, she tried too much with too little.

Anglo-French disagreements over the League have given way to Anglo-American differences regarding collective security in and through the United Nations, with the United States in many respects taking up the French approach to methods and objectives. Yet, though vastly better off in regard to the available means, this country has to contend with a revisionist Power subtle enough to put up with "capitalist" international law and organization as temporary expedients for a holding operation pending a radical refashioning of socio-political relations. In the light of more fundamental conflicts between the United States and the Soviet Union, their divergent ideas on the institutions of collective security appear as merely derivative. If the split prevented the implementation of the Charter, it was further illustrated in connection with the Uniting for Peace Resolution. The United States, in sponsoring the resolution, emphasized the objective of security. Conversely, the Soviet opposition could be rationalized in terms of the equivalence of substantive and procedural aspects. A procedural deadlock would then justify the suspension of the substantive purposes of the system: organs are as important as objectives. The American position prevailed. It was, however, eschewed in the Guatemalan case when distribution of functions between general and regional organization was put before the purpose of calling a halt to the display of force.

The smaller states also contributed their share to the dissonances on ends and means. In the League, the internationally conservative small states were disappointed in their hopes for Anglo-French coördination and their reliance on the organization itself. Their revisionist counterparts disliked the League and relied on kindred Powers. The "consumer" small states, not unlike France, stressed military as well as economic sanctions and mutual assistance among sanctionist and victim states. They sought to strengthen the League but were vulnerable to the charge of aggravating the contrary dynamics by their distaste for peaceful change. In a yet more short-sighted attitude, the less exposed "producer" states sought the reduction of the commitment and favored disarmament and peaceful settlement rather than enforcement, despite multiplying bids for violent change. They either failed to realize that positive security in war was broader and included negative security against war, or else considered the two to be mutually exclusive.

In the United Nations, as in the League, many small states have sought to constitute a "third force" aloof from conflicts, while others are in the tow of either of the major Powers. Yet there is a significant difference from the 1930's: the essentially revisionist Soviet bloc manages now to defy the principle of collective security and pay lip-service to it at one and the same time.

Among themselves, with different degrees of responsibility, the individual great and small states undermined in both periods the collective-security commitment they had given themselves in a pious moment.

THE PRACTICE OF COLLECTIVE SECURITY

As important as their attitude to collective security in principle is the behavior of states in specific cases, which constitutes the practice of collective security. Among the relevant aspects are Great-Power initiative, the response of smaller states to it, their behavior as sanctionists, and their reactions as victims.[23]

If not always sufficient, the initiative and contribution to collective action by one or more Great Powers are a necessary practical condition of an at least temporary equilibrium level of commitment and resulting power preponderance in a particular instance of resistance to aggression. It will surprise no one that such initiative will be vitiated by the conflict over objectives among rival Powers and over methods among broadly coöperative states. Only on secondary issues involving minor offenders are the Great Powers likely to exercise joint initiative in a transient concert. An instance is the use of force allegedly without belligerent intent by Yugoslavia against Albania and by Greece against Bulgaria in the early years of the League. The Powers in the Council called the delinquent states easily to order; the mere suggestion of sanctions was enough. A similar offense by Italy in the Corfu case, however, went unpunished. The case illustrated the power deformation of collective-security principles and the differentiation of their practical application behind a screen of ambiguities surrounding the distinction between "war" and "force short of war." The victim rather than the Great-Power offender was penalized, to the acute resentment of other smaller states. In the war between Bolivia and Paraguay, no direct concern of the League Powers was at stake and the interests of the United States had to be taken into account. Hence, only a half-hearted and belated initiative was displayed. Matters are still worse when there are contrary interests. This has been the case with the Arab-Israeli conflict under the United Nations. Only when the interests of the Great Powers converged in time and purpose could the Security Council threaten enforcement; the actual fighting then stopped almost at once. The situation was similar in the cases of Indonesia and Kashmir.

When a Great Power is the aggressor, the initiative of other Powers is awkwardly hesitant or nonexistent. Even the Covenant proved in two instances inapplicable to a major aggressor. The Corfu case has just been mentioned. In the Sino-Japanese "incident," no serious initiative was taken to institute economic, let alone military, sanctions. The British desired to mediate and compromise; the French conceived of collective security as inapplicable to the Pacific area; and the so-called Stimson Doctrine misconceived "nonrecognition" as a substitute for effective sanctions. The commitment under the Covenant was reduced to moral pressure and the League to impotence. There was no impact of the collective-security principle on the military-political balance in favor of the weaker victim. Aggression by a Great Power seemed to be safe.

In the next instance, the colonial background and the European implications of the Italian aggression in Ethopia conspired to impede effective sanctions. The British hesitated between preference for arrangements outside the League and support for collective security, and settled for collective security with limited liability. At one point, the British Foreign Secretary Sir Samuel Hoare took a strong stand for collective action to save a minor country with the aid of other smaller states. At another point, he tried with his French colleague Laval to make a deal with Italy to partition Ethiopia for allegedly the same purpose. The French opposed all measures, notably military, which might prevent the return of Italy to the work of "European reconstruction." Their conception of the *de facto* limited scope of the League again placed a non-European country outside the "practical" extent of the obligation to effective sanctions. And the intervening remilitarization of the Rhineland extinguished the last remnant of leadership which had survived the confusion of purpose. Henceforth, the initiative of the two leading League Powers was devoted to a rapid dismantling of the economic sanctions.

At last, determined initiative by the United States in the Korean case brought about fairly effective military intervention against aggression under the aegis of collective security. The Korean example can be used to illustrate the whole range from normative theory to a realistically debunked actuality of collective security, from a United Nations collective action to a Great-Power-directed coalition war using the symbolism of a universal organization. At the center is the solid fact of American initiative and major contribution to the nearest approximation of effective collective enforcement on record. The motivation of the United States was as complex as the case itself, and interacted with the instrumental aspect. On the one hand, the motivation comprised collective-security principles as well as the concrete American interest in the security of occupied Japan and the global balance of power. On the other hand, the principles and the organization of collective security were instrumental in legitimizing the American-led intervention and reinforced it institutionally; but the presence and use of the American troops in Japan and the resources of a global Power were the equally indispensable instruments for translating the principles into potent reality.

To be sure, the need for the initiative and leadership of a Great Power injects all kinds of ambiguities into the pure theory of collective security. The full use of the institutional framework of a United Nations is necessary, and hardly sufficient, to counteract the overwhelming military and political weight of the initiating Great Power with respect to the other sanctionist states and the organization itself. Influence does and should correspond to input. A special type of military-political balance which would place "force under policy" collectively defined is necessary, however, to make an action collective "in substance as well as in form." [24] A Great Power must exert initiative if something like power preponderance against the aggressor is to be mustered behind the law of collective security. But the coöperating states in the organization must have a fair, or more than fair, share of codetermination if the political preponderance of the initiating Great Power in the sanctionist group is not to efface the collective character of the action. The Korean action fully realized neither of the two types of preponderance by and for the United States in coöperation with others. As a result — both fortunately and unfortunately — the action was to a reasonable extent collective in character, but remained indecisive in results.

Korea illustrated fairly accurately the unequal interaction of the institutional and the geopolitical factors. Its ambiguities are preferable to the failure in the case of Ethiopia. There, the two categories of factors, instead of reinforcing each other at least in certain respects as motivations and instruments to collective action, tended to frustrate each other in all.

The behavior of the smaller states favorable in principle to collective security is as uncertain as that of the Great Powers. They depend on the leadership of the major states and often press for action; but they lack as frequently the ability and willingness to match their encouragement with corresponding contribution. They like to complain about the hesitations of the Great Powers; but they shrink from the consequences of a too vigorous initiative. *Ad hoc* collective security tends to deepen the maladjustments between them and the major Powers. When it comes to actual performance, the willingness of the smaller states to participate in sanctions must be distinguished from their ability to do so. The margin of power required for a substantial input is not always available to weak countries. Inequality of contribution by differentially powerful states may represent a yet greater but inverse inequality of burden relative to the available resources. This complicates the problem of a fair share. Still, the record of the smaller states is not too good.

Two major classes of cases can be distinguished. Those which involve only smaller countries, such as the Chaco and the Arab-Israeli conflicts, do not raise the issue of collective security as a device for the protection of smaller against decisively more powerful states. It is a radically different matter when a Great Power is the aggressor. The collectivist smaller states pressed for precedent-making action against Japanese aggression in China for both moral and self-interested reasons. Their desire for greater share in relevant decisions, however, was not sustained by their willingness or ability to act economically and militarily in a correspondingly decisive fashion. This did not exactly promote equitable ratios between anticipated actual input, individual and collective advantage from an intervention, and desired influence in decision-making. Moreover, geopolitical realities contended with the desire to see the institutions of collective security strengthened. The small states sheltered by their geographical remoteness from the particular conflict but exposed in their overall security position could be and were the most determined. On the other hand, the generally strongly collectivist New Zealand was more cautious in view of its location in the Pacific area.[25]

In the Ethiopian case, the pro-sanctionist small states were prepared to support a Great-Power lead but afraid to move without a determined guidance. They wished for a telling demonstration against Great-Power aggression, but feared to antagonize Italy and be left holding the bag after the Great Powers had come to terms among themselves. As could be expected in a weakened system, the geopolitical factor reasserted itself over the institutional principle: Austria, Hungary, and Albania failed to participate in sanctions because of their location in the Italian sphere of influence. Conversely, the geographical closeness of politically hostile Yugoslavia, Greece, and Turkey induced these states to proffer a formal pledge of military support to Great Britain as a stimulus to all-out intervention. Even countries not too favorable in principle to a coercive League were prepared to implement economic sanctions, and oil-producing and controlling small states like Rumania, the Netherlands, and Iraq were ready for the vital oil sanctions, if they were decided upon. In due course, the vacillations of the leading sanctionist Powers dampened the élan and provided an excuse for the shortcomings of most smaller states. Such an excuse is not, however, available in the Korean case.

Confronted with the fact of North Korean aggression, the lesser members of the United Nations were again influenced by their location with respect to the conflict itself and, in addition, to the East-West rift in general. Their attitudes ranged from full and active support of the American initiative to a critically detached neutralist position, while the Soviet bloc countries were isolated in their outright opposition to collective action. Actual contributions were in many instances made, gradated, withheld, or opposed in accordance with extraneous considerations rather than in deference to the commitment and the requirements of the concrete case. A major consideration was the particular state's relationship of dependence, would-be "independence," or hostility toward the United States and its policies. A pattern of division of labor between the United States and the other non-Communist member-states emerged. The former assumed primary responsibility and control on the strength of its material input. The latter, alive to the advantages of an implemented guarantee but anxious to limit the extent of their contribution and the armed conflict itself, sought to restrain the United States and to keep the action within jointly defined limits as the price of its collective character. And the United Nations itself was the coactive institutional framework of this multilateralism rather than a mere instrument of American national policy.[26]

However, the influence of member-states over the implementation of the commitment should be in some relation to their actual contribution. This was not always the case in the Korean instance. When the smaller states fail to do their full share in the enforcement, they weaken both the balance against the aggressor, the justice of their claim to more weight in the institutional equilibrium, and their case as the primary "victims" of collective security.

An extreme instance is the reintroduction of neutrality into collective security. It nullifies in law or in fact the commitment of the neutrals. The neutral member-states cling to a passive role and accept the privileges of membership without more serious responsibilities. The Swiss retained their neutrality within the League and were exempted from taking part in military sanctions. A demand by Weimar Germany for a similar status was rejected. If an institutionally recognized neutrality is bad for a collective system, *ad hoc* neutrality with regard to a specific enforcement action is worse. It is both a consequence and a cause of the system's weakness. Immediately before and after the Ethiopian fiasco, a number of smaller countries, including traditionally neutral states, set themselves up as the so-called neutral Powers. Even the sanctionist states sought a middle position as "neither neutrals nor belligerents." The United Nations, too, came to know *ad hoc* neutrals in connection with the Korean situation. Their factual existence was formally sanctioned by the armistice agreement's distinction between belligerents and neutral nations.[27]

Neutrality not only reduces to naught the commitment, but may also upset all equitable ratios between contribution, advantage from collective action, and influence over its course. The so-called neutrals in the United Nations, notably India and other Arab-Asian bloc countries, used their excessive influence to pose as "balancers" between the aggressor and the sanctionist states. In fact, they upset by their attitudes the equilibrium of the organization with respect to both structure and collective-security commitment, and contributed greatly to the failure to array preponderant power and determination against the aggression. Neutrality as a legal status is inconsistent with the law of collective security and the idea of a "just war"; neutralism as a self-centered and relativistic state of mind and political attitude is still less consistent with the ideology of collective security postulating interdependence and active involvement against "unjust aggressors." The ideal attitude for smaller states would seem to be neither extreme neutralism nor satellite dependence but objective impartiality in Great-Power disputes up to the point when a clear case of aggression calls for active participation in collective enforcement. Much of what small states sow as subjects of collective security they may expect to reap as its objects.

As objects of collective security, the smaller states are at a disadvantage in several respects. Collective security tends to be effective only against them and fails to operate for them at all or to protect them adequately. It does not concede sufficient influence to the victim over the course and liquidation of a case.

Offending smaller states are not only the more likely targets of actual or threatened sanctions but are also much more vulnerable to them. Interdependence if backed by all-out sanctions is ultimately a deadly fact for all except global power; but even limited sanctions will demonstrate it promptly and efficiently to a minor country. The Great Powers not only dispose of more resources and bargaining power in their own right; they can also coerce lesser and especially neighboring countries into continued deliveries. Similarly, an embargo applied impartially to both sides is actually partial because it is fatal to the weaker side only. This was true of the general embargo imposed by Britain before the Italian aggression; it was no less true of the American neutrality legislation of the 1930's and the theory of a "revised" neutrality that would institute a general embargo in case of war.[28] Not even the one-sided economic sanctions against Italy could tip the balance in favor of Ethiopia, while a mere threat of sanctions or partial embargo sufficed to bring to terms a Yugoslavia, Paraguay, Israel, and the Netherlands.

A special instance of a victimized culprit is the satellite aggressor acting as proxy for a Great Power. This is the ultimate perversion of the power-responsibility doctrine: the Great Power remains nominally free of its actual responsibility for the offense, and the puppet bears the consequences without collecting the fruits, if any, of the aggression — witness the part of the Soviets in the Greek and Korean "civil wars." To be sure, the phenomenon is not peculiar to any era or system of security; but it is the more damaging to collective security when the guilty Great Power can block action against its pawn-accessory.

Yet all the theoretical and practical shortcomings of collective security notwithstanding, it remains a fact that joint measures were taken against Great Powers, directly against Italy and at least by implication against the Soviet Union and Communist China. In both cases the victims of aggression were small countries.

A victim of aggression can be beneficiary and victim of collective security at the same time. This happens when the expectations aroused by the general guarantee are not realized adequately or at all. Then the small state suffers the consequences of the gap between the promise of the law and actual performance. The League made no real attempt to protect the victim in the case of invaded China, violated Austria, and rump Czechoslovakia. For Ethiopia, inadequate sanctions against the aggressor and the denial of positive assistance to the victim combined to leave virtually intact the "balance" between the two. Military sanctions and assistance enabled South Korea to escape the defeat of Ethiopia but did not produce the preponderance which would compensate sacrifice and destruction with complete success.

In both instances, there was a real disparity between the input of the victim state and its influence over the case. Ethiopia had no voice in the Hoare-Laval plan, and the little voice she had initially in the League was smothered in polite applause when the end of sanctions was being decided over the protests of her Emperor. Where a member of the League fared ill, the nonmember could not expect to fare better in the United Nations. South Korea was heard on crucial occasions but was not really consulted in advance on vital decisions either by the organization or by the principal sanctionist Power. Only the fact of mutual dependence for facilities in joint military operations gives the small victim state some influence.

A small victim nation is not only ignored most of the time; it is likely to be exposed to the balance-of-power type of adjustments within or without the framework of collective security. The succession of plans for unification, partition, and neutralization of Korea in response to changing political situation and fortunes of war was essentially akin to Sir Samuel's varied responses to his Ethiopian dilemma. One may condemn the Hoare-Laval plan as an instance of cynical Great-Power and balance-of-power politics; but it could be and was defended by one of its authors on the high ground of conscience as the only alternative to general war or complete destruction of the attacked small country, misled to expect too much from collective security.[29] Today, many Koreans feel that they were victimized for similar reasons. Others feel that the South Koreans, having been saved by collective security, set out to misuse it for their particular and exorbitant goals. The gap between the ideal and the actual in collective security as in other things is a fertile area for manifold and contradictory feelings of grievance.

The limited amount of historical experience suggests rather grim reflections. First of all, the small victim state must be prepared to fight and face extinction without waiting for collective and specifically Great-Power approval and support. Second, consideration for the small state's viewpoint will grow when it threatens catastrophic, even though self-destructive, behavior if its interests are not taken into account. In more favorable circumstances, to be sure, Syngman Rhee heeded the lesson of Czechoslovakia's submission at Munich to the Great Powers and their interpretation of the general interest. By a diametrically opposite attitude he laid the basis for collective action and extracted significant concessions. In the final analysis, only when it itself accepts battle can a small state hope for others to join in order to avert the otherwise inevitable wider consequences of its defeat.

THE DILEMMA OF COLLECTIVE SECURITY

Tentative conclusions concern, first, the position of individual states in collective security, and second, the system as such.

States as subjects and producers of collective security fall into different categories as all-out supporters, cautious sympathizers, so-called neutrals, and actual opponents of collective enforcement. Moreover, in function of events, they may change from subjects into objects, from actual or potential givers into recipients and targets of mutual assistance. Performance in one capacity does not always match claims advanced in the other. Supporters of the principle of collective security will allow extraneous considerations to qualify their conduct in concrete cases; and delegates of states skeptical about enforcement in principle may argue for more stringent sanctions against a specific aggressor, as Riddell of Canada did in the Ethiopian case. On the whole, states incline to extend their national interest in response to the requirements of collective security by only a small margin. There is little difference in this respect between the minor and the major states; the latter only lack the extenuating circumstance of a limited and uncertain influence over the course of a crisis. Immediate interests and risks contend successfully with the long-range interest in an effective security system; the dictates of ultimate self-dependence are often at variance with those of interdependence, still insufficient to affect decisively an offender with large resources. And the ratios of contribution, advantage, and actual share in decisions with respect to a collective action tend to be too disparate among differently situated states individually and between the smaller and the greater Powers as distinct groups. The less powerful victims of aggression are the first to suffer from the resulting disequilibrium with regard to the collective-security commitment.

Collective security, no less than the balance of power, failed to realize its ideological promise of safeguarding weaker communities. Theoretically, the law of collective security is ideally suited to ensure the survival of smaller states in a world of multiplying contacts and frictions; in fact, it may aggravate their already precarious position.

Membership in a collective-security organization imposes on weaker states additional strains and projects them into active involvement in all major issues of world affairs, frequently characterized by Great-Power conflicts. Additional dangers for smaller states, and ambiguities for collective security, seep into a weakened system through the gap between the promise of the law and actual performance by member-states. This is particularly the case when *ad hoc* collective security lacks an integrational connection between the material factors of power and geography, and the institutional norms. The community-creative expectations of mutual assistance are supplanted by the community-destructive doubts, fears, and suspicions; states which attempt to pursue security on both disconnected planes at once run the risk of tumbling in the chasm; minor countries in an exposed location tend to relapse into a passive status in the geopolitical context as buffers, neutralized states, satellites, or partitioned fragments; member-states do not extend to each other assistance irrespective of the geographic location of the victim or are subject to intimidation by a stronger neighbor-aggressor should they try to do so. And even when instituted, sanctions against the aggressor and assistance to the victim are not necessarily such as to equalize great power differentials between the two. As a result, the less powerful nonaggressive states tend to be suspended in a precarious position between the reactivated "laws" of the balance of power and the promise of a discredited collective security applied *ad hoc* or not at all. They forfeit even the tentative guidance which could be derived from the conventional rules of the traditional principle.

Moreover, the reliance of some of the exposed small countries on collective security in the earlier phases of the new dispensation produced a feeling of security or at least a sense of collective rather than only individual responsibility for defense against aggression. This made such countries ill-equipped to deal with a concrete predicament in terms of their own power, morale, and self-reliance. However, the revisionist small states, opposed to the new principle in the name of the past, suffered in the end a no more enviable fate. Nor would the "independence" and "neutrality" of some countries today survive a collapse of the combination of an imperfect collective security and a global balance of power which now protects them despite themselves.

All the disappointments have not extinguished the interest of smaller states in an effective world organization. One of the reasons is their worsened position in the military-political equilibrium. Technological change since the first days of collective security has been magnifying power differentials at a self-accelerating rate, and the relative efficiency of offensive weapons has increased. Lesser countries can now assert themselves independently and successfully only against another small (or a dispirited great) state.

In the course of the Second World War, most small states were unable to resist for any length of time the full impact of a major opponent. It is prudent to remember this fact, but it is not a sufficient reason for writing off small states altogether as abso-lete strategic hazards in an era when Great Powers go down in swift defeat and a Greece and Yugoslavia were able to contribute significantly to the joint war effort. Impressed by their impor-tance for the security of others, lesser countries like Australia and Canada did not hesitate to claim a privileged role as "middle Powers" in the postwar organization of peace.[30]

Most recently, the difficulty of developing and maintaining a military establishment, however small, equipped with nuclear weapons or capable of resisting them, has deepened the depend-ence of exposed countries with limited means on those with large resources. Moreover, modern conditions of warfare tend to depress weaker and strategically located countries into the more or less passive role of air and naval bases — unless they manage to take refuge in a precarious, if often profitable, neutrality. Their posi-tion has been described as that of mere security zones, atom absorbers, stationary aircraft carriers, and jumping-off grounds for the defense of continents. It is possible to regard bases sym-pathetically as merely the physical expression of membership in a collective-security system, freely consented to by the host country; or they may be attacked by the contained Great Power as contrary to national sovereignty and independence. However evaluated, the number and geographic dispersion of bases for long-range delivery systems available to either of the two super-Powers may be the decisive factor in determining both defensive and offensive superiority in a situation of "atomic stalemate." [31]

Strategic imperatives cannot but press hard against claims to national and political self-determination of smaller communities. When the facilities of a country are required to improve the strategic posture of Great Powers, its external and internal situa-tion may be either strengthened, endangered, or altogether sub-verted according to its withholding capacity and the methods used by the more powerful state. Yet at a time when ultimate power is focused in an inanimate force at least as much as polar-ized in two super-Powers, even they are to some extent its satellites and fear to employ all-out war as the traditional instru-ment of national policy. They contend then for more or less dependent allies as an alternative and deterrent to war rather than as a preliminary to it. The balance of power is consolidated by a balance of terror, pending its control by means of international supervision and reduction of nuclear and conventional armaments.

In a bleak situation, the responsible and politically mature leaders of smaller states anxious to preserve their independence are left with little option. They have to strive on against all odds for an effective collective-security system as an institutional deterrent to aggression, reinforcing and controlling to some extent the primary technological and political deterrents. They may try simultaneously to improve the position of their countries in the military-political equilibrium by means of individual and collective integration of their resources. A hopeful trend for smaller states and collective security generally might be reversion to small and highly specialized armies. This might enable even lesser countries to make significant contributions to a collective security which would realize the idea of limited war under policy. If the new type of armies were not only small but also largely professional, this might facilitate the working of collective security itself: it might set the unifying ethos of professional honor against nationalistic divergencies and reduce emotional popular involvement in a collective action, which impedes the system's requisite flexibility.

Facile skepticism about collective security is as unwarranted as festive optimism. It is futile to deny or ignore geopolitical realities and compulsions in the flush of constitution-making and try to reorder sovereign states as it were alphabetically within an organization based on legal rights and obligations alone; in a period of disillusionment it is rash to discount completely a global institution of security. A working collective security rests on a favorable interaction of the normative ideology of collective security, the partly fulfilled conditions of its effectiveness, and the particularistic tendencies implicit in the concern of states with pressing immediate interests. In themselves, normative precepts and slender organizational devices will not prove sufficient most of the time to channel national purposes and resources reliably toward collective action; fixed divisions among nations introduce all kinds of rigidities into a system depending on an extremely elastic and far-sighed response to the abstract principle; and both governments and peoples tend to weight the anticipated costs and

risks more heavily than the advantages of implemented commitment. These facts will always hamper collective security pending a profound modification of the state system. Yet the available experience does not warrant a definitive judgment either way.

To be sure, the sanctions of a decentralized system may or may not be applied and be forceful enough to counterbalance power differentials between aggressor and victim. The weakening of the collective-security principle entails a concurrent reassertion of unprincipled balance-of-power politics. Too much comes to depend on an unpredictable concert or the uncertain initiative of one or more leading Great Powers. It is no longer possible to distinguish the role of the collective-security principle as a motive and/or instrument of national policy in such an initiative, when forthcoming. The result is "pragmatic" and "permissive" collective security, attended by quasi-parliamentary balancing of influence on the part of sanctionist, aggressor, and neutral states for compromise instead of enforcement. Wilson's "old game" is reintroduced in a new guise into the perennial quest for security. A balancing process of this kind is an indubitable fact and may be an operational theoretical concept; but it is not collective security in any meaningful sense of the term. It is no more than traditional diplomacy in a new institutional setting, which would surround the operation of any principle of security and bedevil its application.[32]

There is, however, no more historical or theoretical justification for the belief that genuine collective security occurs only when the sanctionist nations obey the principle and choose the long-range advantage of collective enforcement "at the expense of immediate security."[33] Few if any interventions, including that in Korea, would live up to so austere a criterion. Nor has one to accept the contention that a collective intervention occurs only when the internationalist precept happens to coincide with a sufficient number of national interests. Rare indeed would be collective interventions of any kind if they depended on such a mechanical coincidence. There is no reason why "mere" compatibility, rather than outright coincidence, of immediate and long-range requirements of national security should not induce participation in collective action; and why the compatibility or even

coincidence of such considerations should efface the collective-security character of an enforcement.

It is self-evident that any political decision and action are the product of a number of considerations which have been weighed in the light of over-all national purposes. A single-minded and absolutely consistent devotion to collective security in complex situations is a mirage, and the line between a pragmatic and an opportunistic application is thin. There is only one demand which may reasonably be made at present on collective security, and in its behalf on countries opposed to violent or subversive curtailment of national independence: that the norms of collective security operate in all relevant instances as one class of motivations of national policy, and that they be flexibly applied when at all compatible with national security of the nonaggressive states. Collective security is not the only principle of international action. Its statesman-like application need not, therefore, imply either going to global war for every local disturbance of the peace or accepting as immutable a pattern of political control over nations which violates the principles of freedom and justice.

Such caution implies that collective security among sovereign states neither has been nor ever can be an assured success, either. Both the League's ideal of legal certainty and spontaneous automatism, and the preference of the United Nations for political discretion circumscribed by the principles of the Charter proved to be avenues to the already familiar dilemma, affecting international organization with respect to the collective-security commitment, too. Realistic, that is to say small, margins of restraint on the autonomy of the Great Powers promote a deadlock of discretionary powers and a discriminatory application of the commitment. Unrealistic, that is to say great, margins of equal restraints on all states produce a high, but disequilibrium, level of commitment as states fail to observe their obligations and attend to their interests by other means. Neither international organization has managed to evolve a compromise commitment which would be neither too low (i.e., be more than permissive), nor too much in disequilibrium. Instead, both organizations fell from disequilibrium or deadlock into at best near equilibrium on a level of commitment too low to guarantee effective preponderance of power against aggression but at least incapable of generating unjustified

reliance on a fictitious promise of the law. They were subject to all kinds of differentiation, decentralization, and evasion. The inducement to, and expectation of, observance of the collective-security commitment on the part of the nonaggressive nations was not such as to nullify the tendency to nonobservance in the form of aggression on the part of states ready to seek violent change.

This was fatal when the balance of power seemed to favor the would-be aggressors. The League fell prey to its institutional disequilibrium reinforced by the imbalance of power. The present internal deadlock or uncertain near equilibrium on a lowered level of the United Nations' commitment is shielded from similar consequences by the reëstablished balance of power and the new balance of terror between the opposing groups of states. Such a state of things depresses to a low estate the standing of the organization as an active component in international politics.

Thus, the only indisputable conclusion about the collective-security commitment and the corresponding institutional equilibrium is that they are not self-sustaining. As a historical fact, this is fairly obvious. When the United States initiated the collective intervention in Korea, it was motivated, among other things, by considerations of the American national interest in the global and local balance of power, and was aided by the necessary minimum of locally available mobile resources. Such more or less accidental support neither annuls the collective-security character of the resulting intervention, nor does it either exclude or guarantee joint intervention against a future aggression in less favorable circumstances. Neither do the balance-of-power considerations involved in the Korean, Ethiopian, and other cases exclude the operation of other factors. British pro-sanctionist public opinion prevailed at least temporarily over the traditionalist outlook of His Majesty's Government in the face of Italian aggression in Ethiopia. But, on the whole, the interwar depression and resulting socio-economic disequilibrium depressed correspondingly the chances of effective collective security. Various aspects of constitutional and psychological equilibrium were a decisive factor in the Korean instance: the suddenness of the North Korean aggression weighted the extensive powers of the American executive in favor of intervention against the anti-interventionist forces in Congress and anti-United Nations pressures at large; the absence of the Soviet delegate from the Security Council removed temporarily the check of the veto from the constitutional equilibrium of the international organization. A collective intervention could be institutionalized. This fact lessened the maladjustments between the West and uncommitted Asians which a unilateral American action would have produced, while intangibles in critical Asian attitudes continued to influence American policies without raising at all the question of a power equilibrium between the "independents" and the United States.

It would be easier to trace the interaction of the domestic and international aspects of the institutional, military-political, and socio-economic equilibrium if the channels of international organization had been used more effectvely. But even if the interrelation can be merely suggested in regard to practice, it can be confidently asserted as a theoretical proposition.

The dynamics of the collective-security commitment must be related to the other facets of the institutional equilibrium and the multiple equilibrium in its entirety. At best, military collective security might shield the consolidation of a socio-economic and political equilibrium, which would in turn lay the long-range bases of more substantial security. *Ad hoc* nonintegrated global collective security has been performing its part of the relationship only inadequately. International organization might promote the larger equilibrium by evolving a satisfactory institutional equilibrium with respect to its functional scope.

CHAPTER 4

THE FUNCTIONAL SCOPE

The issue of functional scope is a focal point in the analysis: it relates international organization directly to the material and social environment of international relations; merges the problem of security into that of general welfare; and leads to the question of geographic scope, concerning global and regional organization.

THE NATURE OF THE ENVIRONMENT

A progressive functional extension of international organization is hampered by nationalistic attitudes of member-states; more fundamentally, it has to cope with diverse precipitants of disequilibrium and a tendency to fragmentation at work in the environment.

Fragmentation occurred in the form of disintegrating European and colonial empires internationally; nationally it was characterized by deepening class divisions within many societies. The search for postimperial reintegration in freedom has in fact amounted to a quest for a new equilibrium: between the nation and the larger international community, between the individual and variously defined groups. The liberal ideal is a dynamic equilibrium between diverse individual and group interests, negotiated into the compromise of a common good. It has had to contend, not always successfully, with ideologies of social and national conflict which reject equilibrium in favor of dictatorial preponderance of a single class or nation, achieved in struggle. The apparently integrative movement from individualism to collectivism only aggravated existing social divisions; the chief claim of nationalism was to resolve them in a larger, national unity. Yet achievement did not always live up to the claim in the domestic sphere and, in triumphing over internationalism, nationalism has definitely deepened divisions among nations. The contest for power preponderance has been anything but eased in an atmosphere of mass psychosis. In the democracies, the interpenetration of domestic with foreign politics has impeded the latter's rationality, continuity, and flexibility. In the totalitarian systems, internal strains always threaten to intensify the attractions of external expansion by the pressure of domestic necessity.

Appeals to — and the appeal of — Social Darwinism, National Socialism, and Marx-Leninism reinforced the conflictual side of the ideologically neutral, ambivalent tendencies in international politics. Such doctrines of conflict — together with the defensive reëmphasis of realism in international dealings on the part of the democracies themselves — have pressed hard to supersede the ideas of men like Cobden, Mazzini, and Wilson. All major modern ideologies deny at least implicitly the adequacy of nationalism by aiming at ultimately global solutions. Idealist or expansionist, they pay tribute to world-wide interdependence. Yet all have shared in the failure to achieve integration above national divisions. Neither an international projection of democracy nor international class solidarity and racial or ideological affinities intertwined with the myth of pan-movements were able to override the limiting boundaries of the nation.

Nationalism has spread and waxed stronger. Instead of liberal internationalism, there emerged the integral nationalism of the "Totalitarian Parochial State." Instead of internationalist socialism, the stage has been occupied by "socialized" nation and nationalized socialism. "National determinism" has in many instances supplanted national self-determination.[1] The reassertion of imperialism, this time compounded with totalitarianism, in Europe and elsewhere coincides with the passing of traditional colonial imperialism in the non-European world. There, the liquidation of the colonial era calls for a new dynamic adjustment between the formerly dominant and dominated cultures as well as within them. The badly shaken imperial nations and the turbulent anti-colonial peoples have yet to arrive at a balanced interpretation of the reciprocal assets and liabilities of the past; only then will genuine moral equality between them facilitate mutually beneficial communication of their particular values and planning for the future.

To add economic to political nationalism proved to be a problematic contribution to the economic aspect of a stable international equilibrium. The proponents of protectionism would have "fair" rather than "free" trade. They would supplant the economic equilibrium of the liberal era with a more equitable adjustment between the requirements of world economy and the needs of national power and security. The less developed countries adopted protectionist devices in order to redress the imbalance between agricultural and industrial resources, and supplement political with economic independence; the totalitarian states sought autarchy as a precondition of external domination; and free-trade Britain embraced a system of discriminatory imperial preferences in the hope of consolidating her commonwealth and empire. In rapid — and partly causal — sequence, the peace settlement of World War I, the interwar economic depression, and post-World War II disruptions dramatized the shortcomings of neo-mercantilism while aggravating its methods.[2]

A special problem confronting international organization is the rise of ever new states. The formal aspects were mentioned in the discussion of recognition; more substantial is the problem of a balance between fragmentation and integration.

The economic implications of political fragmentation have been subject to much fault-finding. Strictures should be qualified by the recognition of the greater effect and frequently lesser enlightenment of the economic and social policies of the Great Powers; yet qualifications must not gloss over the many maladjustments characteristic of smaller countries that emerged from larger empires, be it in Latin America, Eastern Europe, the Near East, or Asia. There, the need is for a postfeudal as well as postimperial socio-economic and political equilibrium. Traditionally static social structures with lopsided economies and, in some instances, a Malthusian imbalance between population and resources are exposed to the simultaneous impact of multiple revolutions. Anti-imperialistic nationalism prompts attempts to defy ultimate dependence on outside assistance; dependence on foreign capital worsens yet further the relationship between the more and the less advanced countries. In many parts of the world today, these and other problems have to be coped with amid the insecurities peculiar to the power vacuum left behind by receding Western imperialism and tempting the imperial Soviets. Far from being complementary, the tasks of building new national communities and organizing the international community at the same time tend to frustrate each other.[3]

The major ideological agency of international fragmentation has been for years the principle of national self-determination. It was never, of course, the only principle governing a settlement; it had always to compete with other political, economic, and strategic requirements. In the first place, the interplay between the balance of power and national self-determination remained; only the aura of legitimacy had been transferred. All major belligerents of the First World War and many of the Second World War proclaimed, more or less sincerely, the right of small nations to self-government; all practiced at one time or another, more or less aptly, the politics of the balance of power in violation of the principle.[4] In the second place, the apparently simple principle, when extended eastward, was brought to bear on areas with ethnically mixed populations and ran into two insoluble antitheses: first, between the dynamics of nationality and the statics of the territorial basis of the state and sovereignty; second, between the monistic implications of nationalism and the pluralistic structure of the societies in European, Asian, and African "Balkans." The resulting territorial and minority issues have unsettled relations within and between the newly independent countries and have encouraged intervention by local and remote Great Powers.

When self-determination is identified with anti-imperialism, the problem becomes even more complicated. The benefit of the principle is then demanded for peoples still under imperial sway; it is denied by recent beneficiaries if an activated minority group asserts it against themselves. The self-accelerating and intrinsically limitless momentum of fragmentation is halted artificially. The dilemma is real, since neither continued disintegration nor the application of a dual standard is likely to produce stability in Asia any more than it did in Central and Eastern Europe.

Continuing national self-determination was not among the

major assumptions of the League Covenant. An exception may be found in the privileged class of mandates; the rule was implicit in the protection of national minorities. The latter was an attempt to contrive a balance between the legitimate rights of individuals, the formerly subject and dominant nationalities, and the new or enlarged states. An internationally supervised equilibrium between the nation-state and its multinational content was to replace the hitherto postulated coincidence of state and nation in ethnically mixed areas and consolidate the foundations of international peace; it was opposed by most of the affected smaller states as a discriminatory device for the perpetuation of domestic instability, external insecurity, and international conflict. Apprehensions of this kind were confirmed when, in the wake of the system's failure, Nazi Germany perverted the idea of national self-determination and protection of minorities into a tool of regional hegemony. After the Second World War, the United Nations sought with little success to universalize the protection of nationality as one of human rights.[5]

A different approach to an adjustment between nationality and state was propagated by advocates of cultural pluralism and national federalism. The theory would restrict the state to nationally indifferent functions, while the several nationalities would enjoy corporate cultural autonomy. If nationality is to be depoliticized, the state would have to be denationalized. The critics would weigh claims to the right of national self-determination, producing ever smaller exclusive units, against the values of international order, security, and welfare, and the capacity to implement the right. They favor a diversified self-determination which would be exercised in favor of larger plural agglomerations for economic and military purposes, capable of meeting more adequately individual and group needs. But the different pluralistic projects and the protection of minorities have common flaws: they are likely to weaken the state in a situation of persisting insecurity; and they underestimate the immanent statism of modern nationalism. The drive of nationality for independent statehood has actually continued and spread into the colonial field, in conformity with the provisions of the Charter for self-determination and despite growing skepticism over its "excesses" both within and outside the United Nations.[6]

Thus, the forces of division and separatism continue to override voluntary integration, and adverse tendencies frustrate attempts at equilibration. Yet both democracy and industrialism generate needs and expectations which will not be permanently reconciled in the formula of nationalism alone. Such temporary compromise has been disrupted in Europe; it can hardly be successfully reproduced in the emergent East. The alternative to a larger framework of purpose is economic stagnation, social conflict, and crisis of democracy. It took two destructive wars for Europe to make the first hesitant and still largely abortive motions toward transcending her nationalisms in federative integration, partly in imitation of the more stable federal societies of the New World; and for member-states of international organization to concede to it at least nominally significant functional scope.

THE DYNAMICS OF FUNCTIONAL SCOPE

An international organization is in equilibrium with respect to its scope when the functional (and geographic) extent of its jurisdiction corresponds to the internationally relevant phenomena of interdependence on the one hand, and the willingness of member-states to yield the requisite measure of domestic jurisdiction or sovereignty on the other. The first part of the criterion stresses the objective need, the second the subjective disposition of the member-states; the two, needless to say, do not always match. The functions to be exercised are in the realm of military-political, social, economic, cultural, and other relations. An organization will be better able to realize its purposes if its scope is both extensive and in an equilibrium position.

The dynamics of functional scope consists of the growth and decline in the actually exercised functions and powers of an international agency. There is, first, the changing and progressively expanding international relevance of diverse phenomena; second, there are the varying responses of member-states to the often contradictory demands of coöperation and immediate self-interest.[7] In a progressive equilibrium movement, a reciprocal stimulation of expanding international activities, needs, and jurisdiction would maximize integration. In a rational world bent on maximizing national and international welfare, the distribution of domestic and international jurisdiction (and the distribution of economic assistance through either national or multilateral channels) would depend on calculations of marginal utility in terms of the rising economic and political liabilities and diminishing returns from unilateral efforts. Yet experience does not quite point to such a pattern.

The League's originally too narrow functional scope was far short of actual requirements. This set off pressures for extending its "technical" activities, as even the limited readiness of members for international regulation in such matters surpassed initial expectations. But the League did not get beyond isolated stop-gap measures of economic aid and reconstruction — implemented by traditional methods of private banking — and expert analyses with only intellectual authority. One economic conference generated another, but none produced long-term programs which would express the interrelation of the domestic and the international aspects of a cumulative global depression. League activities concerning colonial mandates, national minorities, police, and cultural matters, too, were narrowed down by the assertion of national sovereignty on the part of members. Moves initiated in the 1930's to extend the socio-economic functions of the League and make them into the principal concern of a non-coercive universal organization were too one-sided and came too late to matter. As a result, the activities and jurisdiction of the League never became sufficiently extensive to redress its initial functional disequilibrium.

After another war, the founders of the United Nations set out deliberately to learn from the inadequacies of the disowned parent organization. They contemplated a measure of military-political integration for security and provided for functions in socio-economic, colonial, cultural, and human-rights matters sufficiently extensive to be in some relation to objective needs. Yet the actually available jurisdictional powers were curtailed by a counterbalancing reëmphasis of domestic jurisdiction on the part of members unwilling to go too far in international interventionism. United Nations organs were confined to promotion, coördination, and recommendations, and were given little leeway in direct operational activities; the progress over the Covenant with regard to the scope of contemplated functions was seemingly offset by regression to a more arbitrary domestic jurisdiction in matters other than enforcement. In the theory of the Charter, the United Nations received an extensive functional scope with limited international jurisdiction.

At San Francisco, the smaller states especially insisted on the interdependence of the various aspects of the international equilibrium, and stressed the importance of social problems as the "basic factor," constituting the "very essence" of the new organization. Representative statements abounded in expressions like "balance" and "checks and balances." They emphasized organized military enforcement and the right of smaller states to take appropriate part in it; but the "negative side" was to be counterbalanced by the "positive side" of a constructive approach which would reflect a "new conception of international affairs" in a "social century." Freedom from want and freedom from fear of external aggression were considered inseparable.[8]

Attitudes differed in regard to the price of effective internationalism. The United States, prosperous and jealous of its sovereignty, did not wish to have the international organization "penetrate directly into the domestic life and social economy of the member states." The Soviet Union, committed to a social ideology alien to the majority in the organization, was yet more anxious to screen its revolution and impede joint promotion of evolutionary changes elsewhere. And the more self-confident among the smaller states, sensing in their potential the promise of future power, also desired to protect the "classical conception of the exercise of sovereignty" against all interference. Only the more tried smaller states were ready to accept as a hopeful tendency both the abandonment of the principle of unanimity and the discriminatory limitation of sovereignty foreseen by the Charter.[9]

In actual practice, there has been little difference between major and minor states when it came to conceding powers and scope to the organization; their attitude to specific projects has been determined chiefly by calculations of anticipated sacrifice and advantage.[10] Most beneficiaries of international coöperation prefer the multilateral global approach through the United Nations to the bilateral and regional type of economic assistance. Their chief criterion is assurance against economic and political domination; their conclusions agree with those of the experts who favor the United Nations method as a means to more economical spreading of burdens and pooling of resources. Some observers would apply more generally the structural principles of some of the specialized agencies, and formalize in voting procedures and representation the *de facto* unequal contribution and weight of major and minor states in organs like the Economic and Social Council; this might stimulate the use of United Nations channels by the principal industrial Powers. Yet the existing pattern of balancing informal influence and interests of primarily beneficiary and chiefly contributing states within the United Nations seems adequate enough to implement the functional scope conceded to the organization from case to case and limited by considerations of a different order. Weighted representation and vote would become acute issues only at a much higher level of international jurisdiction and integration.

So far, the welfare activities of the United Nations have concerned chiefly the immediate postwar reconstruction and relief, short- and long-range trade and monetary questions, technical and other assistance to underdeveloped countries, promotion of health and education, and the formulation of minimum rights and standards. A growing number of organs, commissions, and specialized agencies has sought to promote a dynamic socio-economic equilibrium on an international scale, in the face of a widening gap between standards of living in the advanced and the less developed countries, and between the world supply of food and the growing world population.

Among the goals is a balanced development of interdependent areas of concern such as food and industrial resources, health and productivity, technical skills and more general education; diffusion and mutual adaptation, rather than unilateral imposition, of skills, techniques, and standards in technical, educational, health, labor, and other matters; and the discovery of a common denominator, rather than a premature synthesis, in the realm of cultural and ideological differences in general, and in matters such as human — including political and social — rights in particular. The problem of method bears on the alternatives of a multilateral or bilateral, regional or global, short-term or long-term approach; rapid industrialization or a balanced development concentrating first on immediate food requirements and informed by the ultimate objective of a diversified international economic equilibrium; and many other questions. In attempting to cope with these tasks, the United Nations agencies have directly operated mainly in the expanded technical assistance program and in relief, refugee aid, and health and educational schemes, continuing the impressive tradition of UNRRA. In most respects, however, the United Nations remains confined to indirectly promotive coördination and recomendations.

The surface reasons are constitutional and financial. In regard to the constitutional reasons, the issue of inward-oriented promotive and outward-oriented preventive national jurisdiction of member-states is of course a factor, although a less serious impediment than might have been expected. United Nations organs have indulged in a fairly broad — some would say too broad — construction of their jurisdiction in matters however remotely affecting international peace; the clause is not meant to apply to specialized agencies; and actual operations and resolutions backed by major states have a practical impact which counteracts the lack of explicit authority over national resources and policies.[11] As to the funds made available for United Nations-sponsored multilateral programs by the member-governments, most particularly the conspicuously involved United States, they have been relatively small. Yet both constitutional and financial limitations only indicate the deeper causes rooted in the contemporary ideological and power conflicts on the one hand, and in vested sectional and national interests in traditional methods and the existing socio-political *status quo* on the other. Where interests meet, the United Nations agencies have been able to initiate and carry through varied socio-economic programs combining self-help and mutual aid on an extensive geographic scale.

When it comes to dependent communities and their rise to self-government, the record of the United Nations is equally ambiguous. Unlike the League, the United Nations is committed to continued national self-determination, especially in the colonial realm, implemented in ways which would not injure the international community as a whole; like the League system of mandates, the United Nations approach to trust and nonself-governing territories registers the interplay of conflicting influences, including the strategic and other concerns of the administering

Powers, pressures of public opinion, and the resurgence of the colonial peoples. At present, the argument between colonial and anti-colonial Powers over national self-determination and international jurisdiction is inseparable from the cold war. That makes for a forcible rather than peaceful and concerted progression toward self-government and independence. It has proved impossible even to define authoritatively to the satisfaction of all concerned the "factors" requisite for either. But the authority of the United Nations in regard to trusteeships and nonself-governing territories has been steadily growing.[12]

As full rights of membership continue to be extended to ever more political communities with larger pretensions than substance, the United Nations itself is in danger of incurring a structural disequilibrium. Already, the delicate balance between the West and the non-Communist East within the organization is awkwardly poised — and antagonized colonial Powers oppose with growing resentment the interference of the General Assembly, swayed by ex-colonial members, in matters reserved in their view to the Trusteeship Council or to domestic concern. It is more and more apparent that the functional scope of the United Nations would profit by combining provisions for fragmentation by way of national self-determination with a complementary concern for the integration of new and old independent political communities on a larger basis.

These and other unruly facts of life have dimmed the wartime dream of security as an "undisturbed social life," and of a peace which would bring nations actively together. The problem of power has not been "tamed." [13] Piecemeal functional coöperation in chiefly economic matters is not a self-sufficient alternative to an authoritative law and organization of collective security. There is no clear separability, priority, or causation, but the lack of military-political adjustment is certain to maximize the intrusion of power considerations into socio-economic relations and reinforce ideological antagonisms. It is therefore crucial that global realization of either an integrational adjustment of the military-political equilibrium into greater conformity with the principles of collective security, or an effective system of international control and limitation of national armaments has been impossible. The perhaps unique opportunity of the year 1919 for the democratic

Powers was missed; since then, there has been no real second chance. The nonaggressive nations failed to preserve preponderant power and purpose which would encourage others to a coöperative rather than expansionist response to growing interdependence; they were no more willing than the aggressive Powers to merge limited resources in a collective military establishment — thus expanding the functional scope of international organization — and continued to rely on strictly national defense potentials and particular alliances. A very real "disarmament" is implicit in international specialization of production; no nation can, however, be the first to undertake it in a situation of competitive balancing of military might.

The pervasive circularity which vitiates attempts to resolve the crucial problems of international relations bars both one-sided disarmament and linear one-factor approaches. A limited advance toward security and welfare, combining the requirements of stability and change, might result only from a pragmatic adjustment of the multiple interactive process, exploiting opportunities for international coöperation and integration as they arise.

THE DILEMMA OF FUNCTIONAL SCOPE — AND OF GLOBAL ORGANIZATION

Hitherto, the functional scope of international organization has been seriously circumscribed. Among the reasons are conflicts of states, ideologies, and cultures; the cult of national sovereignty and vested interests; and the by-passing of existing international facilities in larger undertakings such as the European Recovery Program. International organization thus faces a dilemma in regard to functional scope, too. An objectively unrealistic, or narrow, functional scope means disequilibrium in relation to the actual needs of interdependence; an objectively realistic, or extensive, scope will be frustrated as one group of member-states reacts against the one-sided internationalism of another group by emphasizing domestic against international jurisdiction and employing other channels free from undesired interference. The first horn impaled the League, the other has been hurting the United Nations.

In relating the institutional to the multiple equilibrium, the United Nations was an improvement over the League: it reversed the earlier assumption, that military-political and socio-economic problems were separable, into a recognition of their interrelation and proposed to implement the relationship. It is true that the United Nations has not operated directly in many fields and has tended to intensify at least as much as to integrate the multistate system; modern international law and organization continue to lack both a firm hold over military force and a living basis of widespread emotional allegiance among directly benefited individuals, which would enhance their functional efficiency as instruments of social control and controlled change. Yet, such as they are, the activities of the United Nations in transmuting colonialism into new forms and promoting a more satisfactory distribution of welfare for long-range security are taking shape as an essential, if limited and controversial, function of the organization in world affairs.

The inconclusive over-all record of both the League and the United Nations goes far in explaining why there is such a divergence of attitudes toward the very idea of international organization. It may be seen as the projection of the democratic principle into international relations; or it may be viewed as a new means for implementing the ancient imperial principle of law and order. It is possible to be a zealous advocate and expect from global organization a fundamental reshaping of international politics, view it with skepticism as diminishing the feeling of responsibility on the part of the Great Powers, or reject outright the possibility of an effective organization of the multistate system.[14]

In fact, international organization is only one, more or less active and forceful, factor in the process of international politics; and specific arrangements are in turn only one element in the organization's effectiveness. It is therefore unwise to expect too much and be embittered by less than total achievement; it is only mildly interesting to deliberate whether the conception of this or that organization was a better one. The League has been described as coördinate, the United Nations as organic because it is more centralized.[15] Theoretically, a centralized organic structure with a measure of military-political and socio-economic integration would seem more fit to develop and maintain a multiple equilibrium. Similarly, the eclectic approach of the Charter to the problem of peace and security seems superior to the somewhat formalistic emphases of the Covenant. But the difference between an institutional blueprint and effective institutionalization in actual operation is tremendous. On the face of it, the United Nations was initially closer to an equilibrium position with regard to structure, security commitment, and functional scope. It has been, however, more vulnerable to the described dilemmas and from a deadlock tended to fall back into decentralization, near-equilibrium on a lower level of performance, or outright disequilibrium reminiscent of the League. A major, if somewhat extraneous, point in favor of the United Nations has been the more determined support by at least one Great Power. Yet the price is unpredictability and occasional opportunism.

In the question whether international law and organization can control military-political and socio-economic events and counteract geopolitically rooted tendencies, or are more likely to be subverted by them, the burden of evidence favors the second alternative. Most of the resulting developments have conspired to turn organizing genius from the global to the regional approach to security and welfare. The disequilibrium or deadlock of international organization has encouraged regional decentralization; the trend to horizontally expanding functionalism has been at least equaled by the drive to enlarge the vertical power structures of major states by the addition of dependable allies and dependent satellites. Collective security and national self-determination have failed to reinforce each other as anticipated; their respective power deformations tend to converge in regional patterns centered in a hegemonic Great Power. This applies to the self-determination of the Soviet as well as the French Revolution, to the United Nations as well as the Atlantic Charter and Wilson's League. All experienced, sooner or later, the submergence of many smaller communities in a Great Power's regional orbit of domination, be it Napoleon's continental system, Nazi Germany's *Lebensraum*, Imperial Japan's coprosperity sphere, or Soviet Russia's camp of peace and socialism.

Historical experience backed political analysis in persuading many that regionalism was the natural pivot in the cycles of fragmentation and integration, and, therefore, the obvious focus for international organization as well.

CHAPTER 5

THE GEOGRAPHIC SCOPE

Regionalism is supposed to introduce a touch of realism into international organization. It should narrow the gap between a general system and the particular facts of power and geography; regional organization might serve as a medium for the reciprocal adjustment of the institutional framework, to which it pertains, and geopolitical conditions, to which it can be more easily adapted. Whereas global organization seeks in vain to uphold the principle of general interests and interdependence, its regional offshoot is a frank concession to the limited reach of national interests and capacities and their gradual shading off in geographic space. Advocates of regionalism postulate a more intimate sense of community and of common dangers within a regional compass; this should serve as a basis for closer and more reliable coöperation, and advance integration and planning for security and welfare. In a closer association of only a few partners sharing concrete interests, the growing liabilities and diminishing advantages from each additional given and received commitment should have a better chance than in a general system to cancel themselves out and ensure maximum possible joint security. The same should be true of functional scope with respect to regional welfare. In this fashion, more authoritative regional institutions would stabilize a more specific guarantee of mutual assistance and a more extensive functional scope in a position of equilibrium with the heightened ability and willingness of member-states to perform.[1]

Yet many of the advantages of regionalism and all of its consistency with global organization depend on the extent to which the two organizational forms are in reciprocal equilibrium.

THE GLOBAL-REGIONAL EQUILIBRIUM

The requirements of such equilibrium are similar for all composite organization, and similar to those of the structural equilibrium of organs. They involve, again, two major criteria. First, the different organizational forms — in this case the global and the regional institutions — are in equilibrium individually and reciprocally when the scope of their respective functions corresponds to their geographic scope, the composition of their membership, and the needs they are to serve. Second, the two forms must mutually reinforce each other by a proper differentiation of their functions on the one hand, and their reciprocal integration under the over-all control of the more inclusive body on the other. The differentiation and distribution of functions should be such as to make the two forms complementary and only potentially substitutive; the criterion should be the fitness of either type of organization to perform the allotted tasks more effectively. Ideally, a measure of competition between the central organization and its subdivisions would promote a progressive equilibrium between them and help expand the total functions and powers of the composite organization.

To meet these requirements, the regional organizations must have a primarily internal focus, i.e., must be chiefly concerned with intraregional peace, security, and welfare, leaving priority in inter- and extraregional security and other problems to the world body; the integration of the two forms is furthered by structural and functional dovetailing, mutual checks and overlapping membership, and the ultimate supremacy and control of the central body acting as a coactive framework for regional arrangements. Integration can go with considerable autonomy for the regional bodies; but a virtual substitution of unintegrated regional arrangements for a weakened world organization upsets the reciprocal equilibrium and leaves wide open all gaps.

The architects of the League did not aim deliberately at an equilibrium between the world organization and the regional understandings; in a merely coördinate system there also seemed to be no need for centralized control over an organic integration of the two forms. Their respective functions were neither defined nor differentiated; joint membership of individual states in parallel systems would supply the main, if tenuous and often confusing, link. Later compromises between central authority vested in the Council and regionalized enforcement embodied in the Draft Treaty and the Geneva Protocol were opposed by the world-wide multiregional organization, the British Commonwealth. But together with the inadequacy of the Covenant, these models inspired the framers of the Charter to seek an organically integrated equilibrium between the general organization, the regional arrangements, and the provisions for individual and collective self-defense. It was justly felt that the issue might determine the success or failure of the United Nations as a whole.[2]

A workable compromise between the requisite autonomy for regional arrangements and their equally necessary subordination to central authority would check two undesirable developments: first, the dangers of competitive balancing of power among regional alliances too independent from central authority; second, the spread of paralysis from a deadlocked central authority to too subordinate regional bodies. An important means to that end was a painstaking distribution of powers and differentiation of functions: the world organization was assigned primary responsibility for general security and welfare; the regional arrangements were entrusted with primary responsibility for the pacific settlement of disputes and supplementary responsibility for enforcement. The Security Council and a Military Staff Committee susceptible of regional decentralization were to ensure central control in matters of security. An arbitrary use of the veto in the Security Council would, however, paralyze regional enforcement, too. This imbalance in favor of central authority was redressed by the provision for collective self-defense, itself in turn checked by the requirement of previous "armed attack" and the ultimate authority of an active Security Council. Individual and collective self-defense is authorized until the Council has acted and, by implication, when it fails to act. It is thus only potentially substitutive for general intervention; it reinsures regional autonomy and self-help but does not impair the supremacy of an effective global organization.

Senator Vandenberg's decisive formula was inspired by the desire to find a mean in the interests of the United States as one of the sponsors of an authoritative global organization and as the leader of the regional Inter-American system. The concern continues, but the global-regional equilibrium has been recently interpreted in favor of regional organization. It is therefore useful to remember that the original compromise was intended to reinsure potential victim states rather than to facilitate the side-stepping of the world organization when it is ready and able to act.[3]

The dynamics of the global-regional equilibrium is bounded by the ideal extremes of a universal organization without regional subdivisions and a completely regionalized international organization. A cyclical process registers the recurrent weakening of the global body and attendant proliferation of regional arrangements on the one hand, and subsequent returns to global organization despite tendencies to the contrary on the other. The universalist purists would expunge regionalism and with it the antagonistic features of the balance of power and spheres of influence. Wilson and Hull leaned in that direction, reacting against the regional and particular alliances which had disrupted the Concert and the League systems. On the other hand, during World War II, the French defended regional organization as the basic component rather than infraction of collective security; Churchill and Roosevelt favored a decentralized system of continental organizations; and a whole school, yet to be discussed, agitated for Great-Power-centered regionalism. In fact, a new global organization, the United Nations, was established and has failed, where the League had not even seriously tried, to contain the trend to regional decentralization. A Western system of alliances evolved under the Charter's provision for collective self-defense, and a Soviet network under another of the Charter's escape clauses for centrally unfettered regionalism.[4]

Recurrent regional decentralization thus constitutes the more conspicuous half of the entire cycle. It reflects the declining faith in the general guarantee attending postwar realignments into fixed political divisions. In terms of the equilibrium analysis, regional disintegration occurs under the pressure of converging and intersecting disequilibria and deadlocks in the world organization, manifest in its lopsided structure, reduced and decentralized commitment to mutual assistance, and a functional scope inadequate for military-political and socio-economic integration on a global scale. The ideal of a stable and progressive global-regional equilibrium is then subverted into an unstable equilibrium: there is little or no mutual reinforcement and countervailing self-assertion of the general organization against encroaching regionalism; and the progressive weakening of the global body is accelerated by each successive increase in the number and functional scope of the regional bodies.

In both theory and practice, the original compromise is revised to fit the new position. The symptoms and indices are many. There is, first, an expedient redistribution of functions between the two forms and, second, the relaxing of reciprocal integration and central control. The global organization is superseded as the principal enforcement agency of collective security; the regional bodies cease to be only potentially substitutive and are substituted in fact. Advance military integration and planning are transferred to regional alliances as more likely to ensure certain and timely performance. The world body is depressed from a controlling into a subsidiary and ancillary position. It is to conciliate rather than coerce; legitimize regional systems rather than implement centralized enforcement; and extend *ad hoc* its sanction or delegate authority to states acting in self-defense rather than organize security in a systematic manner. It is to help negotiate political settlements before or after a breach of peace. In a word, it is to serve as a safety valve, a moral force, and should not try to be simultaneously plaintiff, sheriff, and judge. Its major object is supposed to be peaceful development for welfare, not military security.

Not the least attraction of the League for France was its usefulness as a connecting framework and legal basis for her network of alliances. The same role has now been assigned by many to the United Nations with regard to NATO and the rest of the Western security system. Only the minority position of the Soviet bloc countries prevents them from trying to appropriate the League's successor for a similar purpose. Both organizations shifted their focus gradually to functions other than the enforcement of security. There is a tendency to forget, however, that the theory of the revised global-regional balance appears valid only from the vantage point of one particular regional system. Applied generally, it leads to competitive claims on the legitimizing authority of the general organization, weakened in its capacity to determine impartially guilt and innocence in a breach of peace. Besides, the trend reduces the prestige and vitality of the global body, alienates from it all but fitful support and respect of crucial states, and threatens to deliver it into the hands of members enamored of mediation and appeasement.[5]

There are other adverse consequences. The revised balance, or rather disequilibrium, is likely to involve competition among regional alliances and inconsistencies between the general and the regional security system. Competitive regional systems may be the necessary instruments for maintaining a disturbed global equilibrium of power; their rise certainly aggravates the disequilibrium of the general organization with respect to both its security commitments and the regional organizations themselves. The ideal of Great-Power concert for a collective security controlling the balance-of-power dynamics yields to the fact of Great-Power-centered antagonistic alliances. There, the shift is from internal to external focus. A regional arrangement is no longer meant to make concrete the abstract general commitment for states within a region and to localize a possible conflict by delimiting in advance the area of additional obligations; it specifies in effect the general commitment against a suspected aggressor from outside the region. The term "collective security" is used loosely to denote any military system jointly organized by several states. Integration of such particular systems into a controlling world organization is out of the question, inasmuch as it would acquaint the suspected fellow-member with measures actually taken against him.

Such a state of things reduces to the vanishing point the always problematic political and ideological, as distinct from nominal legal, consistency of the two forms. If a frozen *status quo* discredits the abstract morality of the idea of collective security, frozen alliance ties can inhibit as seriously a flexible and impartial response to the abstract imperatives of the general commitment; active participation of major states in both organizational forms distorts then the implementation of their reallocated functions, which it was supposed to coördinate. Theoretical incompatibility may be resolved when a specific case of aggression happens to make complementary the nominally consistent terms of the general and the regional treaties. Such a convergence is assumed for the Western system of alliances and its relation to the United Nations. A contrary aggressor-victim relation may, however, turn theoretical inconsistency into actual contradiction, and reveal a particular arrangement as an instrumentality of aggression or support for aggression against the general system. This was substantially the case with the Soviet system in regard to the North Korean and Communist Chinese aggression. A less flagrant contradiction between regionalism and general collective security appeared in the Guatemalan case; it will be discussed presently.

To be sure, a regionally promoted balance of power may ultimately encourage resort to the larger organization by making aggression unattractive and raising the costs of competitive armaments to the point of uneconomically diminished returns. Yet the recurrent rebound to a general organization, the second movement of the cyclical fluctuation between the two forms, is due not only to calculations of marginal utility and to the actual or potential usefulness of a world body. It is caused also by the inadequacies of the narrower and allegedly much more effective organizational form. An inquiry into the internal equilibrium of regional organizations and alliances will disprove some of the facile assumptions about regionalism as the best practicable approach to security and the necessary preliminary stage to global community integration.

First about the structure of regional organizations. Practically none has surpassed the powers which would accrue to the Security Council under a fully implemented Charter. This is true of the Organization of American States, the British Commonwealth, if it can be described as a regional organization, the Little Entente, and in the final analysis, of NATO, too. A structural equilibrium among unequally powerful states is more difficult to evolve in a narrow Great-Power-centered arrangement. Formal affirmations of state equality and nonintervention cannot offset the fact of unilateral ascendancy in the absence of enough Great Powers to counterbalance each other. Too much comes to depend on the self-restraint of the dominant partner. This may intensify strains on the group's cohesion; it certainly gives rise to a real difficulty. On the one hand, an arrangement including several more or less competitive Great Powers in addition to smaller states will not materialize at all or will be unsuccessful, as witnessed by the various attempts to apply the Locarno idea in the interwar period and more recently. On the other hand, a regional alliance system centered in one preponderant Power will be subject to special dangers; it may only too easily serve as a disguise for a sphere of influence, relieving the hegemonic Power of the risks and the odium implicit in a direct assault on the independence of the affected smaller states. The regionally patterned, bilateral non-aggression and mutual-assistance pacts of Nazi Germany and Soviet Russia supplied the most flagrant instances. But any regional arrangement, be it an OAS or a NATO, will be beset by some of the suggested problems.

The odds are no more favorable in regard to the mutual-assistance commitment. First of all, it will tend to be on a relatively low level. The mutual-assistance treaties underlying the Little Entente had a very limited bearing, and the Arab League featured at first no security commitment at all. The Locarno guarantees were qualified, distrusted as not impartial in implementation, and in the end were ineffective. Even ambitiously conceived instruments like the Rio Treaty, the recent Manila and Baghdad Pacts setting up a Southeast Asian and a Middle Eastern Treaty Organization respectively, and the North Atlantic Treaty itself, do not provide for completely automatic military and other intervention in support of an ally subjected to armed attack or internal subversion. In many instances, the unfolding costs, divergent orientations and fears, antagonisms and sympathies are more influential than the parallel interests and anticipated advantages which bring neighbors into an alliance in the first place. It is both fair and safe to expect performance only when the actual occasion for invoking the alliance and the initial purpose of the treaty coincide precisely in character and follow each other rapidly in time. The temptation to evade the engagement will grow with the gap in either respect, and internal equilibrium with respect to the mutual-assistance commitment will lapse. Few allies fight and wars rarely spread as a result of particular commitments of long standing. Nor have regional alliances displayed heretofore any significant measure of military-political integration, with the exception of NATO and the "integration" of the Soviet system under the Warsaw Treaty.

All these inadequacies point to the weakest point of regionalism, its insufficient geographic scope. It is difficult and often impossible to define a geographic region; and a region is mostly unable to accommodate the requirements of larger supraregional interdependence. Few regions possess sufficient materials for the development of a multiple equilibrium among nations whose proximity is in fact rarely the source of coöperative harmony. The diversity among regions is rarely paralleled by complementary diversity within them. Neither do security areas and welfare areas as a rule coincide; the resulting overlaps call for larger coördination. The Charter recognized this and opted in principle against regionalism in socio-economic activities. And finally, members are not willing to concede to a less than global organization significantly greater functional scope and jurisdiction at the expense of their sovereignty; even a NATO and the British Commonwealth depend in this respect on fluctuating spontaneities, and the supranational powers conceded to the European Coal and Steel Community remain largely on paper.

As a result, the quest for security and welfare through regional organization alone is hedged in with limitations. The functional and the geographic scope are inadequate individually and do not correspond either to each other or to the needs of members and the objective requirements of global interdependence. Regional organization is in and by itself no absolute or virtual substitute for a world organization. Self-contained regional arrangements endure only rarely: they have to evolve toward still closer federative integration, which is rare; or disintegrate, which is common. Nor has an unequal balance between global and regional organization proved to be a lasting compromise.

A complete cycle consists thus of a movement between the two forms, as world organization is weakened by or succumbs to disequilibrium particularly with regard to general commitment and functional scope, regional organization runs into limitations chiefly with respect to geographic scope, and both forms fail to find the internal and reciprocal equilibrium necessary for greater security and welfare.

In what follows, these propositions about regionalism and its interdependence with global organization will be applied to regional arrangements as diverse as the Little Entente and the Arab

League, the Inter-American System and the British Commonwealth, the noninstitutionalized regionalism of Great-Power spheres, and to NATO and the actual and planned institutions of Western European integration.

TYPES OF REGIONALISM

To what extent are regional associations fit to adjust an intraregional equilibrium among unequally powerful states, improve the position of the relatively weaker states in the balance of power, and promote institutionally a multiple equilibrium within the region? There are different types of situations and responses. A relatively trusted Great Power may extend regional protection to not too resentful lesser associates; smaller states may have to pursue security and welfare in an area exposed to many conflicting pressures; and finally, such states may either accept active involvement or try to preserve a neutral position.

Smaller states exposed to the pressures of several major Powers find it most difficult to reconcile regionalism with membership in a general organization, national security, and genuine independence. This has been the situation of most smaller countries in Europe and, increasingly, in the Middle East and South Asia.

Weaker states ready or impelled to participate actively in the quest for national and international security value the greater independence and dignity of membership in a general organization; they are also attracted by the promise of more certain security from a regional alliance, based on concrete interests and backed by one or more Great Powers. They both desire and resent the need for alliance with a major state and seek to lean on a remote rather than a local Power. They would wish to receive the intervention of the powerful ally only when claimed and then with certainty; the Great-Power ally is likely to prefer the exact opposite. From the respective advantages of general and regional organization the smaller states wish, not unnaturally, to retain both. Only doubts about the effectiveness of the general system will tip the balance toward the regional pattern. But smaller nations that are anxious to avoid absorption in a Great-Power-centered alliance will wish for the regional pact to stay related to the general system of collective security and underpin rather than supersede it.

A new situation arises when the general system is discredited. Then even formerly activist smaller states may prefer to become buffers between contending Great Powers rather than participate in a regional pact. After 1933, Poland chose to be a "barrier of peace" between Germany and Russia instead of joining an Eastern Locarno; Belgium resumed her neutrality after the unpunished breach of Western Locarno and the Covenant. Or, for domestic as well as external reasons, neutralism may be elevated into a creed and generate a corresponding conception of regionalism.

Contemporary Asian neutralism typifies the preference of smaller states for regional organization without Great Powers. According to this school of thought, the global character of security requires a global approach through a general collective security system. It is there that the Great Powers should perform their functions and counterbalance each other in the process. Regional arrangements around a Great Power are merely disguises for domination over weaker associates; they could not enforce sanctions against another Great Power if they conformed literally with the Charter. Instead, regional organizations should be set up among states with approximately equal resources and development, certain to respect each other's sovereignty and independence. They should concentrate on socio-economic and cultural tasks and stay aloof from Great-Power conflicts.[6]

Such a doctrine cannot but appeal to youthful nationalism anxious for both economic development and political independence. The influence of the Asian-African bloc in the United Nations makes it safe to emphasize general organization as the principal instrument of security, forum of mediatory activities, and agency for economic assistance. Consistently enough, India and a number of other Southeast Asian countries, with the exception of the Philippines and Thailand, refused to join the security pact for the area sponsored by the Western Powers. But the implementation of the alternative program has run into difficulties, too. Among them are insufficiency of local resources, divergent orientations in regard to the "cold war" intertwined with mutual territorial and other conflicts, and distrust of real or suspected leadership aspirations on the part of regionally prominent states like India, the Philippines, and, increasingly, Communist China.

It is a sad fact that all areas of any scope comprise states with highly unequal resources and corresponding claims to influence; and that the exclusion of Great Powers, local or remote, is not always possible (even supposing it were always desirable) since most countries are unable to ensure regional security and welfare with their limited resources alone. The Bandung Conference produced chiefly verbal results; the Colombo Plan is inseparable from British and American support; and a "Marshall Plan" for South Asia would be sure to vitalize the languid SEATO into more than literal resemblance to NATO.

Convenient and strikingly comparable examples of the virtues and the limitations of small-state regionalism are the Little Entente and the Arab League, emerging from the First and the Second World War respectively. It is worth while to look at the similarities and limitations, without denying the differences and accomplishments.[7]

The similarities are many. Both associations brought together relatively minor communities formerly belonging to large empires, situated in contested geopolitical areas with considerable strategic importance and resources but inadequate local power for successful defense. The decisive incentive to association was a negative one, opposition to revisionist neighbors — Hungary and to a lesser extent Bulgaria in the case of Yugoslavia, Rumania, and Czechoslovakia; the Jews in Palestine in the case of the Arab countries. Beyond this, the partners desired to keep down Great-Power interference in the region: the founders of the Arab League were anxious to expel first the French and then the others, and to create a self-contained Arab world in the Near East; the Little Entente statesmen were chiefly concerned about Germany, Italy, and Russia. Both groups needed, however, the aid of friendly Powers as a means to stability and development. At the outset, all the Little Entente countries found a unifying safeguard against their local antagonists in France's blanket support for the *status quo*. The Arabs depended, however resentfully at times, on Great Britain and, more recently, the United States for revenues, welfare, and security, using in the latest phase both the overt advances and the latent threat of the Soviet Union as a counter to a too exclusive Western sway. The positive, if vague, inspiration of both associations was the desire to build from the fragments of a "balkanized" area the nucleus of a larger union.

Attempts to cope with a critical regional position engaged all aspects of the international equilibrium. The coördinate structure of both organizations rested on the postulate of undiminished national sovereignty under international law; neither of them possessed internal constitutional homogeneity; but both leagues displayed on many occasions considerable diplomatic unity. The Little Entente states sought deliberately to integrate their particular system into the League in order to reinforce it and demonstrate its defensive character; the paramount object of the Arab League seemed to be less consistent with the principles and purposes of the Charter. Both groups increased their international weight and internal cohesion by common action in global institutions. The Little Entente acquired a permanent representation in fact on the League Council and frequently had one member express a concerted view in the Assembly; it was described as a virtual diplomatic federation, an organic union, and the most perfect form of a regional understanding on record; at times it might fancy itself as constituting something like a collective Great Power with respect to external relations. There were attendant dangers. The group's institutional influence depended greatly on France's backing and did not rest on effective military-political and socio-economic regional integration; the disparity between the position in the institutional equilibrium and the balance of power gave rise to ambiguities and to eventually disappointed expectations. Much the same applies to the disparity between the weight of the Arab bloc in the United Nations General Assembly, the Arab League as a military force, and the Middle East as an economically lopsided area.

The level of the mutual-security commitment was low in both instances. The Little Entente rested on only a gradually consolidated network of bilateral treaties of mutual assistance providing for joint defense against Hungary and, in the case of Yugoslavia and Rumania, against Bulgaria. All members had a treaty with France, but only the Franco-Czechoslovak Treaty had a convincingly military character. No mutual-security provisions adorned the original Arab League Pact, and the lack was remedied only reluctantly after the conflict with Israel. Neither of the two associations developed an integrated collective force which would sustain their position in the region and in the global security system. In regard to the latter, the Little Entente supported collective enforcement in both principle and practice, whereas the Arab League states — with the exception of Lebanon — adopted a neutralist attitude to the United Nations action in Korea and to collective security generally.

In the actual military-political balance, the Entente could assert itself successfully against the largely disarmed Hungary, particularly as long as she lacked the backing of a determined Power; the Arab League states failed to tip in their favor even the local balance of power with regard to Israel. In 1948 they placed themselves very much in the position of aggressors under the collective-security system and had to be saved by that system from a still greater defeat. Since then, they have gone to great lengths to improve their relative military posture. The Little Entente was in a worse position in relation to the local Great Powers; perhaps characteristically, it was not meant to operate against them in the first place. Among the local Powers, Czechoslovakia feared most Germany, Rumania's main apprehensions were focused on Soviet Russia, and Yugoslavia was at odds with Italy. Centrifugal anxieties were translated into divergent orientations when the Hungarian threat had passed and Germany again emerged into the position of power and influence; by that time the initial unifying basis was eroded by France's changing policies toward Italy and Soviet Russia, and by her own growing dependence on a Great Britain opposed much too long to Central-Eastern European commitments. The Arab states have been no more effectively united in matters of regional defense. Under the jealous if contested leadership of nationalistic Egypt, the Arab League did anything but complement the various Middle Eastern defense schemes put forward by the far from harmonious Anglo-Saxon Powers. Torn by conflicting rights and competing demands of intra- and interregional balance of power, the Middle Eastern area beyond the Turkish borders of NATO would fare no better than Central-Eastern Europe in case of an unfavorable shift in the global equilibrium.

Both the Little Entente and the Arab League pacts provided for many-sided functional coöperation through appropriate organs; but accomplishments were limited by subjective attitudes as well as by actual inadequacy of resources. The predominantly agricultural economies of Yugoslavia and Rumania could not be adequately complemented by industrialized Czechoslovakia alone; in the most favorable conditions the entire Danube area would hardly be a sufficient basis for self-sustaining economic integration and development among politically sovereign states. As for the Arab states, they are patently unable to overcome on their own the many economic, socio-political, and cultural obstacles to the growth of their one-sided, underdeveloped economies; Israel's industrial potential is completely dependent on outside assistance; and plans for a joint Jordan River Valley development languish in the absence of a political settlement.

In both areas, indecisive and rival gestures toward political and economic integration have been frustrated by divisive separatisms. In the Arab Middle East as well as in Central-Eastern Europe, separatism has been fed by vested interests of the élites, dynastic and personal feuds, and the overcompensating nationalism of plural societies split along cultural and social lines and confused rather than fused by various pan-movements; the Little Entente and the Arab League states were kept from closer ties with their neighbors by additional interrelated conflicts over national minorities, irredentist revisionism, and claims to regional leadership, all residues of the shifting tides of historic empires. In such a situation, a judicious combination of Great-Power intervention and aid may be decisive. France, however, was unable to induce a larger association of the Danubian states. Her own economic structure barred other than financial backing for immediate and chiefly military requirements; and no scheme for Central-Eastern European integration could overcome the contradiction of a political orientation against the German Reich and economic dependence on the German market and product. In the critical period following the Second World War, the United States had more means but no more consistency and success with a parallel socio-economic and military-political approach to Middle Eastern problems; and the Soviet Union is now bestirring itself in both respects to end the Anglo-American monopoly and succeed Germany in the Middle East as well.

On the whole, despite more hopeful isolated signs, seemingly imperative preoccupations of the moment militated in both instances against a concerted attack on long-range regional problems, thus perpetuating conditions inimical to internal as well as external security and welfare.[8]

It would appear that a loose regional grouping of smaller states has but limited merits. In matters of security and the military-political balance, the addition of small-state weights must be qualified by a drastic deduction on account of insufficient coördination and divergent purpose. Only still weaker states of the region can be contained. The Little Entente was not really put to a conclusive test, but the evidence is not encouraging; the Arab League has been anything but a convincing success militarily and otherwise. Neither of the two organizations was in equilibrium with respect to a sufficiently centralized institutional structure, exacting mutual-security commitment, and functionally and geographically extensive scope. They did not realize for their members, let alone the respective regions as a whole, closer integration in terms of a favorably adjusted multiple equilibrium. The desire to contain Great-Power contests for a monopoly of regional sway came to naught over the apparently irresoluble conflicts among the revisionists and the anti-revisionist smaller states. Yet for ultimate success any comparable organization must transcend its original negative impetus in a broader community. In the final analysis, the fortunes of the Little Entente were tied to the fate of the general organization; and any Arab regional system will depend on a favorable configuration of global factors at least as much as on closer ties of language, religion, and shared past.

In no way are, of course, these limitations peculiar to the two regions: they apply to Western Europe almost as much as to Central-Eastern Europe, and the similarities of the latter with Southeast Asia are even more pronounced than those with the Middle East.

THE THEORY AND PRACTICE OF GREAT-POWER ORBITS

Smaller countries are hardly able to contrive regional integration and stability on their own; a more promising alternative might be regional groupings anchored in the superior resources of a nuclear Great Power. This idea was worked out during World War II in theories contemplating a world order based on such regions; the vision has been realized since in some places. It is therefore both necessary and fair to distinguish between the intrinsic validity of the conception and its deformation in the Soviet and to a lesser extent Chinese orbits, between its ideological roots in the experience of British and American dominion over lesser communities and its derivation from the circumstances of the wartime alliance.[9]

According to the idea, regional groupings of small states ought to cluster around the local Great Power and pool military, economic, and other resources in peace and in war. Such an arrangement would implement the fact of interdependence and the need for integration of resources and advance planning for defense. The smaller communities would extend to the focal Great Power facilities and amicable coöperation, and receive in return a realistic measure of independence, aid, and protection. They stand to gain by transferring into stronger hands the chief responsibility for organizing regional security; and the Great Powers would also profit from having dependable allies within their strategic area. There would be more security and prosperity both intra- and interregionally.

Among the more or less explicit premises is a gloomy view of the "mirage" of collective security, its feasibility and implications. Instead of a general and abstract commitment there should be a realistic balance between national power and commitments confined to areas of vital interests.[10] There should be no more all-out application of the principle of national self-determination generating insecure and insecurity-producing small national states. Instead, diversified self-determination should satisfy the needs for intimate cultural life of an ethnic community on the one hand, and for larger association for economic and military purposes on the other. Within a Great-Power-centered area of regional integration, modified collective security and modified self-determination would produce a more realistic pattern of organization. Logically enough, the theory is informed by skepticism about smaller states. Their validity, viability, and capacity to conduct independent foreign policy, defend themselves, or maintain their neutrality is questioned; their obsolete practices of economic nationalism and balance-of-power politics are condemned. By contrast, assumptions concerning the Great Powers are favorable. The authors of the idea emphasize the primacy of Great-Power strategic interests, their special ability and responsibility to ensure general security, and the ultimate dependence of the smaller states on their behavior. The legitimate interests of the major Powers and the legitimate rights of the lesser states are held to be compatible; so is national independence with strategic and economic interdependence. To concede bases to the protecting Great Power in no way infringes national independence and state equality. A cardinal assumption is that in their own interests the Great Powers will pursue liberal and nonaggressive policies toward the smaller states and each other. There is a connection: without self-restraint and respect for the rights of smaller states there can be no enduring accord among the Powers. Yet a nuclear coalition of the Great Powers must sustain the global order as necessarily as a nuclear Great Power must provide the magnetic core for regional integration.[11]

A general international organization is reduced to a secondary role or renounced altogether. It is pronounced "forever dead," not mentioned at all, or half-heartedly restored to life as a framework for globally ramified socio-economic functions and, somewhat illogically, the regulation of relations between the smaller and the greater states. A general system of collective security could hardly be admitted. A commitment which might require the intervention of an associated smaller country against the nuclear Great Power or another regionally associated state could not be honestly undertaken in law and honored in fact. There could be no organic connection between the global organization and the regional pattern even if the former were admitted to inferior coexistence. The Great-Power protectors interpose themselves in varying degrees between their dependents and the organization. This is more than a reasserted international hierarchy of the Concert type; the League's ideal of international democracy is replaced by international feudalism, a system of bilateral duties and rights rooted in territorial relationships, without the moral climate requisite for an equitable functioning of the system.[12]

On the one hand, the theory represents a deliberate concession verging on surrender to geopolitical determinism in world affairs; on the other, it half-consciously attempts to liberalize elements of the *Wehrwirtschaftsraum* doctrines of Nazism and the co-prosperity-sphere slogan of the Japanese in the light of British and

American experience. Unwittingly, the Western writers returned the compliment of the Nazi and Japanese apologists who had appealed to the admired and supposedly legitimizing precedent of the Monroe Doctrine; their reservations and inconsistencies show also how hard it is to reconcile liberal and totalitarian precepts in international politics. The difficulties did not seem insuperable in the glow of wartime alliance with the Soviet Union; but no attempt to extrapolate the "Good Neighbor Principle" and the idea of the Commonwealth from their particular contexts and elevate them into a general principle of international organization can assign due weight to a fundamental point which disqualifies the Anglo-American precedent from broader application.

The point is that international politics, being power-normative, comprises the interaction of power and purpose. The former has its rules and "laws" which no Power may and dare disregard; but the latter is affected by the projection into foreign policies of a nation's value system, ideology, social and governmental structure, and other variables. These influence objectives, methods of dealing with other nations, and the evaluation of the outside world in the same way as the nature of a nation's international involvement reacts on its domestic order. There are thus obvious differences in the type of control "natural" to different systems. A major difference between the totalitarian and the liberal Powers is the latter's capacity for transcending in an evolutionary fashion the coercive origins and aspects of control over weaker communities into a more consensual type of relationship. A totalitarian system seems unable either to maintain control on the basis of consent alone or still less to relax coercion without seeing its pattern of control disintegrate. If a liberal Power can rise above the limitations of domestic politics, it is in a better position to combine self-restraint based on more sensitive moral propensities with self-control derived from a pragmatic calculation of long-range advantage. A totalitarian system, with its haunting concern with survival, and equation of survival with expansion, prefers the absolute and immediate certainties of complete domination. In that sense it is always to some extent irrational.

Thus relations among unequal countries depend not only on the existing power situation; they are greatly influenced by the structure and purpose of the greater Powers as well. Each Power within its sphere faces the choice between the crude combination of imperialism and satellitism, and a more subtle reconciliation of its legitimate regional interests with the rights of the smaller nations. Even for a nontotalitarian Great Power the tendency to dominate rather than strive for consent will be difficult to resist in the absence of external countervailing restraints.

Accordingly, the unique evolution of the British Empire and the transient character of American imperialism in the Western Hemisphere were due in large part to the predominantly liberal values of the two societies. Both imperial systems avoided the self-aggravating momentum of deepening coercion, peculiar to their situation; instead, they have evolved in a process of self-determination for the smaller countries toward a new basis in consent, equality of status, and interdependence. In its imperialistic phase, the Monroe Doctrine embodied the major traits of the Great-Power-zone species: isolation of a regionally dominant nation's security area from the outside world and the maintenance therein of greatest possible political and economic conformity. Yet the more galling corollaries and uses of the Doctrine, notably in the Caribbean, were overcome in the Good Neighbor Policy as reciprocal pledges of nonintervention and mutual assistance for security and welfare extended outward the principles of American colonial and constitutional tradition; the growth of the Inter-American system is the tale of gradual multilateralization and institutionalization of North American hegemony into pan-American solidarity. Similarly, the originally coercive British Empire was progressively liberalized into the Commonwealth in an outward projection of British conventional constitutionalism with its aptitude for organic growth and adjustment. In both instances, although not with equal consistency, the greater Powers have shouldered ever more of the duties and retained less of the privileges of the association; by the same token, the smaller communities have been moving toward a position which is almost the reverse of a satellite's.[13]

The peculiar liberal ethos of the two English-speaking nations was not the only factor favorable to self-restraint; another was their geopolitical situation, in many respects unique. A deliberately manipulated balance of power in Europe freed the extra-European spheres of control of the insular Great Britain and the remote United States from large-scale competitive interference. If the United States was the incidental beneficiary of British balancing, it was also its occasional if secondary object — when Canning extended the technique into the New World to shield the young Latin American republics; and its opponent — when the senior North American Republic frustrated the attempts of the British as well as those of other non-American Powers to counterbalance its sway in the Western Hemisphere. By that time, however, the preponderance of the United States could not be really challenged from within the region and it could soon afford to be generous. Basically the same was true of Great Britain when she relaxed her control over the white settlements at the height of her nineteenth-century power and let them reinforce theirs by helping them federate. Factors of distance, too, favored moderation by making rigid control either unnecessary or too onerous; and the naval character of both nations' power called for only a limited claim on the resources and facilities of dependent communities.[14]

In neither case has all been sweetness and light. Both leading nations have tried with varying intensity and success to promote regional partnership rather than reinforce their own predominance. In the case of the Americas, the task has been impeded by the very economic and political superiority of the United States — not always wisely employed; in that of the British Commonwealth, by the decline in the resources and power of the mother country. In both instances, common ties of interest and sentiment have been strained by divisive pulls for greater independence or rival predominance in the Americas, for neutrality in Britain's wars or outright secession in the Commonwealth and Empire. Ireland and more than one Latin American republic gave the Anglo-Saxon Powers an opportunity to show unique self-restraint during the Second World War; they continue to demonstrate the failures of liberalized association between greater and smaller nations joined by geography but separated by nationality and the feelings of grievance. Argentina tried to find counterweights in hostile European Powers; outlying Dominions such as Canada and Australia could not but gravitate into the sphere of the United States, trying to keep in balance their relations with Washington and with the mother country. On the whole, it has been often difficult and sometimes impossible to span the many political, cultural, economic, and strategic divergences among geographically and racially differentiated segments within the Western Hemisphere and the Commonwealth.[15]

In the face of such shortcomings and maladjustments, both particular systems have found in global organization a useful means for a larger equilibrium.

The ambivalence of the smaller members of the Inter-American system in regard to general and regional organization reflects their attitude toward the United States, and is an inverted replica of this country's own dualism as a regional and a global Power. On the one hand, Latin Americans rely on the United States for security and welfare, and are jealous of its commitments outside the hemisphere; hence they sought at San Francisco to strengthen regional organization in relation to the global body. On the other hand, they continue to be uneasy about unilateral intervention by the United States within the hemisphere and value the general organization as a forum of their own extra-hemispheric self-affirmation. The regional collective-security pact of Rio, the Bogotá Charter's repudiation of even collective intervention in internal affairs, and the weight of the Latin American states in the United Nations constitute a coherent institutional basis for the resolution of their dilemma. Their massive collective vote provides the Latin American states with an additional potential check on the Colossus of the North. Washington's frequent dependence on this vote offsets at least partly in the eyes of the Latin Americans their real dependence on this country for their physical security and much of their welfare. In this fashion a not unimportant psychological equipoise is promoted in a situation surcharged with the familiar manifestations of rankling inferiority feelings.

Broadly comparable are the attitudes of the lesser members of the British Commonwealth. They, too, have sought to reconcile regional interests, association with a global Power, and the desire for independent status in world affairs by way of a favorable adjustment of the privileges and obligations which go with participation in both the general and the more restricted system. Membership in the League implemented internationally their independence; their stature grew further in the United Nations. For some smaller countries, like Ireland, membership in the general organization could serve to counterbalance the British connection; for all it provided an additional source of security, a framework for economic welfare larger than the imperial preference system and the sterling bloc, and a formal basis of resistance to undesired imperial entanglements. Conversely, the flexible Commonwealth tie gave the lesser members a higher standing in the world bodies; it preserved for them the more concrete safeguards of Britain's might as supplementary and if need be substitutive to general collective security; and, before SEATO, when British power was at a particularly low ebb, it even allowed that the regional ANZUS pact associate Australia and New Zealand with the United States under the aegis of the United Nations Charter, without including Great Britain herself.[16]

There is thus a definite interrelation between regional and global organization. Depending on policies and predispositions, it may be turned into mutual reinforcement advantageous to all parties; into merely one-sided advantage, for instance when regional systems keep the general organization out of some intra-regional affairs and purge themselves of others by passing them on to the world body; or into outright incompatibility. The Inter-American and the British Commonwealth systems cover mainly the first two possibilities; the Soviet bloc is a glaring instance of the fundamental conflict between self-contained territorial regionalism and the structure and spirit of global institutions. A less shocking incompatibility may be revealed in a specific event involving the application of collective security. In this respect the United States collaborated unwittingly with the Soviet Union to provide a striking illustration.

It revolves around the relevant features of the Korean and the Guatemalan cases. The two constitute a kind of inverted parallel. It may not be too far-fetched to say that the Communist-infiltrated Guatemalan government in the Western Hemisphere meant about the same to the United States as the pro-American South Korea on the mainland of Asia to Communist China and Soviet Russia. The common denominator was the existence in a small country of a political regime antagonistic to the local Great Power, which regarded the area as part of its geopolitical and historical orbit. It might be argued that the United States by its position in Japan was a local Power with regard to Korea, too;

the argument would hardly be admitted by the Communist Powers. If anything, the ambiguity highlights the theoretical weakness and the political dangers inherent in the unavoidable overlaps of the Great-Power-zone pattern. In both instances, the desire for ideological and political homogeneity within its security sphere induced the regional Great Power to look favorably, to say the least, on a forcible attempt to eliminate the discordant feature. The local Great Power interpreted as civil war what the remote Great Power, desirous of maintaining its foothold, described as international aggression. When the two breaches of the peace were brought before the United Nations, both the United States and the Soviet Union adopted in each case an attitude to collective enforcement almost diametrically opposite to that taken in the previous case. The only consistency in the situation was that the remote Great Power in both instances favored action, and the local Power inaction, on the part of the United Nations.

In both contrast and opposition to the complexities of the groupings around the United States and Great Britain stands the would-be monolithic unity of the Soviet bloc. There the question of an interaction between the smaller countries and the dominant Great Power as members of regional and world organization does not even arise. Instead, the Soviet system raises the issue, and the spectre, of the satellite as the typical status for smaller states in a Great-Power zone of the totalitarian variety.

An order based on satellitism is at the opposite pole to the premises of flexible equilibrium. Its fundamental principle is preponderance on one side and subjection on all others. A satellite cannot exert even vestigial political self-direction and international codetermination. Its nominal independence and sovereignty are revocable conveniences of the dominant Great Power and a concession to the principle of national self-determination inimical to outright annexation. The Great Power has absolute control without corresponding responsibility; the small states retain duties without correlative rights, the liabilities without the assets of international status. Satellitism has transposed into modern Europe the most reactionary manifestations of colonialism, including a perverted form of "indirect rule." The dependent community is an instrument for the dominant Power's security, prosperity, and expansion. At best, it can hope to collect the incidental perquisites of its ancillary status.

Institutionally, the relationship finds expression in a more or less enforced alliance — a *foedus iniquum* constituting a *societas leonina* — which is further reinforced by a "supranational" apparatus of party and secret police as the outreaching tentacles of the controlling totalitarian body politic. A two-level approach is facilitated by the very nature of the "dual state": a kind of federation between the Great Power and the small-state satellites on the party level, and the continuation of separate international status — far from unprofitable to the hegemonic Power — on the formal institutional plane. Actual federative strengthening among the satellites themselves is vetoed. In the socio-economic sphere, the techniques of exploitation will differ according to whether the Great Power practices private or state capitalism and places itself in the posture of creditor or debtor. Whatever the specific method, the captive economies will be anything but balanced internally, and regional coördination will be governed by immediate or long-range military needs of the imperialistic taskmaster. Any incidental industrial development of the satellite will be used to increase its economic, military, and political dependence. Finally, in the military-political security zone of the dominant state, the satellite will function as an expendable armed buffer, "ally," or proxy aggressor.

Being itself largely the result of previous global imbalance of power, the enforced satellite status of smaller countries will perpetuate global instability. A malaise settles over international affairs as majorities in the captive communities strain away from the local totalitarian to the more cognate remote Great Powers, who in turn contest the legitimacy of the local Power's coercive control. The interplay of power and conscience as the essence of politics reaches an agonizing climax.

As long as it lasts, the character of Soviet regional hegemony in Eastern Europe illustrates the *telos* of the Soviet concept of the balance of power, while the global picture reflects the ideologically tolerated temporary acceptance of military-political equilibrium, pending the destruction of all "hostile" forces and the real peace of Communist utopia. The Soviet doctrine of the balance of power does in its essentials little more than explicitly radicalize the drive for preponderance, always implicit in the balancing process, by the Marxist-Leninist postulates of necessary conflict and ultimate Communist domination. Consequently, the widespread failure in the West generally and among the American military in particular to apply any balance-of-power thinking at all to the Soviet ally in a single-minded campaign against the Fascist Powers was much more serious than the ignorance of the not at all startling peculiarities of the doctrine. The Soviets found it relatively easy to establish their regional hegemony; and, when the Soviet ally had to be branded as an enemy before it was countered as an unbalancer, the shift of Western policies from concessions to counter-offensive must have appeared to the more ideologically minded among the Soviet policy-makers as a delayed manifestation of only temporarily subdued "necessary" anti-Soviet hostility, vindicating *ex post facto* Soviet expansionism in the first place.

In the perspective of history, the tendency of local Powers to assert regional control appears as natural and the freedom of exposed smaller countries as a compound of fiction and accident. The United States eliminated progressively all outside interference in its orbit; so did or tried to do Germany and Soviet Russia more recently. This country escaped on the whole the need for satellite control; the two totalitarian Powers did not. Yet, however recurrent the pattern, the satellite technique has never been permanently successful in the modern state system.[17]

In pronouncing on problems of international organization, it is thus necessary to take into account not only the actual or desired balance of power among states, and the balance between the several nations' power and commitments, but also the likely balance between the power of the principal Great Powers and their sense of responsibility and self-restraint. If a great nation's ideology does not counteract the expansionist and coercive tendencies implicit in superior power, but stimulates them instead, the smaller communities within its reach are doomed to extinction or to satellite status unless otherwise protected.

Such protection is certainly not provided for in the theory of Great-Power orbits. Smaller countries, by being irrevocably assigned to regional power blocs, are denied even the measure of safeguards they may derive from the balance of power. Henceforth, only an interregional balance makes sense. A puzzling question is against whom are regional defenses organized if the Great Powers are expected to exercise self-restraint and respect their separate preserves — an assumption more "utopian" in a regional configuration of power than in the conceptual universe of the United Nations Charter. Security zones are practically certain to overlap, making contests over intermediate smaller countries at least as likely. This will increase the pressure on the nuclear Powers to tighten control over "their" allies, and to consolidate intraregionally a fusion of power rather than implement a diversified pluralism. To expect the spontaneous adherence of the smaller nations to such a scheme is to mix would-be realism with considerable blindness to any organism's natural response to the threat of extinction. There is thus no need to invoke moral considerations or special factors, such as historical and ethnic antagonisms among neighbors, to invalidate the proposition that regional zones are desirable as a general principle of international organization, and that they would freely coalesce and remain cohesive without being made exclusive.

Moreover, it is fallacious to assume that Great Powers with mutually alien social ideologies, which have to organize regionally their military-political defenses, would coöperate globally in socio-economic matters. The reverse proposition is more plausible. As an alternative to global coöperation, the several groupings would have to contrive a socio-economic equilibrium from limited intraregional resources and even more limited, if any, interregional exchanges. But regionalism came too late to catch up with the sudden leap from national to global economic interdependence; it cannot supply the basis for a balanced economy, planned or free. Complementary resources and diverse functional needs, constituting not a few self-sufficient but many overlapping regions, might weave together existing communities into larger ones if they were left to spontaneous organic growth; they confound attempts at coördination in overlapping institutions; and they are the source of unrest when they cut across the boundaries of reciprocally hostile security areas. Interregional needs tear then at the concentric pull of regionally organized power systems. Results will vary depending on the geographic scope and degree of self-sufficiency of the region, the expansionist or conservative phase and ideology of the regional Great Power, and the pressure applied to the region from outside.

Three main types of responses are possible. First, the Great Power may let the horizontal relationships of interdependence dissolve, as it were, the regional power structure and pursue the objective of a larger equilibrium. It will do so more easily if its potential is such that the relationships will serve as channels of influence abroad rather than as avenues of encroachment from the outside. Great Britain and the United States came closest to adopting this course. Or, as in the case of Nazi Germany and Imperial Japan, a Great Power may set out to conquer the interdependence pressing beyond too narrow regional confines, disrupt an already badly shaken global equilibrium, and be defeated by the world-wide reaction. Finally, a Great Power may attempt to seal off interdependence within a larger region organized against other Powers. In the effort to repress global interdependence it will depress the small states of the region into the position of tributary dependence. This has been the case with the Soviet Union. Thus if any determinism is involved, war and satellitism are much more the necessary consequence of integral regionalism than such regionalism is the necessary and enduring pattern of world organization.

In its implications, the theory as well as the practice of Great-Power spheres is essentially illiberal. It stands for the enlargement of the vertical power structure of the nuclear state, typical of imperialism, rather than for the release of institutional, socio-economic, and military-political forces and relationships into the equilibrium interplay of reciprocal adjustment and restraint, which constitutes the nearest equivalent of constitutionalism in the international community. By the same token, regional compression of broader interdependence will put a premium on dictatorial rationing of security, welfare, and prestige among dependent satellites; it will not allow international exchange and communications to dissolve local restrictions and sustain an equitable distribution of these values among independent parties to authoritative general institutions.

This does not mean that the theory is all wrong. In the first place, the organization of security around several Great Powers is a recurrent if objectionable makeshift in international relations. And in the second place, the theory is correct in emphasizing the need for economic and military integration to counteract nationalistic fragmentation, the primary role of major states in any security scheme, and the dangers of neglecting particular facts of geography and power in an abstract system. As an alternative to the fusion of power in the focal state, however, intraregional relations between major and minor states should at least be multilateralized in an institutional equilibrium extending into a complementary global organization. Moreover, the relatively smaller states within the region should be free to strengthen themselves by means of federative integration rather than be kept in separate dependence.

It is not intended to examine in detail the extent to which the Soviet system realizes the illiberal potential of Great-Power spheres. Instead, the following chapter will explore the application of the remedial features in the Western regional association.

CHAPTER 6   THE PATTERN OF
            INTEGRATION

According to the density of institutional,
functional, and communal ties, patterns of international organization can be distributed along an integrative continuum from an
unorganized congeries of isolated states to a unitary global super-
state. As preparation for an inquiry into the ways and means of
employing the United Nations to promote regional integration,
the hitherto implied pattern of integration will now be explicated
and exemplified in relation to the North Atlantic Treaty Organization as a framework for different levels of integration and a
potential balancer in the Western European federalizing process.

THE INTEGRATIVE PROCESS

Integration translates into functional and institutional terms the
awareness of larger interdependence for security and welfare.
It can be a matter of spontaneous growth, be deliberately instituted, or, most likely, be a compound of the two. Interdependence does not ensure integration, it merely constitutes a challenge.

International integration may be seen as a dynamic process
involving emerging community ties, functional and treaty relationships, and organs that range along an ideal continuum from
more or less sporadic connections between sovereign states under
international law to federal and unitary supranational institutions
governed by constitutional law. Conceptually, there is no dramatic break; it is therefore often difficult to determine where
international organs cease and supranational ones begin. Nor does
the denial of *de jure* supranational powers necessarily exclude the
de facto supranational character of institutions formally ruled by
international law and sovereignty. When the integrative process

passes into the federalizing stage, however, political and juridical sovereignty is definitely pooled and some of it transferred to joint institutions. There emerge into coördinate status interrelated central and component state organs, reciprocally autonomous within their defined spheres; and the federative institutional structure corresponds to a similarly composite pattern of inclusive and exclusive community feelings, needs, and interests. Traditional dichotomies between international, federal, and confederal systems are dissolved.[1]

Any form of integration presents thus two major aspects at any particular moment. It constitutes, first, a static quantity or density of integration within the continuum. Second, it is a phase in the dynamic integrative process, progressive or regressive in relation to its own evolutionary potential and to other more or less advanced forms.

It is impossible to square the idea of an integrative continuum and process with a static view of sovereignty. On the one hand, it is still the rule to regard sovereignty as an intrinsic, fixed, and equal quantity of rights and immunities accruing automatically to any state. Sovereignty stands then for "complete freedom of action regarding peace and war" and is a "symbol for concentrated power." It is tempting to reject completely such an idea. On the other hand, one may prefer the notion of differential sovereignty as a variable aggregate of legal rights and claims, and try to preserve the concept of sovereignty as a functionally divisible and juridically unifying normative principle of a consistent organization of power. This seems to be the more constructive procedure. Some kind of order is preferable to the legal anarchy of uncoordinated powers, which would logically result both from rejecting altogether the idea of sovereignty as an ordering principle and from subscribing to the absolutist pretensions made on its behalf.[2]

Unlike Austin, Grotius believed that sovereignty retained its essential character despite limitations and disabilities imposed on its subject. And in fact, no state in reciprocally dependent relations with other states can preserve an absolute and unlimited sovereignty. Rather, it employs its autonomy to render less onerous its adjustment to other states. This is inevitably truer of weaker states whose diminishing power implies increasing power deformation of their sovereignty no less than of other institutions. Unless the contact of a sovereign self-will with another self-will produces a collective will, the alternative will be curtailment for the weaker self. It is thus impossible to uphold absolute, equal, and indivisible sovereignty against the facts of power differentials and the pressures of interdependent needs. Instead, substantial or effective sovereignty appears as a dynamic function following, as it were, the shifting point at which intersect the two continua of greater or lesser national power and *de facto* international integration. To elaborate, effective sovereignty is, on the one hand, a variable on the scale of actual coördination of policies and resources among states, corresponding to a range of attitudes from extreme ethnocentrism to coöperative internationalism reflecting the recognition of interdependence; on the other hand, effective sovereignty is a variable depending on the power of a state and its role and responsibility in international relations and organization. This may mean actual dissovereignty for weaker states and actual or institutional extension of the effective sovereignty of greater Powers as contemplated, for instance, by the United Nations Charter.

Such a view may imply graduation of differential sovereignty among factually unequal states; it certainly implies the pooling of divisible sovereignty in a way which would distribute national and international or supranational functions and powers in conformity with the structure of individual and group needs, and the progressive transfer of such functions and powers from domestic to international and supranational jurisdiction. This brings together the juridical-normative view of sovereignty and a realistic interpretation of international society. The former points to functionally diversified organization of institutional powers as a prerequisite of national, federal, and international legal order. The latter points out the basis of such an order in actual facts about national power and international interdependence. In a power-normative situation, the two approaches join to provide a rationale for a growing scope of international organization and integration as an alternative to legal and political anarchy.

To the extent that it is deliberate, integration represents a manipulative approach to order, security, and welfare. It supplements, to say the least, the discredited automatism of the "laws" of political balance of power and economic equilibrium on the one hand, and of the normative laws of collective security on the other. It is supposed to stabilize (but not freeze) the operation of these laws among the integrated parties and, in the case of only regional integration, consolidate the joint position of the parties in the global equilibrium and security system. This is, to be sure, only the barest skeleton of integration, which is overlaid by the softer tissue of community feelings in a finished organic whole. Yet, like the theory of sovereignty, the theory of integration, too, must place into a unifying focus not only the element of community and institutions, but also of power and, in addition, military security and socio-economic well-being. This is especially true of integration among unequal communities with a tradition of personal and group insecurity, which stimulates the naturally anti-integrative tendencies implicit in nationalism.

Nations may be pulled together, among other things, by an active sense of larger community, needs of interdependence, and the anticipation of advantages flowing from a more inclusive union. They may seek joint security against common external threat. But nations with an antagonistic past and fears for the future may be induced to closer integration, including federation, also by the desire to be secure against each other. Security has been traditionally sought by means of a successful war or alliance, producing a favorable balance of power. Collective security was designed to modify this pattern. Yet within a menaced fragment of the state system, like Western Europe today, internal war may be out of the question and the area for diplomatic maneuver too narrow. Security by means of federal association with the feared neighbor may then appear as the alternative to his containment by war, alliance with countervailing states, or disarmament. Still more obviously, federalism as a vehicle of expansion may be substituted for warlike conquest. And in the realm of economics, a coöperatively integrated economy is a fairly close alternative to competitive trade war. Mutual attraction and repulsion characteristic of so many neighbors is thus paralleled by an equally ambivalent relation between federation and war. Nations in an intense contact may have no option but to be joined. The question then is whether they are to be joined in recurrent struggle or in a federal embrace.

If federation, or any other type of integration, is to fulfill its security function and be protected against its hegemonic potential, it must provide effective safeguards for the weaker parties. This is essential. Preoccupation with security will not promote forms of integration which fail to implement their *raison d'être*. Insecurity in separate diversity will be preferred to a union which is merely a medium for the aggrandizement of the nuclear nation. Just as there is only a narrow dividing line between federation and war, so is there only a thin partition between the anti- and the pro-federalizing effect of apprehensions among many unequal communities. A paralyzing concern about the future is less easily submerged than past antagonisms, and tends to cling to the known if precarious *status quo*. Hence, military-security arrangements and trusted safeguards against political, economic, and other peaceful penetration may easily be the decisive factor in the equation. They must counterbalance the threat of intrafederal supremacy by stronger partners or an extrafederal regional Great Power.

All this points to a proposition in terms of our conceptual framework. A successful integrative and federalizing process requires that military-political and socio-economic equilibrium in the larger security and welfare area be promoted through institutions in equilibrium with respect to their structure, security commitment, and both functional and geographic scope, as a means to an expanding functional and moral community. A reliable equilibrium cannot be always established from elements within the prospective area. Then, an external balancer or equilibrator may be required to intervene as a *deus ex machina* in the crisis and break through the dilemma. His function is to guarantee the crucial period of consolidation and thus to tip the balance of negative security fears from their natural anti-integrative to a pro-integrative expression.

It is, therefore, futile to deny the ultimate unity of politics by postulating an antithesis between the balance of power and the federal principle of equal rights in a "coördinate state." Quite to the contrary, federation may be the necessary condition of maintaining safe equilibrium among democratically governed nations; and internal equilibrium is essential for reinsuring the coördinate autonomy and legal equality of member-states, especially in incipient federations.[3]

SECURITY THROUGH REGIONAL COMMUNITY

If the North Atlantic Treaty Organization is the main framework for the integration of the North Atlantic Community, it is in the first place an institutionalized regional coalition for the maintenance of the global balance of power, formally related to the United Nations as an agency for collective self-defense. As such it illustrates the fusion of security, community, and welfare in the revised idea of collective security as a "community security system," pooling national resources in an integrated defense effort against a suspected aggressor. A drastic departure from the early League ideals attempts to adjust to the contemporary schism the integrative approach of the Charter; effective collective security is now coterminous with an integration area and expands or shrinks with the latter.[4]

NATO displays a particular kind of integration and institutional equilibrium. As an organization of sovereign states, NATO is located at a relatively low point on the integrative continuum. It has no supranational organs and shows no federative tendencies; yet a noticeable organic growth has been stimulated by the interacting responses to specific functional tasks within a "two-chamber system" of expert and political bodies. The Council is the seat of national representation and multilateral high policy. In the Permanent Organization, the International Secretariat is the central fortress of the collective NATO spirit. Between the nationalist and the internationalist extremes of the institutional spectrum, the Permanent Representatives of the member-states constitute an intermediary link. But the balance is uneven because the Secretariat — the most highly integrated civilian organ — is endowed with only advisory and mediatory powers, and the authority delegated to the Representatives is scant. On the other hand, the Permanent Organization is an effective civilian counterweight to the more tightly integrated military structure of NATO headed by a Supreme Commander. This enables the Permanent Organization to coördinate the economic and military aspects of security and give continuity to the sporadic action of the national Ministers, who constitute the ultimate check on the military.

NATO's integration is thus primarily operational. First, delegation of authority has gone to the standing operational organs rather than to political organs. Second, integration has resulted from the actual operation of the national and international organs rather than from a unique constituent act establishing a supranational authority. Interallied relations have been greatly institutionalized by the so-called "NATO method" of multilateral consultation aiming at unanimous recommendations without resort to vote. A rather progressive structural equilibrium between the military and civilian standing organs has stimulated the growth of NATO's modest powers; another factor for increased efficiency has been the continual adjustment between the "supra-national NATO view" and the "national views." This informal interplay has kept in bounds the imbalance between the limited jurisdiction of the integrated organs and the extensive domestic jurisdiction of members assembled in the Council. On the whole, NATO shows that any closely coördinated military and economic undertaking among materially interdependent nations will result in *de facto* supranational character of the joint organs and some derogation of effective national sovereignty.[5]

Such as they are, NATO institutions have served as a coactive framework for military-political and, to some extent, economic integration. Integration and balance were the watchwords of NATO's first concern, joint equitable rearmament. Among allies with greatly disparate resources, contributions must be properly adjusted to "politico-economic capabilities"; a balance must be evolved between joint military needs and the requirements of economic, social, and political stability of member-nations. The aim was to develop "balanced collective forces" and later "an integrated force under centralized command." The "community power" of jointly trained and strategically directed national units is to replace separate national potentials as the foundation of security; and a measure of integration is to narrow within NATO's regional scope the fatal gap between a collective-security commitment and the actual ability and willingness of states to perform. Anticipation of performance should strengthen the community of tradition and interests among the allies. Thus, a *casus foederis* should find NATO in equilibrium with respect to the mutual-assistance commitment of its members. Yet final evaluation depends on NATO's fitness to implement its long-range community function.[6]

In this respect, the organization has been subject to a number of limitations. Treaty provisions and statements of intention must be distinguished from actual means and accomplishments. The provisions are broad enough, but their implementation has lagged. Military-political equilibrium has been established more effectively against the Soviet bloc than internally: it is not easy for unequal partners to develop integrated, balanced forces, and international specialization is not favored by continued sovereignty; furthermore, military integration is still not matched by correspondingly intimate coördination of foreign policies. It has proved no less difficult to adjust the organization's short-range and long-range purposes. The initially legitimate concentration on the military-defense problems has grown one-sided as NATO passed from the emergency stage into the "long haul." It is difficult to strike the right balance. On the one hand, the primary task of NATO was to redress the "serious imbalance of military strength" in Europe into a balance or even "preponderance of power." This contributed to general stability and a sense of community in the West. In that sense "economic measures are not enough." But, on the other hand, neither is military balance or preponderance. And as international tensions relax, even reduced burdens of military preparedness are borne with growing reluctance by societies which have a narrow margin of expendable economic resources and social peace.[7]

NATO's limitations have been also geographical. In spite of the vast resources and overseas connections of its members, NATO lacks scope for a diversified equilibrium and flexible defensive strategy in depth. It has had to be extended beyond the North Atlantic region proper, and interallied relations have suffered from larger needs, chiefly economic and strategic, and wider problems, mainly colonial. Since the regional alliance has not been able to relate itself organically to the world organization, it looked at times as if it would supersede the United Nations under the impetus of expanding pressures.

Hence, if NATO may be presumed to be in fair equilibrium with respect to the commitment to military assistance, it is not in that position with respect to its functional and geographic scope, and to the global organization. Today, the idea of the Atlantic Community is alive primarily in the method and the spirit of the quest for a fair ratio of burdens and advantages flowing from the alliance. Yet there is a growing feeling, most recently taken up by the United States, that the alliance must develop more positive and extensive nonmilitary activities. Otherwise, it will become brittle, the equilibrium will be lopsided, and the tissues of regional community will not grow. The very existence of the alliance might be jeopardized as an all-out war of annihilation comes to be considered less likely; "massive retaliation" yields in popularity to "graduated deterrence" and limitation of peripheral conflicts; and strategic thinking catches up with the revolution in weapons and long-range delivery systems.[8]

One factor that has hitherto obstructed more extensive delegation and integration is the problem of a "balance of influence between the small and the large countries." In bare outline, the present compromise consists of the exclusive representation of the three Great Powers in the authoritative military Standing Group, and an equal vote and formal veto for even the smaller nations in the ultimately decisive NATO Council. An informal play of pressures and influence assures the requisite supremacy for the major Powers and the equally necessary safeguards for the lesser states within this arrangement. It may be argued that structural equilibrium as well as further integration would benefit from a political standing group where fewer members with higher average power could properly exert greater powers. Yet the smaller states, far from disposed to abdicate more authority, wish to compensate for the predominance of the Great Powers in the military organization by retaining the greatest possible role in multilateral policy-making. They, like Great Britain and France when bypassed by the United States, insist on consultation prior to irrevocable decisions that might have equally irrevocable consequences for all in the age of nuclear weapons. Conversely, the Great Powers wish to preserve some of the advantages of bilateral diplomacy and more intimate consultations among themselves. They do not wish to be exposed to too many "organizational pressures." The situation is reflected in the uneven employment of the NATO Council, ranging from consultations of all or only the major members to their unilateral decisions, not least so by the United States.[9]

In the long run, the internal equilibrium of the alliance would be served best by moves toward equalizing resources among its component units. American aid is to mutual advantage and is partly compensated for by the strategic and other facilities made available by others. But it cannot redress the imbalance of strength among the allies and, when combined with greatly unequal contributions, tends to upset the vital psychological equilibrium. It might be argued that a federatively integrated Western Europe together with Great Britain would constitute a desirable counterpart to the United States within the alliance, improve relations among partners, and increase the security and welfare of all concerned. For a time NATO seemed to be assisting the process.

THE FEDERAL BALANCER

Federative integration among unequal and heterogeneous partners raises two interconnected issues: first, the effect of differentials on the integrative process; second, the equilibration of disparities by appropriate means.

All central features of federalism are usually involved in the task of evolving the necessary, if not sufficient, structural equilibrium, not only among the states but also between the states and the federal government. The latter must not fall under the control of the greater states, or be hamstrung by excessive safeguards for the lesser members, especially in the absence of a unifying party system. A written constitution sets up the organizational structure and defines substantive powers. Next, a bicameral legislative system may be employed to counterbalance the proportionate composition of the lower chamber with an upper chamber embodying the principle of state equality. This is not always so; the Great Compromise of Philadelphia was followed by other compromises between equality and proportionality elsewhere.[10] When the powers of the upper chamber are small, the efficiency of the check decreases; this raises the importance of an impartial self-restrained federal executive and still more, of the federal judiciary as the most striking intrafederal balancer. An impartial federal judiciary with review functions can maintain and adjust to changing conditions a dynamic constitutional equilibrium of powers and rights among individuals, the states, and the central government itself. Its judicial activity can thus have a constructive influence toward closer integration, not least by lessening the impact of a rigid amending process and other safeguards.

If federal institutions are also in equilibrium with respect to a sufficiently extensive functional scope, they will be in a position to balance integration among member-states by more tangible means. Control of decisive or all military force enables a federal government to enforce the various rights and duties, if necessary; administrative, legislative, and judicial regulation, and other federal resources including grants-in-aid, may be used to promote internal socio-economic equilibrium by coördinating disparate economic potentials, needs, and interests, and by containing particularistic cultural and other tendencies. American federalism illustrates the daily performance as well as a tragic breakdown of this function.

The more heterogeneous the federation, the more vital and difficult is the role of the federal government as equilibrator; it may be impossible among hitherto sovereign communities indulging in ambivalent attitudes to each other. A central authority then can hardly induce the integration from which it is to result, nor can it be a sufficiently powerful and detached balancer to restrain possible bids for supremacy in the crucial period of consolidation. The history of German federalism is instructive in this respect. A remedy is not easy to devise. Federation among equal members with identical interests is a utopia contrary to the very purpose of federalism, which is to reconcile diversity in a larger unity. A greater number of member-states might help to supply more elements for internal equilibration. Or internal elements might be supplemented from outside, which might reduce the need for internal safeguards to a point where they would not fatally impede federal integration. An external balancer may not be always necessary and should be in any case temporary. In many situations, however, it might be the missing component of a successful federalizing process. Such an external balancer might be a Great Power, a broader association like NATO, or the world organization itself, encouraging and guaranteeing the federation by a proper use of larger resources.

First about the Great Powers. Their attitude to federation, like that of the smaller states, varies with its effect on their own position and interests. They favor the federation of remote countries that promises to create a situation of strength against another Great Power. They discourage the federation of adjacent states if it threatens to lessen their own influence and benefit another Power. They will consider joining a federation only if it preserves or improves their standing in the order of regional and global power. Bismarck did not work to submerge Prussia, and Briand France, in a larger whole. Both France and Prussia favored at one time or another federation for Germany: France supported a loose one as an alternative to a unitary state; Prussia enforced a tight one to replace the multiplicity of independent states. After the dissolution of the Austro-Hungarian Empire, the Western Powers encouraged a closer association of the smaller states of Central-Eastern Europe so as to reinforce the eastern wing of the continental equilibrium, but Italy, Germany, and Soviet Russia in succession used their local power to frustrate such an association for identical reasons. Great Britain never supported European combinations which she could not control, nor did the United States with respect to Latin America. But the two Anglo-Saxon Powers did act on occasion as balancers toward federative integration of other communities.

For Great Britain to be a pro-federative balancer is just a special manifestation of her traditional role. She held the balance in Europe for the safety of the Empire. Within the Empire, she has tried to hold the balance between antagonistic groups and interests, sometimes toward federation. The best illustration is Canada, wherein Great Britain tipped the unequal balance between what Lord Durham called "the two nations warring within the bosom of a single State" toward federation by the British North America Act of 1867 and guaranteed the resulting constitutional equilibrium. The major institutional safeguards were the right of appeal to the independent and impartial Judicial Committee of the Privy Council; constitutional amendment by an

Act of Parliament at Westminster alone; and the over-all moderating influence of the Crown. In addition, the unwritten guarantee of the British Navy provided for military security, and free trade under the aegis of the London Exchange for the economic side of the equilibrium. The "two nations" passed from "war" to a fairly sociable coexistence preserving cherished diversities under a central government with expanding powers. The federal balancer has gradually relaxed or completely abandoned its temporary functions. In the Central African Federation more recently, the imperial arbiter has been trying to contain by comparable means but with less success the differences between the indigenous and the local white populations. To assist the federalizing process of lesser communities need not injure the enlightened self-interest of a major Power, and may implement the idea of trust and self-government in an integrative rather than divisive fashion.[11]

The United States also encouraged federative integration of other countries as part of a larger scheme. Great Britain used to be identified with the balance of power, and interwar France with collective security; the United States must make the best of a more complicated equilibrium situation. The flexible conventions of the balance of power suited to perfection British national empiricism and conventional domestic politics. Free hand was the political next-of-kin of free trade. The larger equilibrium of the *Pax Britannica* was due to unique spontaneities more than to deliberate coördination. When these broke down, Great Britain made only half-hearted moves toward fundamental international reconstruction. As for France, her juridical and, in international relations, primarily military-political orientation was mirrored in the championship of a correspondingly conceived collective security. Among the fragments of the earlier policies scattered by two wars, the United States has been groping toward what may yet be their confusion, pragmatic combination, or a kind of dialectical synthesis.

In the historical balance of power, the United States has figured alternately as both a weight and a balancer; its attitude varied even more with respect to collective security. By sponsoring the United Nations and later NATO, this country has given tokens of support for a newly conceived collective security which would rest on a progressively integrated world-wide or regional multiple equilibrium and would institutionalize a reliable global balance of power. The superior resources as well as the internationally conservative temper of the United States dictate for it today the role of equilibrator in an unstable world facing the extremes of violent upheaval and would-be monolithic rigidity characteristic of the totalitarian systems. Immersed in a complex interaction of often conflicting requirements, values, and objectives, the United States must try as best it can to transcend and control the interaction so as to ensure the survival and expansion of freedom in the world. Some of its responses to socio-economic problems could be seen as an international extension of the New Deal, its advocacy of trade liberalization as that of American free enterprise. Insofar as this country conducted its foreign policy amidst the institutional checks and balances of international organization, this has supplied — apart from occasional frustrations — a convenient link between American constitutional tradition and the less familiar ground of international politics. External and internal stresses have now and then overshadowed the socio-economic by the military-political approach and jeopardized a judicious use of international organization. But the need is stronger than the shifting currents of moods and politics.[12]

American performance as equilibrator found special application in the support for federative integration in Western Europe. This country favored Western European unification in the belief that it would promote intraregional security and welfare, sustain the NATO system of collective security, and reinforce the Western wing of the global equilibrium against the Soviet threat. Moreover, the principle of supranationality would extend to problems of international politics the federative approach that had proved successful in American national experience. Rightly or wrongly, with or without appropriate methods and timing, the government of the United States employed its influence and resources to encourage and in effect guarantee the European integrative process, while resolutely stopping short of a supranational integration of the entire North Atlantic area.

Great Britain, too, remained content to adjust rather than revise completely her traditional position with regard to the continent. She joined in the guarantee of the European Defense

Community, which must have appeared to her as merely a more elaborate implementation of the Locarno concept, but refused to join the integrative process as the decisive impetus and possibly indispensable weight. On the continent, the Franco-German issue reflects most of the tendencies involved in the problem of European integration. Distrust and fears, vested political and economic interests, but also a sense of interdependence and a still timid European spirit have contended over the ultimate direction of their cumulative impact. Intermingling concerns for security, equality, or preponderance through new organizational forms influence attitudes in both countries. France has been held back by concern over the best conditions of her national recovery, security, and prestige, her Great-Power status, national army, and the relationship between integration and the colonial empire, between a European and the French Union. As long as Germany is not offset by British participation, France will shy away from the "risk of hegemony, the risk of an internal disequilibrium" and of German secession. Germany in her turn is uncertain whether the larger unity in the West is the best way of recovering national unity in the East. Her hopes are France's fears.[13]

In such a situation, the success of the Western European process depended in large part on the possibility to contrive from available factors an institutionalized multiple equilibrium within the prospective area of integration. Institutional checks and balances were most pronounced in the Draft Treaty of the European Political Community. Provisions concerning executive, legislative, and judicial organs aimed at a structural equilibrium of the several branches, of the powers reserved to the member-states and conceded to the Community, and of the rights and interests of the materially unequal members. In the complete scheme, the Political Community was to integrate institutionally the other functional Communities, and stimulate the sense of moral and political community through popular elections to the lower chamber. The European Coal and Steel Community contributed a nucleus for closer socio-economic integration and equilibrium between Germany and her neighbors. And, finally, the European Defense Community was designed to supplement institutional and socio-economic with military-political equilibrium. It, too, was not self-sufficient: its organizational devices alone could not permanently redress the imbalance in potential military strength of the several parties, and the EDC Treaty did not provide for centralized foreign-policy control. Yet integration which intertwines members militarily and leaves them free politically might open a still more dangerous gap than that between promise and performance in an unintegrated collective-security system. In order to be successful, the Defense Community needed thus a Political Community for the coördination of foreign policies, and further reinforcements for purposes of both military and economic equilibrium.[14]

NATO supplied to this end, first, the presence of Anglo-American forces in Europe as a counterweight to Soviet and potential German preponderance; second, the reciprocal commitments and integration between NATO and EDC; and third, a measure of joint foreign-policy determination.

In a joint declaration, issued in connection with the signing of the EDC Treaty and of conventions aiming at virtual restoration of German sovereignty, the Western Big Three agreed to consider as a threat to their security any threat to the EDC from "whatever quarter," and to station in Europe forces "necessary and appropriate to contribute to the joint defense of the North Atlantic Area." The stated object was to "prevent the resurgence of former tensions and conflicts among the free nations of Europe and any future revival of aggressive nationalism." Additional American and British pledges concerned equal duration of NATO and EDC, continued stay of the troops of the two Powers in Europe, and the coördination of British contingents with those of the EDC.

Military integration within the EDC and of the EDC into NATO was to make it impossible for any single nation to mount an independent operation. The EDC Treaty provided for much tighter military integration than is practiced within NATO, aiming at carefully balanced national quotas and international command — in fact, nothing short of "a common, supra-national, European, quasi-federal army." A nonautonomous EDC was to be further integrated into the NATO structure with respect to supreme command, training, strategy, and operations. Its supranational executive organ, the Commissariat, was made dependent in many respects on NATO for over-all direction. Finally, pending the establishment of a Political Community, the only available if inadequate agency for the coördination of foreign policies is the NATO Council.[15]

Thus NATO itself was to serve as an institutionalized balancer among newly integrated Western European nations and add its organizational resources to those of the two guarantor Powers. A comparable adjustment was necessary to pave the way for a substitute for the rejected EDC: the so-called Western European Union, including Germany in a traditional type of alliance without supranational powers and directly in NATO; it is likely to prove useful or even indispensable for the success of future federative integration confined to Western Europe or any other area where local resources are insufficient for a self-sustaining equilibrium.

In the meantime, the existence of NATO may actually have helped defeat the EDC project. The impact of the alliance on the global balance of forces created the security necessary for federative experiments, but, by reducing the threat from without and providing alternative framework for integration, it lessened the drive to more cohesion within a more limited area. NATO's capacity either to reinforce or to drain the vitality of both a smaller regional association and the larger global organization, the United Nations, points to it as the central focus of regional and global equilibrium available to the West at the present time. NATO includes Great Britain and the United States as actual weights rather than mere balancers. In the eyes of many, more integration and policy coördination within NATO would dispense with elaborate arrangements for NATO's aid toward integration in Western Europe and affect equally all parties. It would dispose of the feeling that the two English-speaking nations favor supranational institutions for others but refuse to give up the least whit of their own sovereignty. A larger area may be expected not only to comprise more elements for a self-sustaining equilibrium, but also to reconcile local antagonisms more easily in a higher allegiance. And a balance of loyalties to the old divisive and the new unifying symbols and values is, of course, the indispensable spiritual basis of genuine community no less than of general equilibrium.

Any future efforts will be faced with the by now familiar

problems. One of them is the optimum area for integration. Here, the option might seem to be between geographic and functional scope: the larger the area, the less intense the integration. But no general law is involved. Achievements like the Coal and Steel Community seem to support the conclusion, certain failures discredit it. Global interdependence calls for ever wider areas of viable integration. Even a NATO must reach outside itself in peace or war. The insufficiency of Europe for balanced integration is widely argued. A theoretical and practical solution has been sought in differently defined areas with different levels of integration and identification for different functional purposes. Such a pluralistic approach may reinforce, but is not immune to obstructing, effective integration in the smaller or the more inclusive areas. NATO's ambivalence in this respect has been described; similarly, an integrated "little Europe" might strengthen the Atlantic Community or weaken it by protectionist and neutralist policies.

A related question concerns the best institutional arrangement. Some students would sharply distinguish between federative institutions set up by a single constituent act and piecemeal functional integration preserving national sovereignties at least *de jure*. In different circumstances different combinations of the two approaches will apply. The functionalist argument in favor of a gradual organic growth has merits. But some institutional pooling of sovereignty is likely to be necessary at a relatively early stage of functional integration. Nations will not disarm through functional interpenetration and specialization without reinsuring their security by corresponding political organization. Customs unions like the Benelux, leaving national sovereignty intact, have not been too successful. And the EDC project suggests the risks of military integration without complementary political union. Besides, functionalism caters to concrete needs but fails to provide the unifying symbols of a larger community.

This raises the issue of the ideal sequence of integration. It is plausible to assign primacy to either economic or political integration. Or, one may emphasize military integration as extending automatically into political and economic coöperation. Switzerland experienced the impetus military integration can give to federative institutions; constitutional and economic steps toward

German unification faltered until brought to fruition by blood and iron. But military associations among nations are ephemeral unless cemented by additional ties. If it is difficult to regulate supranationally only one sector of the economy, it is still more difficult to integrate only one aspect of the state. The conceptions of the European Coal and Steel Community and the Defense Community were strikingly similar; both were suspended on the vision of a supranational political authority; neither of the three could be really successful without the two others. The threads of security and welfare are intertwined in the fabric of a shared political community. Isolated as an economic fragment of European integration, the Coal and Steel Community has hitherto failed to put into effect its supranational features. It has suffered from a narrow scope and survived largely on the hope for eventual extension of the integrative pattern, at the very least into additional economic areas.[16]

Accordingly, the mechanism of the integrative process consists of a chain-reacting equilibrium movement. In a balanced process more integration in one, say military, sphere will stimulate countervailing integration in the socio-economic and institutional spheres until the multiple equilibrium is reëstablished on a higher level of over-all integration. Within the institutional sphere itself, a progressive equilibrium movement between the different inter- or supranational organs, too, may promote a rising level of integration. If the equilibrium response fails to occur, integration in the lone, say economic, field will run grave risks of relapsing to the lower common level. The unifying form of the process is an emerging sense of community. A policy aiming at progressive integration has to adjust the materials at its disposal to the pattern of the integrative process. This is essential because the theoretically distinguishable interaction can be easily diverted from actualizing its integrative potential by pressures implicit in national and group interests.

In an interlocking integrative process, neither need regional federative integration be at variance with global international integration. Sovereign states tried to promote supranational institutions for Western Europe through the instrumentalities of NATO, itself a regional community arrangement for collective self-defense within the global United Nations system. Ideally, not only a highly integrated Great Power or a loose regional association, but the world organization itself might act, where needed, as the equilibrator-guarantor facilitating closer regional union; in so doing, it would help implement on a global scale the wartime prescription of a peculiarly farsighted, if since maligned, statesman:

The first thing to be secured in the new postwar organization of Europe . . . must be a permanent and general European equilibrium. This equilibrium must be based both politically and economically upon the balance of forces between a number of . . . large, individual and balanced organisms, each of them sufficiently powerful territorially, politically, and economically. The weakness of small states must not in the future tempt large states to fall upon them.[17]

A NEW ROLE FOR THE UNITED NATIONS

In the suggested capacity, global international organization might help equilibrate differential resources and interests of member-communities, and guarantee them against domination from within and without. Such assistance might be decisive in tipping the scales of otherwise indecisive factors toward federative integration; it would in any event be temporary, pending consolidation of joint resources and shared loyalties. The objective would be an intermediate position for lesser political communities, combining as far as possible the advantages of international status and of larger supranational association.

In the first place, the global organization would guarantee mutual security and supervise balanced military-political integration among members. It would also supervise the economic "disarmament" of members through specialization of production and serve as a channel for skills and resources contributing to balanced integrative development. This would minimize the disturbing effects of unilateral foreign aid, especially in communities emerging from dependent colonial status, without ruling out a larger role for particularly interested Powers. Lastly, the associated communities as well as the central authority would be appropriately represented in the various international institutions. Final appeal and determination on questions concerning the federal constitution might be lifted to the International Court of Justice, pending the development of confidence in an impartial federal judiciary. This would implement the desire for community in some respects and for separateness in others, implicit in the federal idea, and keep safely open for all the access to the centers of international facilities and guarantees. A structure of powers, functions, and controls extending all the way to the world organization might profitably supplement the strictly federal checks and balances, and counteract dangers of excessively centralized regulation and intervention. Complete dependence on the state for security and welfare is a powerful stimulus to nationalism; a diffusion of functions might promote an equally salutary diffusion of allegiance.

It is possible to isolate elements of a precedent. Among them is the relation of Briand's project of a United States of Europe to the League, and the League's role in the protection of national minorities, the self-government of Danzig, and temporary direct government over the Saar. Also relevant are the supervisory and other powers of the United Nations over trusteeships — particularly if and when a trusteeship is constituted into a "customs, fiscal or administrative union or federation with adjacent territories" — the competence of the United Nations to act itself as administering authority, and the plans for entrusting to the Security Council supreme authority with extensive powers over the Free Trieste Territory.[18] Failures and shortcomings highlight the practical prerequisite: operative responsible organs and collective-security machinery for at least a special guarantee. Yet even a far from effective Security Council upheld in the Trieste case a potentially significant theory of implied powers and thus capacity of international organs to accept additional responsibilities. And, according to an advisory opinion of the International Court of Justice, enunciated in a different connection, the rights and duties of international organization "depend upon its purposes and functions as specified or implied in its constituent documents and developed in practice." In other words, the United Nations has powers conferred upon it by "necessary implication as being essential to the performance of its duties." [19]

It would not be without advantage to use such implied powers or amend the Charter in the suggested direction, supplementing in a constructive fashion the provisions for collective security, functional coöperation, and national self-determination. International guarantees of security and promotional welfare activities would be employed to stimulate political communities into merging sovereign independence in federative integration. A functional dovetailing of global and regional organization would promote equilibrium and dampen disturbing oscillations between the two forms, exploit their interdependence for full efficiency of either, and mitigate the overlaps and insufficiencies of self-contained regionalism. Two converging developments would reduce the gap between too abstractly conceived institutions and the dynamics of power in a concrete geographical setting: first, international and supranational institutions would be adjusted more closely to factual conditions and diversities; second, by strengthening fragmented areas of weakness and instability, the pattern would adjust also the material facts so as to sustain rather than strain the premises and promises of international law and organization. On the whole, the arrangement would occupy a middle ground between the contrary assumptions — emphasizing different aspects of an ambiguous reality — of natural community of interests within a region on the one hand, and of intra- as well as interregional conflicts on the other.

Internationally supported regional integration might improve the chances of general collective security and institutional equilibrium. A more even structuring of the global balance of power might in itself encourage coöperative responses to interdependence, discourage aggression, and decrease the need while increasing the ability and willingness for applying sanctions. The new regional associations would not, moreover, constitute just another "Great Power." They would be restrained, and if necessary encouraged into taking part in enforcement action, by means of the powers reserved to the global organization, while rigidities in the general system resulting from uninhibited competitive regional alliances would be minimized. Integration might thus strengthen intra- and interregional deterrence and enforcement; it might also promote the long-range bases of security and facilitate peaceful change. Furthermore, it should be easier to implement the principle of equality among materially less unequal subjects without violating the structural requirement of an equitable ratio of actual power and institutional influence. And in its new role, international organization would extend its functional scope and control over regional organizations, promoting thus its equilibrium in the last two respects as well. If it performed successfully a creative function in however limited a sphere, global organization might be revitalized and develop both the powers and the resources for adequate performance as balancer in the general system of collective security and a really coactive framework for regional and global multiple equilibrium.

And finally, the arrangement would protect lesser communities and restrain drives for regional hegemony by perpetuating in new forms the traditional concepts of the balancer and the Concert of Powers. All or most of the local and remote Great Powers, balanced against each other in the global organization, would play a major role in the guarantee and supervision of the newly federated countries, subject to the additional checks implicit in international law and organization. Their joint control would be undoubtedly hampered by frictions; yet it might eventually mitigate contests for unilateral control over intermediate areas of small countries. And, for the associated lesser communities, to concede controlled powers of collective intervention to the international guarantor would be a reasonable compromise between the undesirable extremes of arbitrary unilateral intervention and dogmatic noninterventionism, often concealing satellitism and misrule behind the screen of sovereign domestic jurisdiction. International organization would constitutionalize the imperial function apparently indispensable for some areas, and put into effect Jan Smuts' neglected interpretation of the League as the residuary legatee of defunct empires.[20]

Many of the issues raised in these pages converge in the theory of international organization as potential equilibrator-guarantor for regional integration. But the propositions are necessarily hypothetical and largely circular. Any such function, like effective international organization of security and disarmament itself, is likely to be successfully implemented only in conditions so favorable as to make it no longer vitally necessary. A major practical question is whether jointly supervised federative integration of strategically important areas of socio-political fragmentation would reduce contests among the Great Powers for at least this limited purpose and make them tolerate a measure of independence of the smaller communities which could not be used against any one of them.

This does not mean that integrative coalescence of political communities with or without outside assistance is a panacea for its members or for the world order. It is desirable only in conditions which promise to realize the expected advantages. In most such instances, however, a closer federative integration is preferable to a loose association, if it is to strengthen the individually weak component communities, make them less dependent on the major states and an unpredictable collective security, and help resolve existing differences among members. An important task of federalism is to reintegrate self-determined nationality in a framework of government which would reconcile the creative effect of diversity with the measure of cohesion requisite for internal and external security. Needs of the latter may limit the degree of permissible pluralistic decentralization of the component communities along lines of ethnic and socio-economic distinctions: separatism and corporativism are the deformations lurking behind pluralism based on corporate autonomies. Instead, an adjustment between the ethnic nationality of individuals and the state should be aimed at indirectly. Federative integration and equilibrium among ethnically intermixed states, with or without international guarantees, might produce a feeling of mutual security, lessen nationalistic pressures in an atmosphere of shared prosperity, and supersede the petty local balance-of-power politics breeding insecurity, economic waste, and subservience to greater Powers. Only when this is the case, and hitherto controversial national minority and related issues can be pragmatically and peacefully resolved in new ways made possible between members of a federative association, will that association have a chance to succeed.

The task is not easy nor the prospects too bright. With some justice, the nucleus theory of integration posits the necessity of a federating Power attracting the lesser communities by various means into closer association. In fact, German unification was achieved around Prussia alone, and a federation of the "third force" of smaller states between Prussia and Austria never materialized; neither did the diverse federative projects concerning the smaller states between Germany and Russia in more recent times.

If achieved, a federation of smaller countries might fall victim to feuds and divergencies of interests difficult to fuse into new loyalties within a too narrow compass. Then, instead of strengthening its members, a federative association would become the medium for reciprocal exportation of problems and outside interference by one or more Great Powers. Even among smaller communities a federation may disguise actual or desired control by the relatively stronger community, as shown recently by the Indonesian example. Such a federation may then follow the law of the species and either be rapidly centralized by the predominant partner or else disintegrate under the pressures released by resistance to the hegemonic drive. Finally, it might be argued, the fusion of smaller states into a larger regional state is no real solution of the problem of the small state in a situation of global interdependence and tremendous cost of really impressive power in world affairs.

In effect, the conditions of freedom and good life depend not so much on the size of a community or association as on the constitutional ordering of relations within and among nations. Aristotle suggested this with respect to the internal affairs of the *polis;* Kant and Wilson extended the insight to the larger framework of the cosmopolis. The problem must be always viewed within the concrete historical setting. When Plato and Aristotle were exalting the Greek city-state, greater forces were already gathering outside its orbits to supersede and engulf it. At the moment of its philosophical apotheosis, the city-state had already become an anachronism in interstate relations. With due differences, a like fate overtook or threatens the smaller states arising in the aftermath of the two world wars. A smaller state has still its peculiar advantages, but in modern conditions smallness is certainly not a good in itself. Whether it be an anachronism in international politics of the twentieth century will depend on the principles of organization which will emerge from the contemporary ferment. The ability or inability of smaller communities to offset by corresponding reintegration the effects of continuing ethnic fragmentation will provide only one, if important, part of the answer.

CONCLUSION   AND BACK TO THE
BALANCE OF POWER —
WITH A DIFFERENCE

In the final analysis, states depend for security,·
welfare, and legitimate prestige under law on the ideal and material structure of the world order at least as much as on any local
arrangement. The interrelation of domestic and foreign politics
can work itself out without detriment to the democratic self-government of any country only insofar as the essential traits of
constitutionalism are extended into the areas of anarchy among
nations.

INTERNATIONAL (DIS-)EQUILIBRIUM IN RETROSPECT

An important component of a constitutional order is effective
international organization which would institutionalize international politics. To this end, it is necessary to narrow the ever
threatening gap between general institutional norms and particular factual conditions, and to expand coöperatively the security,
welfare, and prestige actually available for distribution. This pre-
supposes that the international organization be able to promote
military-political and socio-economic equilibrium, by being itself
in internal equilibrium especially with respect to an extensive
functional scope and particular regional arrangements. Only then
can the collective-security commitment be stabilized on a sufficiently high but still equilibrium level and the organization become a major factor for long-range security, combining stability
with progressive peaceful change.

International organization has not yet succeeded in meeting
these requirements. It has been able only exceptionally and to a

limited extent to assert itself as the coactive framework of international politics which would counteract differentials among states, coordinate national policies, and integrate the state system. Failing to concede in time its due to the changing character of the world which gave it birth, the state system is entrapped in the intricate web of interrelationships which, unintegrated, constitute a standing invitation to conquest by the more "dynamic" members. Man has been unable to counterbalance his revolutionary achievements in the technological realm by corresponding attainments in the field of political organization. He thus condemns himself to live in a perpetual state of war or fear of war.

It was seen that the Concert of Europe, while initially in a fair equilibrium, failed to adjust itself to the new forces released by the industrial and national revolutions. The post-World War I order reversed the traditional assumption of self-help into one of collective enforcement of a law proscribing unilateral use of force in war, and replaced the discretionary Concert of Great Powers with an organization designed to embody the new international democracy under the new law. Subsequently, the pendulum swung back from the comparatively equalitarian and decentralized structure of the League toward institutionalized hierarchy in a United Nations combining elements of state equality with the legal primacy of the Great Powers. Yet conflicts among these Powers soon brought into the open the always latent contradiction between the coöperative premises of hierarchy and the competitive balancing of power; the combination of the two conflicts made apparently irresoluble the dilemmas posed for all international organization by the question of more or less ambitious structure, security commitment, and functional scope.

There has been a rebound from deadlock into jurisdictional and regional decentralization, disclosing ominous parallels with the evolution of the League. The tendency to unstable equilibrium or cumulative disequilibrium with respect to the collective-security commitment — a tendency fatal to the League — was temporarily contained in the United Nations without making certain the collective defense of victims of aggression in the future. The actually operative functional scope of the United Nations has been expanding as compared with the League, but again not enough to counteract the many disturbances in the material and social environment. Actual needs have tended to outrun the functions and powers of the organization, and these in turn anticipated the actual readiness of member-states to implement them. The seesaw movement between decentralized equalitarian and authoritative hierarchical structure has been intertwined with a similar movement between global and regional organization, as the alternatives clashed with political realities and the natural facts of interdependence, and ran into their peculiar limitations and disequilibria. Both international law and organization continued to lack an adequate basis in functional and political community.

As a result, elements of authoritative distribution of security, welfare, and influence within international organization have been more than matched by a haphazard pursuit of these values by more or less independent states on the one hand, and their dictatorial rationing among satellite states by a dominant Great Power on the other. The Great Powers tended to sidestep the organization as ineffective, after having made it so, or to use it indiscriminately as an instrument of national policies against each other. Many of the smaller states used a disproportionately great institutional influence to adapt to their views the purposes of the organization. The behavior of no state has been such as to promote consistently the working of the new international system of action. This impeded the institutionalization of relations in a multilateral process as well as a coöperative expansion of the universally desired goal values. Judging by rough indices — such as the willingness of states to participate in the more onerous tasks of general organization, or the content of communications between states differently oriented toward the central problems of the East-West conflict, the colonial question, and the problem of economic development — only the fear of universal destruction from a clash of equipoised nuclear power has kept the nation-state system in a state of precarious general equilibrium, i.e., a distribution of security, welfare, and prestige which could not be significantly improved for individual states by resort to forcible action.

When states can neither jointly pursue shared interests nor assert too forcibly national ambitions, they will accentuate a familiar technique of politics in conditions of scarcity: the balancing against each other of more or less conflicting aims, claims and counterclaims, and of supporting and opposing influences. In contemporary international relations, such a balancing process revolves around the three major issues of collective security, economic development, and colonialism; it takes place among Western, noncommitted, and Soviet-bloc countries within and between the regional and the global organizations; and it weakens at once the cohesion of regional alliances as inadequate to contain and coördinate conflicts of interest and orientations, and the position of the divided Great Powers, unable to dominate collectively and forced to buy individually the support, or at least neutrality, of politically strategic minor countries.[1]

The traditional balance of power, as encountered at the outset, has been modified by its contact with collective security. At first, an attempt was made to institutionalize the dynamics of the balance into normatively more reliable operation by means of the law and ideology of collective security within the framework of the League. Superior collective power was expected to coalesce *ad hoc* behind the law and oppose in the last resort all aggression anywhere. After the Second World War, an integrational approach to collective security sought to bring about a more reliable preponderance of power against renewed aggression. The law of the Charter was to be supported by correspondingly adjusted military-political and socio-economic factors. The failure to implement the concept on a global scale released two compensating developments. First and foremost, regionally integrated "collective security" is now relied upon to sustain a still ultimately bipolar global balance, deter large-scale aggression, and crush the far from anonymous suspected aggressor if necessary. A decentralized general system of collective security continues to extend permissive authority for a pragmatic application of collective sanctions. The second development is a reëmphasis on the quest for ways and means of reducing and supervising national armaments so as to control at least in this fashion the competetive dynamics of the reactivated global balance of power.

Thus, the balance of power was not so much recast by collective-security ideology as the symbols and institutions of collective security have been employed to buttress the military-political equilibrium as part of a larger, multiple equilibrium. This is adequate enough for an emergency. It promotes, however, only incidentally the growth of international constitutionalism. The balance of power in its traditional form, without a well-defined normative principle apart from the standard of quantitative equipoise, constitutes only an unreliable restraint on power. The interplay of power to be held in balance can safeguard but also consumes rights. If the balance of power is unreliable, the formal guarantees of collective security have been in themselves inadequate: legal rules regarding international conduct cannot have an assured normative effect in an imperfect community. In international relations, a kind of communal constitutionalism consists instead of a restraining interplay and proper equilibration of military-political and socio-economic as well as purely institutional factors. Changing configuration of the balance of power, the policies and ideologies of chiefly the great nations, and the moral temper of a period are among the conditions which, in a power-normative situation, codetermine the ultimate effect of the relations of interdependence and the effectiveness of institutional safeguards, including those of collective security. A particularly forbidding deadlock of military power is today called upon to contain the disturbing impact of anarchic practices within and outside international organization.

Historically, this state of things can be traced to three major developments. The growth and spread of economic nationalism and statism in the wake of waning *laissez-faire* and free-trade capitalism have intensified an outdated mercantilistic outlook, and have failed to substitute for spontaneous economic equilibrium a deliberately integrated international economy; modern totalitarianism is committed to rigid domination rather than to flexible pluralistic interaction, and projects — as motives or disguises — incongruous ideologies of conflict into the coöperative normative universe of international organization; and lastly, the triumph of anti-colonialism, in giving rise to ever new, often irresponsible and mostly weak sovereignties, has not only upset the last remnants of the imperialistic economic and political order, unhinged the structural equilibrium of the United Nations and created vacua in the military balance, but has also introduced into international agencies still unassimilated cultural and legal preconceptions, combined with large claims on international organization as a forum of political influence, agent of radical colonial emancipation, and fount of economic assistance.

Such upheavals cannot but aggravate the difficulties which would confront international organization in any event. Among them are the divergent ideas of differently situated, revolutionary or conservative, peripheral or exposed, would-be monolithic or pluralistic, states as to what constitutes a "favorable" equilibrium; different assumptions about the role and nature of international organization and of the problems — such as war, economic scarcity, social and political injustice — with which it is supposed to deal; and the different criteria for, and appreciation of, rational decision-making aimed at maximizing security and welfare by the best available means at the lowest possible cost to other values and to individuals and groups. All this thwarts the needed high degree of rational, long-range, responsive, and defensive attitudes on the part of members of international organization in general, and collective security in particular, which would assign the greatest value to its success as a relief, among other things, from the diminishingly profitable process of balancing national military power. Yet unless such a high value is assigned, international organization of collective security will be a dubious proposition, both uneconomical and unpredictable: either it will fail at the very outset to command acquiescence because of the high marginal cost — in terms of involvement and lessened certainty of performance all around — and small marginal advantage of the last unit of high-level commitment to and from any, even a weak and remote, state; or, it will fail to be implemented in an actual case of aggression in view of the high total cost and often not clearly compelling advantage of participation in a remote conflict. As a result, the belief in collective security as an economical and predictable safeguard against aggression will be weakened for friend and foe alike, reducing thus to a minimum both its attractive and its deterrent force.

And, in fact, the inconclusive record of the world organizations established at Paris and San Francisco has stimulated a number of alternative or supplementary schemes. In terms of scope, they advocate either a global or a regional basis. As regards method, the prescription is either for more authoritative international institutions, preferably bearing directly on the individual, or else a deëmphasis of institutions in favor of a practically coöperative world order. Primacy is assigned now to a judicial approach, now to military organization and enforcement, or to economics. The regionalists differ from world federalists, who in turn do not see eye to eye with the functionalists. Some would wish to depoliticize economics, others to legalize politics. It is felt that "deeper insights" and "new conceptual foundations" for international organization are necessary if it is to contribute substantially to the solution of the problem of security.[2] Basically, the question is how to channel the interplay of socioeconomic, military-political, and institutional factors and processes so that they perform their restraining constitutional function; and how to generate in coöperative practical experience new interests, values, and rewards, which would counteract the deepseated presumption of irreparable scarcity and thus conflict. To shield a necessarily slow process, the irreducible requirement continues to be a global equilibrium of power favoring the great nations which are themselves favorably disposed toward the rights of less powerful communities. Beyond that, nonaggressive states may find it wise to implement their concern for an increased share of security, welfare, and influence in ways compatible with an expanding institutional equilibrium.

Signs are not lacking that the most extreme point had already been reached in the post-World War II swing away from general organization to self-contained regionalism. It is an open question whether, when, and how, in radically changed conditions, a return movement will acquire a perceptible momentum and revitalize the United Nations as a coactive framework of international relations.

THE PROSPECTS OF AN EQUILIBRIUM THEORY

One fact emerges clearly from the analysis: it is the persistent reassertion of the balance or equilibrium of power as the irreducible if changing central dynamics of international relations. It changes internally as developing technology subordinates balance or preponderance of conventional military forces to relative offensive and defensive strength in nuclear weapons, long-range ballistic missiles, and strategic aircraft; and it changes externally as balancing of vertically organized and territorially based national military power structures is ever more intertwined with, and seeks vainly to override, larger socio-economic and political needs and aspirations, cultural idiosyncrasies, and institutional norms and practices. Both major Powers of today have experienced the consequences of obsolete policies as Soviet territorial encroachments and one-sided American emphases on military factors have provoked hostile reactions of a kind reserved for political behavior out of keeping with the mood of the day. Victory in the rising and falling global crisis, which has not been resolved in open war, will ultimately come to the Power learning soonest and best how to manipulate to its advantage the compensatory, non-military elements of the larger equilibrium that fluctuates uncertainly over the thermonuclear stalemate.

Such a state of things has theoretical implications which carry on the ideas put forward in the introductory chapter.

It is now more than suggestive to represent schematically the full scope of power-normative international reality as consisting of an inner hard core, or central dynamics, of continually balanced military power, shading off into militarily and politically ever less directly relevant factors, processes, interests, and values. All influence in their multiple interaction the behavior of politically significant individuals on national and international plane; but different, more or less forcible, components of the spectrum become relatively more efficacious depending on the degree of crisis, i.e., the extent to which the survival of one or more states as independent political societies is at stake. It is impossible to overemphasize the theoretical significance for all politics of the differentiation between a crisis situation — implying conflict over sheer physical or political survival as the minimum immediate objective of policy — and a noncrisis situation (in times and conditions of relaxed competition and tensions) — implying an often coöperative quest for additional goals, such as individual freedoms, general welfare, and justice, as the maximum and long-range political objectives. Failure to make the differentiation explicit has been responsible for much confusion in theoretical debate.

Some of it has concerned the problem of scope, symbolized in the terminological question of international "politics" versus "relations." The analyst confining himself self-consciously to the strictly political (meaning power) phenomena tends to reject all else as irrelevant to a realistic inquiry. His strength is a cogent doctrine of political dynamics reducible to a fairly simple and exciting formula, attractive to the student who is unwilling or unable to cope with the complex and changing interrelationships in the social and political world. The success of this kind of analysis in the United States after the Second World War is due to an intellectual need at least as much as to the historic conditions of post-Wilsonian disenchantment and the Soviet threat. Conversely, the advocate of a broader scope for international relations, including the social, cultural, and institutional factors, will see in the narrowness of the strictly political approach a major weakness. He admits the centrality of the strictly political, however conceived, but wishes to include the other factors as a condition of genuine realism. He can insist that this is no innovation or sign of liberal fuzziness, but rather a return to Aristotle in a situation of total politics reminiscent of the Greek *polis*. The weakness of the more inclusive inquiry is an almost inevitable loss of cogency, as the great methodological difficulties confronting the social sciences and their integration threaten to cause a relapse into the diffuseness (now aggravated by jargon) afflicting the study of international relations in the interwar period.

A theoretical analysis need not choose sides. To deal with the hard core of military-power dynamics, the determining influence of which grows with the rising level of crisis, the analysis will seek to develop and refine a "pure" power and equilibrium model, positing rational weighing of alternative means for maximizing chosen values; and it will relate this hard core to the less tangible modifying outer phenomena, chiefly socio-economic and institutional, which have grown in importance over time and become relatively more significant in situations of lessened crisis. This book has essayed such an approach between the Scylla of traditional realism, mistakenly representing the dynamics of too broadly conceived national power as being the whole of international relations, and the Charybdis of apolitical sociologism and legalism, which would miss the distinctive features of international politics. An attempt to account for as much as possible in terms of institutional equilibrium in no way precludes and in many respects supplements other methods and concepts of the behavioral sciences focusing attention on individual and group action, attitudes, ideologies, personality in culture, the role of élites, social communication, or decision-making. Pending further progress along these lines, the outline given in these pages may have some merits despite its own particular pitfalls and limitations.

It is anything but easy to analyze an equilibrium situation with respect to nonquantitative relationships and noncomparable, if related, factors. The resulting statement is not conclusively verifiable. This may offend the uncompromising empiricist, prone to mistake illustrations for clinching verifications and loath to accept a measure of inner consistency and over-all plausibility of a theory resting on sympathetic understanding of the subject-matter as a valuable feature in its favor. A necessarily simplified construct, however dynamic, can besides present only a lifeless approximation to the complex and changing interplay of real forces and events. Yet as a generalization stands for no specific instance, so an abstraction may correspond to nothing actual without ceasing therefore to denote something real. Impressive critics would make the scientific use of the equilibrium concept depend on the development of methods for measuring the power and other variables whose equilibrium makes for stability, and for defining operationally the conditions which produce them. The objection has force, but would be decisive only if measurements in social sciences were clearly established as possible and really fruitful in producing crucial insights into social processes. As it is, some precision can be introduced into an equilibrium analysis by the use of rough indices that point inferentially from qualitative and quantitative symptoms to underlying structures. For instance, abstention from war despite aggressive tendencies may serve as an index of military-political equilibrium; the frequency with which especially Great Powers act through international organization and the kind of business which they transact there are a possible index of the state of the institutional equilibrium, and, as regards socio-economic equilibrium, the well-developed economic measurements may be supplemented by quantifying the extent and evaluating the content of social communication within and between groups.

In mentioning economics, it is possible to derive some comfort (without ceasing to deplore the difference in possible accomplishment) from the continued use of the concept in economic theory despite its shortcomings, including a limited analytical and predictive value, and the loss of specificity when too many data are included in a "general equilibrium." Nor is the economic world at all immune to disequilibrium, approximating at best the "neighborhood of equilibrium," or unaffected by the existence of oligopoly — broadly comparable in the political world to the concentration of power in a few members of the international oligarchy — which mars the assumptions of the equilibrium theory, as much as those of the classical theory of collective security, by enabling a few players to change in their favor the terms of the game.[3]

To the extent that it focuses the resultants of individual behavior, our theory tends to reify such social processes and phenomena as the state, international institutions, and power. The drawback is minimized in approaches that put at the center individual human beings, their behavior and motives. Since the members of the general public are as a rule not sufficiently involved and articulate to have an identifiable direct influence on policy, it is both tempting and wise to seek meaningful statements of actual interrelations by the study of élites, i.e., politically crucial individuals. Yet, apart from the dangers of arbitrary selection, the élites which can be subjected to intensive inquiry are too few, their communications too largely inaccessible, and their behavior too variable to produce safe generalizations. Without at least a hypothesis (such as that of equilibrium) concerning the principles and dynamics of international relations and organization, which both govern and result from the interactive behavior of actors in the social and material environment, behavioral approaches will not do. A good instance is the approach from decision-making, which, though promising as a focus for the subjective-attitudinal and objective-environmental aspects, depends too much on an impossible historical reconstruction of situations, communications, and motives, often imperfectly known to the actors themselves.[4]

As an alternative, this essay has rooted the equilibrium analysis in a corresponding idea of rational decision-making: it posits as a guide to policy behavior the weighing of means, marginal and total costs and advantages, with the view toward maximizing chosen values like security, welfare, and prestige. Such a balancing procedure affects foreign policy not only when it is applied to relations with other states by the ideal detached foreign-policy maker, but also as it (ever less rationally) impinges on such policy from the interplay of particular, variously intensive and influential calculations and decisions within and between the different specialized publics, interest-groups, and branches and agencies of government. A rational, utilitarian pattern of decision-making may be of limited significance in modern international relations, yet it does gain ground whenever there is a weakening of the ideological, mass psychological, and other "irrational" modifiers of the fairly rational rules of traditional diplomatic statecraft.

Moreover, reification, rationalism, and relative deëmphasis of the domestic political process of the states-actors are less grievous shortcomings in a study concentrating on the over-all process of international relations resulting from the interaction of foreign policies of the members of the state system, rather than on the foreign policy of one or several nations. Not only would the opposite procedure multiply variables to the point where they defy any but a taxonomic theoretical statement; but also, quite apart from the question of feasibility, the now fashionable treatment of the domestic political process as the major determinant of foreign policy and international relations can be vastly overdone.

No one will deny that there is a relationship between domestic and international politics with regard to their principles and actual practice. And where there is a relationship, there is a problem; in this case the problem of conceptual and functional unity or disparity between the two branches of politics.

The liberal idealist and the conservative realist are superficially agreed upon the conceptual identity of all politics, domestic and international. However, the realist will castigate the liberal's tendency to transfer mechanically the principles of domestic, constitutional politics to the international sphere. He will deride liberal ideas about the feasible scope and function of law as an instrument of social control among states. The critique will rightly point out the confusion of cause and effect implicit in the attempts to extend the ideal of an unaided "rule of law" to interstate relations. It will emphasize the differences in the nature of the actors and their relations, and the lack of a firm supporting fabric of shared convictions in a primitive international community. The realist will, therefore, reject as fallacious and naïve the tendency to set up constitutional principles as an easily reproducible model for international politics, and to attribute to domestic politics legitimate priority over foreign affairs. Instead, the realist will see the unity of political phenomena in the pervasive role of power and will incline to assert the primacy of external over internal politics in a situation of chronic international crisis. Yet his tendency to treat nations as homogeneous units with a definable national interest will be rejected in turn as unrealistic by students who emphasize the determining influence on foreign policy of heterogeneous interest-groups in a pluralistic political community.

There is room for an intermediate position. As regards the conceptual identity or else disparity of domestic and international politics, an inquiry may attempt to isolate relevant principles and other variables common to all politics, and to differentiate their respective place, weight, and manifestation in the different types of the two major areas of politics. In a general way, such an inquiry is facilitated if one assumes a continuum in the forms of possible control relationships, passing from coercive or competitive application of physical power to a complex interaction of normatively ordered competitive and coöperative responses, regulated by a fundamental consensus and a generally recognized authority. Any actual political system, democratic or totalitarian, domestic or international, will approximate in an imperfect fashion the one or the other extreme type of control. Or, more specifically, a theory can assume the operation in all politics of an essentially identical principle, for instance that of equilibrium. The difference between various political systems ceases then to appear as one of basic principle and becomes one of the principle's implementation: while interstate and preconstitutional domestic politics revolve around a relatively unregulated balance of power in inchoate institutions for the coördination of interests, constitutional domestic politics rests on an equilibrium of interest groups within an elaborate system of institutional and other checks and balances.

As for the question of functional interdependence, few will deny that the predominant values of a political society influence foreign-policy attitudes. Nor is there any doubt about the growing interrelation of practical domestic and foreign politics. But, on the latter score, it is necessary to avoid extremes. A sound theoretical outlook will not worship at the altar of an irresistibly self-evident and morally absolute national interest. Neither will it see foreign policy as a mechanical resultant of the interplay of domestic political forces. To the extent that the slogan is true, foreign-policy analysis may and often has to start where domestic politics ends, that is to say, at the watershed. There are two major reasons. First, international politics of the state system has its conventions, techniques, and requirements which, embedded in tradition and existing conditions, are relatively independent of the internal political system of any one participant nation. These are the international equivalents of the generally supported "rules of the game" which even the most determined special-interest-group analyst must introduce as a vitiating exception into his scheme of the domestic political process. At the very least, an informed interpretation of the conventions and requirements of the international game will rule out certain foreign-policy ideas of special interest-groups as patently absurd and weight others as more plausible. This will affect decisively the balance of domestic pressures on foreign policy-making — notably when these pressures cancel themselves out into a deadlock or are overwhelmed by the impact of international crisis — and ensure considerable continuity in the foreign affairs of a plural society within the broad framework of majority consensus, strikingly demonstrated whenever political parties abandon or substantially modify their foreign-policy nostrums once they have attained the responsibilities of executive office.

The second and related reason for drawing a line, however thin, between domestic and foreign politics is the persistence of national "self-preservation" and "survival" as the necessary and in themselves sufficient goals of foreign policy. To say that they are teleologically ambigious since they beg the question of the values to be preserved is to miss the point. The irreducible minimum objective of foreign policy is precisely to safeguard the integrity of the state so that the values of the surviving society can be determined by domestic political processes independently of external pressures. Where this objective is realized, the diminished role of domestic politics in foreign policy-making is compensated by an enlarged autonomy in all other matters. The deeper the crisis and more difficult sheer survival, the greater will be the predominance of foreign over domestic politics. According to their security position and, secondarily, their domestic political system, countries have thus to work out their individual compromises between the two extremes of domestic determinism of foreign policies on the one hand, and international determinism of domestic policies on the other.

In such a situation, policy-makers may profit by theories that place in a unifying focus the factors and processes to be taken into account in the pursuit of security and welfare; and a policy-oriented bias puts high premium on a theory organized around a basic principle which the makers of policy are familiar with and actually apply in daily decisions. As the empty boxes of conceptual frameworks are piled up and move in the opposite direction, the gap between theory and foreign policy-formulation widens to the detriment of maker and student alike.

If, finally, one makes the most of the institutional aspect, such an approach has its merits provided it remains in close touch with international realities. First, the norms of international law and organization constitute one scientifically ascertainable variable and one of the elements in the definition of the institutional equilibrium. Second, and more important, the various actors in, factors for, and relations of international politics are subjected to analysis while they pass through an organizational framework, and the produced effects can be translated into qualitative and quantitative indices. In addition, a theory emphasizing institutions supplements otherwise focused theories with the inquiry into some of the means, other than national power, of implementing desired values. It is not impossible that well-chosen instrumentalities might enlarge the "quantity" of security and welfare to be distributed, relieving thus the mercantilistic mentality which continues to pervade much of international politics.

There are many approaches and intermediate objectives under different names and symbols; the ultimate goal remains the good life of individual men in free communities, great or small.

NOTES

Introduction: *Toward an Equilibrium Theory of International Relations and Institutions*

1. Cf. Hans J. Morgenthau, *Scientific Man versus Power Politics* (1946), pp. 168 ff. In his *Inevitable Peace* (1948), p. 30, Carl J. Friedrich observes that the "convergence of the ideal and material motivation constitutes the complete reality." William Y. Elliott develops in his *Pragmatic Revolt in Politics* (1928) a dualistic theory of a "co-organic" character of societies, consisting of the limiting physical environment, or ecology, and the realm of value and purpose. Frederick Watkins makes the persistent dualism of the Western conception of politics into the central theme of his *Political Tradition of the West* (1948). Concerning the relationship of power and norm, Reinhold Niebuhr sees in politics "an area where conscience and power meet, where the ethical and coercive factors of human life will interpenetrate and work out their tentative compromises"; *Moral Man and Immoral Society: A Study in Ethics and Politics* (1932), p. 4. Even E. H. Carr, certainly no "utopian," grants that "Political action must be based on a co-ordination of morality and power." *The Twenty Years' Crisis 1919–1939* (1949), p. 97.

2. On the question of power see Charles E. Merriam, *Political Power: Its Composition and Incidence* (1934), pp. 15 ff., 46; Carl J. Friedrich, *Constitutional Government and Democracy* (rev. ed., 1950), pp. 22 ff.; Harold D. Lasswell and Abraham Kaplan, *Power and Society: A Framework for Political Inquiry* (1950), pp. xvii, 75 ff., 92 ff.; Bertrand Russell, *Power: A New Social Analysis* (1938), pp. 13–14, 35, 135; V. O. Key, Jr., *Politics, Parties, and Pressure Groups* (3rd ed., 1952), p. 4; and Morgenthau, *Politics among Nations: The Struggle for Power and Peace* (1949), pp. 14, 80 ff.

3. Cf. especially his comprehensive article, "Another 'Great Debate': The National Interest of the United States," *American Political Science Review* (December 1952), pp. 961–988.

4. In addition to G. E. G. Catlin, *A Study of the Principles of Politics* (1930), the discussion draws chiefly on Lasswell's *World Politics and Personal Insecurity* (1935); Lasswell and Kaplan, *Power and Society*; Daniel Lerner and H. D. Lasswell, *The Policy Sciences:*

Recent Developments in Scope and Method (1951); Talcott Parsons, *Essays in Sociological Theory Pure and Applied* (1949); Parsons and Edward Shils, *Toward a General Theory of Action* (2nd ed., 1949); David Easton, *The Political System* (1953); Quincy Wright, *The Study of International Relations* (1955); and Karl W. Deutsch, *Nationalism and Social Communication* (1953).

5. Cf. Joseph A. Schumpeter, *Business Cycles* (1939), Vol. I, ch. 2; A. C. Pigou, *Economics of Welfare* (4th ed., 1932), pp. 794–795; George J. Stigler, *The Theory of Price* (1946), pp. 26 ff., on the idea of equilibrium in economics; and Robert W. MacIver, *Social Causation* (1942), p. 169, for the concept of the "precipitant."

6. See Catlin, pp. 114, 197, and *passim*; Lasswell, *World Politics and Personal Insecurity*, pp. 52 ff.; Lasswell and Kaplan, pp. xiv ff., 250 ff.; Parsons and Shils, pp. 107–108, 230. Also see M. Fortes and E. E. Evans Pritchard, eds., *African Political Systems* (1940), pp. xxii–iii, 14, 17–18, 271; and Eliot D. Chapple and Carleton S. Coon, *Principles of Anthropology* (1942), pp. 44 ff., 362, 462.

7. Cf. Carl J. Friedrich, *Foreign Policy in the Making: The Search for a New Balance of Power* (1938); and Chester I. Barnard, *The Functions of the Executive* (1940).

8. Cf. H. W. V. Temperley, *The Foreign Policy of Canning: 1822–1827* (1925), p. 466. Canning had in mind the enlargement of the balance of power to include the newly arising Latin American states.

9. Cf. Melville J. Herskovits, *Man and his Works: The Science of Cultural Anthropology* (1948), pp. 522 ff.

10. Cf. Robert K. Merton, *Social Theory and Social Structure* (1949), pp. 21 ff.

11. Reinhold Niebuhr, *Christian Realism and Political Problems* (1953), p. 51.

12. Cf. Eugen Ehrlich, *Fundamental Principles of the Sociology of Law* (1936), with an introduction by Roscoe Pound; Julius Stone, *The Province and Function of Law: Law as Logic, Justice, and Social Control* (1950); Nicholas S. Timasheff, *An Introduction to the Sociology of Law* (1939); Léon Duguit, *Law in the Modern State* (1919); and, more specifically on international law, Gerhart Niemeyer, *Law Without Force: The Function of Politics in International Law* (1941); Herbert W. Briggs, "New Dimensions of International Law," *American Political Science Review* (September 1952), pp. 677–698; and I. L. Claude, Jr., "Individuals and World Law," *Harvard Studies in International Affairs* (June 1952), pp. 10–22.

13. On the geographic aspect, see Nicholas J. Spykman, *The Geography of the Peace*, ed. by H. R. Nicholl (1944), pp. 3 ff., and Robert Strausz-Hupé, *Geopolitics: The Struggle for Space and Power* (1942); on international institutions C. Easton Rothwell, "International Organization and World Politics," *International Organization* (November 1949), pp. 605–619.

Chapter 1. *The Traditional Balance-of-Power System*

1. On intervention, see Ellery C. Stowell, *Intervention in International Law* (1921), pp. 317, 414 ff.; J. L. Brierly, *The Law of Nations* (4th ed., 1949), pp. 284, 287–288; Philip C. Jessup, *A Modern Law of Nations* (1949), p. 172. On recognition, see H. Lauterpacht, *Recognition in International Law* (1948), pp. 2–3, 27 ff., 358, 362–363; and Brierly, pp. 122, 124.

2. Cf. Sir James Headlam-Morley, *Studies in Diplomatic History* (1930), pp. 109 ff., 121; and Canning's paper in Temperley, *The Foreign Policy of Canning*, Appendix II, p. 539.

3. The quoted phrases are from Art. 22 of the Guarantee of Wallachia and Moldavia. Cf. E. Hertslet, *The Map of Europe by Treaty* (1875–91), Vol. II, p. 1260.

4. According to a *mot* attributed to Talleyrand, "non-intervention was a metaphysical and political phrase meaning almost the same thing as intervention." Cf. C. K. Webster, *The Foreign Policy of Palmerston 1830–1841* (1951), Vol. I, p. 99.

5. Brierly, p. 38. The preceding quotes refer to Emerich de Vattel's contention that a dwarf is as much a man as a giant is; a small republic is no less a sovereign state than the most powerful kingdom (*Le droit des gens*, ed. 1758, préliminaires, p. 11), and to Hobbes' justification of natural equality of men by the fact that "as to the strength of body, the weakest has strength enough to kill he srongest. . . ." *Leviathan* (Everyman's Edition), ch. 12, p. 63. For a positivistic assertion of state equality, cf. Lassa Oppenheim, *International Law*, ed. by Arnold D. McNair (4th ed., 1928), Vol. I, par. 115, p. 238.

6. Cf. Payson S. Wild, Jr., "What is the Trouble with International Law?" *American Political Science Review* (June 1938), p. 482.

7. Cf. Edwin deW. Dickinson, *The Equality of States in International Law* (1920), pp. 3 ff. and 334–335; Jessup, p. 28; Brierly, pp. 115 ff.; Nicolas Politis, *The New Aspects of International Law* (1928), pp. 8–9; David Mitrany, *A Working Peace System* (4th ed., 1946), pp. 35–39, 49; Carr, *Nationalism and After* (1945), p. 64; and *Cmd.* 2768 (1926), p. 14, for the so-called Balfour formula distinguishing equality of status and function.

8. Frederick Gentz, *Fragments upon the Balance of Power in Europe* (1806), p. 58; his italics. See also Gentz, pp. x, 63–64; Henry Saint-John Bolingbroke, *Works* (1754), Vol. II, Letter vii, p. 374; *The Correspondence of Prince Talleyrand and King Louis XVIII During the Congress of Vienna*, preface by M. G. Pallain (1881), pp. xi–xii; David Hume, "Of the Balance of Power," *Essays Moral, Political, and Literary* (1854), pp. 348–356; Sir A. W. Ward and G. P. Gooch, eds., *The Cambridge History of British Foreign Policy 1783–1919* (1923), Vol. II, p. 3; and Sir Geoffrey G. Butler and Simon Macoby, *The Development of International Law* (1928), p. 66.

9. Cf. Maurice A. Asch, "An Analysis of Power, with Special Reference to International Politics," *World Politics* (January 1951), pp. 218–237.

10. Cf. Vattel, *Le droit des gens*, livre III, ch. 3, pp. 39–40; Gentz, pp. 55, 57; and W. H. Dawson, *Richard Cobden and Foreign Policy* (1926), p. 48.

11. The quoted phrases are from Gentz, pp. 72–77. Historical illustrations on the period between the Congress of Vienna and the First World War are based mainly on W. A. Phillips, *The Confederation of Europe* (2nd ed., 1920); Charles Dupuis, *Le principe d'équilibre et le concert européen* (1909); Webster, *The Foreign Policy of Castlereagh, 1815–1822* (1925), and *The Foreign Policy of Palmerston*, 2 vols.; Temperley, *The Foreign Policy of Canning;* Robert C. Binkley, *Realism and Nationalism 1852–1871* (1935); William L. Langer, *European Alliances and Alignments 1871–1890* (2nd ed., 1950); and Sidney B. Fay, *The Origins of the World War*, 2 vols. (1928).

12. Cf. his "Memorandum on the Present State of British Relations with France and Germany," *British Documents on the Origins of the War*, ed. by G. P. Gooch and H. Temperley (1928), Vol. III, pp. 402–403. See also Sir Austen Chamberlain's essay on the foundations of British foreign policy in *The Foreign Policy of the Powers* (1935), pp. 29, 60.

13. Headlam-Morley, pp. 183–185. But see also Headlam-Morley, p. 124, regarding the effectiveness of British guarantees in regard to the Low Countries alone. A later statement on the lack of British interest in the eastern frontiers by Lloyd George is recorded in W. M. Jordan, *Great Britain, France, and the German Problem 1918–1939* (1934), p. 201.

14. Lord Castlereagh gave classic expression to a theme which is still with us: "When the Territorial Balance of Power is disturbed, [Great Britain] can interfere with effect, but She is the last Govt. in Europe, which can be expected, or can venture to commit Herself on any Question of an abstract character"; Confidential State Paper of May 5th, 1850, *Cambridge History of British Foreign Policy*, Vol. II, Appendix A, p. 632.

15. Cf. Oppenheim, par. 51 and 136, pp. 99, 268. Conversely, Quincy Wright asserts complete incompatibility between international law and the balance of power: cf. "International Law and the Balance of Power," *American Journal of International Law* (January 1943), p. 102. On the preceding points, see Gentz, pp. 56 ff.; Talleyrand to Louis XIII, December 28, 1814, *Correspondence*, p. 201; and John Stuart Mill, *Utilitarianism, Liberty, and Representative Government* (Everyman's Library, 1950), p. 426.

16. Guglielmo Ferrero, *The Reconstruction of Europe: Talleyrand and the Congress of Vienna 1814–1815* (1941), p. 35, uses the quoted phrase.

17. Cf. J. H. Beale, Jr., "The Development of Jurisprudence During

the Past Century," *Harvard Law Review* (February 1905), pp. 275–276; T. J. Lawrence, "The Primacy of the Great Powers," *Essays on Some Disputed Questions in Modern International Law* (1885), pp. 206–213; M. W. Graham, "Great Powers and Small States," in Morgenthau, ed., *Peace, Security and the United Nations* (1946), pp. 62–63; Harold Nicolson, *The Congress of Vienna: A Study in Allied Unity 1812–1822* (1945), p. 137; and T. E. Holland, *The European Concert in the Eastern Question* (1885), p. 2.

18. Cf. Winston S. Churchill, *Triumph and Tragedy*, Vol. VI of *The Second World War* (1953), pp. 227–228.

19. Sir Alfred Zimmern, *The League of Nations and the Rule of Law 1918–1935* (1936), p. 75. Typical commitments can be read in Article XVI of the Treaty of Chaumont and Art VI of the Treaty of Quadruple Alliance. Cf. Webster, *The Congress of Vienna 1814–1815* (1919), pp. 32, 144, and *passim* on the system in general.

20. Cf. Langer, pp. 195–196.

21. See Phillips, pp. 208–209, for the text of the Preliminary Protocol of Troppau. The undertaking of the members of the Neo-Holy Alliance, Austria, Russia, and Prussia, to render each other automatically mutual assistance against revolution anywhere, reads, *mutatis mutandis*, like an article from the League Covenant.

22. Cf. Gaetano Mosca, *The Ruling Class*, edited and revised with introduction by Arthur Livingston (1939), pp. 50, 70, 130; Robert Michels, *Political Parties* (1949), pp. 136 ff.; and C. W. Cassinelli, "The Law of Oligarchy," *American Political Science Review* (September 1953), pp. 773–784.

Chapter 2. *The Structure of International Organization*

1. Cf. W. W. Kaufmann, "The Organization of Responsibility," *World Politics* (July 1949), pp. 511–532; William E. Rappard, *The Geneva Experiment* (1931), p. 49; Arnold Wolfers, "The Small Powers and the Enforcement of Peace," *Memorandum No. 3*, Yale Institute of International Studies (August 1943), pp. 12 ff.; William T. R. Fox, *The Super-Powers* (1944), pp. 153–155; and *Documents of the United Nations Conference on International Organization San Francisco 1945*, Vols. I–XII (1945), Vol. I, pp. 125, 135, 138, 360, 362–363, 562 (hereafter cited as UNCIO, *Documents*).

2. Cf. Walter Schücking, *The International Union of the Hague Conferences* (1918), pp. 223 ff.; F. C. Hicks, "The Equality of States and the Hague Conferences," *American Journal of International Law* (July 1908), pp. 535–536; Dickinson, *The Equality of States in International Law*, pp. 286–289; and Graham, "Great Powers and Small States," p. 68.

3. The phrase is quoted by Zimmern, *The League of Nations and the Rule of Law*, p. 289. On the background see Miller, *The Drafting of the Covenant*, Vol. I, pp. 64, 146–162, 248, 313, 315, and Vol. II, p.

566; and Rappard, "Small States in the League of Nations," *Political Science Quarterly* (December 1934), pp. 561, 557–558.

4. Cf. the statements of the American, British, and Soviet delegations, UNCIO, *Documents*, Vol. XII, pp. 296, 316; 307; and 306, respectively.

5. Cf. UNCIO, *Documents*, Vol. I, pp. 369–370, and Vol. XII, pp. 296 ff., 490, 503. See also *Report to the President on the Results of the San Francisco Conference by the Chairman of the U.S. Delegation, the Secretary of State*, Department of State Publication 2349, Conference Series 71 (1945), pp. 17–19; and Leland M. Goodrich, "Development of the General Assembly," *International Conciliation* (May 1951), pp. 262–265.

6. The first cited phrase is from the Israeli delegate in the United Nations (see J. Maclaurin, *The United Nations and Power Politics*, p. 217, for full quotation); the second is from Field Marshal Smuts. Cf. UNCIO, *Documents*, Vol. I, p. 423.

7. See UNCIO, *Documents*, Vol. XI, pp. 321–322, 710–714, 129, 319, 327, 330, and Vol. XII, pp. 297, 316, 317, 504. Also Herbert V. Evatt, *The Task of Nations* (1949), pp. 29–30, 46.

8. Cf. Margaret E. Burton, *The Assembly of the League of Nations* (1941), pp. 50, 206 ff., and Goodrich, "Development of the General Assembly," pp. 259, 277.

9. Cf. M. Margaret Ball, "Bloc Voting in the General Assembly," *International Organization* (February 1951), pp. 3–31.

10. Cf. Maclaurin, p. 100; Rappard, "Small States in the League of Nations," pp. 572–573; and Paul Hasluck, *The Workshop of Security* (1948), pp. 177 ff.

Chapter 3. *The Collective-Security Commitment*

1. Cf. Jessup, *A Modern Law of Nations*, pp. 47 ff.; Lauterpacht, *Recognition in International Law*, p. 6; and Briggs, "Community Interest in the Emergence of New States: The Problem of Recognition," *1950 Proceedings, American Society of International Law*, pp. 169–181. More conservative are the Secretariat General Memorandum on the Legal Aspects of the Problem of Representation in the United Nations, *U.N. Doc. S/1466*, March 9, 1950, and P. M. Brown, "Legal Effects of Recognition," *American Journal of International Law* (October 1950), pp. 621, 625.

2. On the problem of force short of war before and under the League, see Albert E. Hindmarsh, *Force in Peace* (1932). According to Brierly, there is no "rule of law" in the literal sense. Only force can rule and the problem is put to it behind the law in a constitutional order; *The Outlook for International Law* (1944), p. 74.

3. Hans Kelsen, *Law and Peace in International Relations* (1942), pp. 35 ff., conceives of "just war" as a sanction against the international delict of aggression.

4. The phrase was authored by the Italian Premier Orlando. Cf. David Hunter Miller, *The Drafting of the Covenant* (1928), Vol. II, p. 569. Miller, p. 563, records Wilson's idea of the Covenant as a "living thing" adjustable to changing circumstances. Cf. also Viscount Cecil, *The Way of Peace* (1929), pp. 82, 89, 103–106.

5. For a realistic critique of collective security, see Carr, *The Twenty Years' Crisis*, and *Conditions of Peace* (1942); Walter Lippmann, *U.S. Foreign Policy: Shield of the Republic* (1943), and *U.S. War Aims* (1944); and Morgenthau, *Politics among Nations*. Cf. also Heinrich Rogge, *Kollektivsicherheit, Bündnispolitik, Völkerbund* (1937).

6. Cf. *International Sanctions*, A Report by a Group of Members of the Royal Institute of International Affairs (1938), pp. 178 ff. At San Francisco, many smaller states opposed a rigid definition of aggression because "it might be difficult to determine the invader if there had been provocation on one side which forced action by the other"; UNCIO, *Documents*, Vol. XII, p. 342.

7. See, for instance, Payson S. Wild, Jr., *Sanctions and Treaty Enforcement* (1934), pp. 211 ff.

8. Cf. John Foster Dulles, *War, Peace and Change* (1939), pp. 82–84, 168, and *passim;* Dino Grandi in *Foreign Policy of the Powers*, p. 86; Dr. Charles Malik and General Romulo in UNCIO, *Documents*, Vol. I, pp. 251–252 and 293, respectively. The issue is not peculiar to collective security. In the heyday of the balance of power, Castlereagh opposed force "collectively prostituted" to support abused power and rights in a general guarantee of the *status quo*. Cf. Webster, *The Foreign Policy of Castlereagh*, p. 151. On peaceful change in general, see Frederick S. Dunn, *Peaceful Change* (1937).

9. On peaceful settlement, cf. H. Lauterpacht, *The Function of Law in the International Community* (1933), pp. 139 ff. and *passim;* and Carr, *The Twenty Years' Crisis*, pp. 193 ff.

10. Cf., for example, Georg Schwarzenberger, *Power Politics* (1951), pp. 492–494, and (1941), pp. 243 ff.; Morgenthau, pp. 332 ff.; Kenneth W. Thompson, "Collective Security Reexamined," *American Political Science Review* (September 1953), pp. 758–766; and Werner Levi, *Fundamentals of World Organization* (1950), pp. 74–75.

11. Cf. Ray S. Baker and William E. Dodd, eds., *The Public Papers of Woodrow Wilson, War and Peace* (1927), Vol. I, pp. 179, 182–183, 234, 342, 343; and Miller, Vol. I, p. 42 (italics in the original). According to the present Lord Salisbury, the crucial assumption of the framers of the Covenant was "great, even overwhelming strength" on the side of the *status quo*. Cf. *The Cranborne Report on Participation of all States in the League of Nations*, pp. 46–47, quoted in Salo Engel, *League Reform*, Geneva Studies, Vol. XI (August 1940).

12. Cf. Jordan, *Great Britain, France, and the German Problem*, p. 37, on Clemenceau; *The Times* (London), July 29, 1931, p. 12, for the statement by Ramsay MacDonald; and Friedrich, *Foreign Policy*

in the Making, p. 14, and Nicolson, *Peacemaking, 1919* (1939), p. 210, on the views of the Czechoslovak statesman.

13. Cf. Jessup, *Neutrality: Its History, Economics and Law* (1936), Vol. IV, pp. v, 156 ff., and Vol. III, pp. 101 ff. and 132 ff.; Charles G. Fenwick, "Neutrality and International Organization," *American Journal of International Law* (April 1934), pp. 334–339; Arnold Brecht, "The Idea of a 'Safety Belt,'" *American Political Science Review* (October 1949), p. 1005; Brierly, *The Outlook for International Law,* p. 30; and Carr, *Conditions of Peace,* p. 58.

14. Cf. UNCIO, *Documents,* Vol. XII, p. 505.

15. Cf. *U.N. Doc. S/336,* April 30, 1947, pp. 32–33, 37; and UNCIO, *Documents,* Vol. XII, pp. 381–382

16. Cf. Miller, *The Drafting of the Covenant,* Vol. I, pp. 209–210, 243–254; and UNCIO, *Documents,* Vol. XII, p. 279.

17. See Gwendolen M. Carter, *The British Commonwealth and International Security* (1947), pp. 8, 105 ff., and Jordan, *Great Britain, France, and the German Problem,* p. 204, for the quoted phrases. The latter statement is by Nicolas Politis.

18. Cf. Carter, pp. 36 (note 37), 102; J. C. Smuts, *The League of Nations: A Practical Suggestion* (1918), pp. 62–63; and Engel, *League Reform,* pp. 77, 79.

19. *Ibid.,* pp. 137–151. The quote is from a statement by the Norwegian delegate on p. 142.

20. For the distinction between negative and positive security, see Headlam-Morley, *Studies in Diplomatic History,* p. 8, Jordan, pp. 196, 202, and Carter, pp. 100–101, 114.

21. See Sir Austen Chamberlain, *A Peace in Our Time* (1928), p. 184, for the cited phrase.

22. The quoted formulation of the idea is from the French Foreign Minister Pichon. Cf. Wolfers, *Britain and France Between Two Wars* (1940), pp. 99–100.

23. The historical data of the following discussion are drawn mainly from F. P. Walters, *A History of the League of Nations,* 2 vols. (1952); Rappard, *The Quest for Peace Since the World War* (1940); Hindmarsh, *Force in Peace;* Goodrich, "Korea: Collective Measures Against Aggression," *International Conciliation* (October 1953); and the cited works by Carter, Wolfers, and Maclaurin.

24. See Elliott et al., *United States Foreign Policy: Its Organization and Control* (1952), p. 161, and Goodrich, p. 189, for the quoted phrases.

25. See Henry L. Stimson, *The Far Eastern Crisis* (1936), pp. 200–201; and Sean Lester, "The Far Eastern Dispute from the Point of View of the Small States," *The Problems of Peace,* Eighth Series (1934), pp. 120–135.

26. For a breakdown on contributions, see *United States Participation in the United Nations,* Department of State Publication 4583

(1952). The U.S. and South Korea provided about 90 per cent of ground forces, and the U.S. itself about 50 per cent of ground, 86 of naval, and 94 of air forces.

27. Cf. Jessup, Vol. IV, p. 123; Carr, p. 55; Appendix IV in *International Sanctions;* and Goodrich, p. 182.

28. See Ch. 6, "The Revision of Neutrality," in Jessup, Vol. IV, pp. 156 ff.

29. See Sir Samuel Hoare's speech after his resignation, quoted in Carter, p. 226.

30. Cf. Strausz-Hupé, *Geopolitics,* p. 191, and Carr, p. viii. Herbert Evatt made himself into a champion of the smaller and the middle Powers: see his *Task of Nations,* and *Australia in World Affairs* (1946).

31. Cf. Schwarzenberger, *Power Politics* (1951), p. 125; John Foster Dulles, "Policy for Security and Peace," *Foreign Affairs* (April 1954), p. 357; and Paul H. Nitze, "Atoms, Strategy and Policy," *Foreign Affairs* (January 1956), pp. 187–198.

32. For the quoted labels, see Thompson, "Collective Security Reexamined," pp. 770 ff., and Ernest B. Haas, "Types of Collective Security: An Examination of Operational Concepts," *American Political Science Review* (March 1955), pp. 47 ff.

33. Cf. Wolfers, "Collective Security and the War in Korea," *Yale Review* (June 1954), p. 485.

Chapter 4. *The Functional Scope*

1. The quoted phrases are from Arnold J. Toynbee, *A Study of History,* Vol. IV (1935), p. 179, Carr, *Nationalism and After,* p. 63, and C. A. Macartney, *National States and National Minorities* (1934), pp. 100, 278.

2. Cf. Langer, *The Diplomacy of Imperialism 1890-1902* (1935), Vol. I, p. 75; E. M. Earle, "Adam Smith, Alexander Hamilton, Friedrich List: The Economic Foundations of Military Power," in Earle, ed., *Makers of Modern Strategy* (1944); Frederick Hertz, *The Economic Problem of the Danubian Basin: A Study in Economic Nationalism* (1947), pp. 218 ff.; and Maurice Zinkin, *Asia and the West* (1951), pp. 208 ff.

3. In addition to the cited sources, see Rupert Emerson et al., *Government and Nationalism in Southeast Asia* (1942), pp. 77 ff.; Emerson, "Paradoxes of Asian Nationalism," *Far Eastern Quarterly* (February 1954), pp. 131–143; J. K. Fairbank, "The Problems of Revolutionary Asia," *Foreign Affairs* (October 1950), pp. 101–113; and Laurence Duggan, *The Americas: The Search for Hemisphere Security* (1949), pp. 215–216.

4. Cf. Temperley ed., *A History of the Peace Conference of Paris* (1920), Vol. I, pp. 167–168; Baker and Dodd, *The Public Papers of*

Woodrow Wilson, Vol. I, pp. 16, 180–181, 233–234; Alfred Cobban, *National Self-Determination* (1947), pp. 16 ff., 20, 22; and Paul Birdsall, *Versailles Twenty Years After* (1941), p. 34 and *passim*.

5. On the controversial question of the protection of minorities, see La Documentation Internationale, *La Paix de Versailles*, Vol. X, Commission des Nouveaux Etats et des Minorités, pp. 69, 129–30, 161–2, 265, 320, 383; Pablo de Azcarate, *League of Nations and National Minorities, an Experiment* (1945); Macartney, *National States and National Minorities;* and Inis L. Claude, Jr., *National Minorities: An International Problem* (1955). The calculated use of "hackneyed and well-trimmed maxims as 'right of self-determination' " against Czechoslovakia in 1938 was advocated in a Memorandum of the German State Secretary von Weizsäcker, dated June 20, 1938. Cf. *Documents on German Foreign Policy 1918–1945* (1949–51), Vol. II, pp. 420–422.

6. Cf. Clyde Eagleton, "Excesses of Self-Determination," *Foreign Affairs* (July 1953), pp. 592–604. See also Lord Acton's essay on Nationality in *The History of Freedom and Other Essays* (1907); Otto Bauer, *Die Nationalitätenfrage und die Sozialdemokratie* (2nd ed., 1924); Oscar I. Janowsky, *Nationalities and National Minorities* (1945), p. 9 and *passim;* Cobban, pp. 173 ff., Carr, *Conditions of Peace*, pp. 39 ff., and *Nationalism and After;* Erich Hula, "National Self-Determination Reconsidered," *Social Research* (February 1943), pp. 1–21; and Francis B. Sayre, "The Quest for Independence," *Foreign Affairs* (July 1952), pp. 564–579.

7. In its advisory opinion concerning the Tunis-Morocco Nationality Decrees, the Permanent Court of International Justice stated: "The question whether a certain matter is or is not solely within the jurisdiction of a State is an essentially relative question; it depends upon the development of international relations." Cf. *P.C.I.J.*, Series B, No. 4.

8. Cf. UNCIO, *Documents*, Vol. I, pp. 171–177, 181–184, 232–238, 244–245, 250, 252, and 422–424.

9. Cf. UNCIO, *Documents*, Vol. I, p. 191, and Vol. VI, pp. 597–598.

10. The following summary of United Nations practice draws heavily on the detailed discussion in Daniel S. Cheever and H. Field Haviland, Jr., *Organizing for Peace: International Organization in World Affairs* (1954), pp. 507 ff. See also Trygve Lie, *In the Cause of Peace: Seven Years with the United Nations* (1954), pp. 142 ff.

11. Cf. Goodrich, "United Nations and Domestic Jurisdiction," *International Organization* (February 1949), pp. 19 ff. and 26 ff.

12. Cf. Goodrich and Edvard Hambro, *Charter of the United Nations* (1949), pp. 406 ff., 423–425; Josef L. Kunz, "Chapter XI of the United Nations Charter in Action," *American Journal of International Law* (January 1954), pp. 103–110; and Haas, "The Attempt to Terminate Colonialism: Acceptance of the United Nations Trustee-

ship System," *International Organization* (February 1953), pp. 1–21.
13. Cf. Mitrany, *A Working Peace System*, pp. 35, 59, and *passim*.
14. Cf. Beneš, *Democracy To-day and To-morrow* (1939), p. 117;
Smuts, *The League of Nations*, p. 25; Wolfers, "In Defense of the
Small Countries," *Yale Review* (Winter 1944), pp. 216–217; Fox, *The
Super-Powers*, pp. 144–145; Carr, *The Twenty Years' Crisis*, p. viii;
Friedrich, *Inevitable Peace*, pp. 10–11, 30; and Claude, "Theoretical
Bases of International Organization," *Harvard Studies in International
Affairs* (June 1953), p. 11.
15. Brierly, *The Law of Nations*, pp. 92 ff.

Chapter 5. The Geographic Scope

1. On regionalism in general, see *Regional Arrangements for
Security and the United Nations*, Commission to Study the Organization of Peace (1953); and B. Boutros Ghali, *Contribution à l'étude des
ententes régionales* (1949).
2. Cf. Goodrich and Hambro, *Charter of the United Nations*, p.
310, and UNCIO, *Documents*, Vol. XII, pp. 682, 766, 783–784.
3. UNCIO, *Documents*, Vol. XII, p. 680, for Senator Vandenberg's
proposal, and *New York Times*, June 26, 1954, pp. 1–2, for statements
by Ambassador Henry Cabot Lodge, Jr. in the Security Council in
connection with the use of force in Guatemala.
4. Cf. H. N. Howard, "The Soviet Alliance System and the
Charter of the United Nations," in *Regional Arrangements for Security and the United Nations*, pp. 65–79; Eagleton, "North Atlantic
Treaty Organization," *ibid.*, p. 97. On the background, see Miller,
The Drafting of the Covenant, Vol. I, pp. 448–450, 458; Lippmann,
U. S. War Aims, pp. 174, 180; Cordell Hull, *The Memoirs of Cordell
Hull* (1948), p. 1646; and UNCIO, *Documents*, Vol. XII, pp. 777–778.
5. Cf. Sir Gladwyn Jebb, "The Free World and the UN," *Foreign
Affairs* (April 1953), pp. 382–391; R. G. Mackay, "NATO and U.N.,"
The Annals of the American Academy of Political and Social Science
(July 1953), pp. 119–125. In defense of the United Nations, Hamilton
Fish Armstrong wrote "The World Is Round," *Foreign Affairs*
(January 1953), pp. 175–199; and Byron Dexter, "Locarno Again,"
Foreign Affairs (October 1953), pp. 34–47.
6. See K. M. Panikkar, "Regionalism and World Security," in
Panikkar, ed., *Regionalism and Security*, p. 4 and *passim*; K. San-
thanam, "A Regional Authority for South-East Asia," *Regionalism
and Security*, pp. 26–27; P. Talbot, "South and Southeast Asia,"
Regional Arrangements for Security and the United Nations, pp.
126–130; L. A. Mills and associates, *The New World of Southeast
Asia* (1949), pp. 376, 379 ff., 412; and A. Appadorai, "The Bandung
Conference," *India Quarterly* (July-September 1955), pp. 207–235.
7. See Howard, "The Little Entente and the Balkan Entente," in
Robert J. Kerner, ed., *Czechoslovakia* (1949), pp. 368–386; Paul

Seabury, "The League of Arab States: Debacle of a Regional Arrangement," *International Organization* (November 1949), pp. 633–642; M. Khadduri, "Regional and Collective Defense Arrangements in the Middle East," *Regional Arrangements for Security and the United Nations*, pp. 100–117; Charles Malik, "The Near East Between East and West," in R. N. Frye, ed., *The Near East and the Great Powers* (1951); Halford L. Hoskins, *The Middle East: Problem Area in World Politics* (1954); and Dankwart A. Rustow, "Defense of the Near East," *Foreign Affairs* (January 1956), pp. 271–286.

8. Cf. V. Reisky-Dubnic, "The Idea of a Central and Eastern European Regional Federation," *Regional Arrangements for Security and the United Nations*, pp. 133 ff.; Hugh Seton-Watson, *Eastern Europe Between the Wars 1918–1941* (1945), pp. 35 ff.; Khadduri, "The Scheme of Fertile Crescent Unity: A Study in Inter-Arab Relations," in Frye, pp. 168, 173; A. E. Ebban, "The Future of Arab-Jewish Relations," *Commentary* (September 1948), p. 206; and Don Peretz, "Development of the Jordan Valley Waters," *Middle East Journal* (Autumn 1955), pp. 397–412.

9. The following synthesis is based on Carr, *Conditions of Peace*, esp. pp. 7–8, 51–52, 56–58, 67–69; Carr, *The Twenty Years' Crisis*, pp. 228–231; Lippmann, *U.S. War Aims*, pp. 80–85; Cobban, *National Self-Determination*, esp. pp. xi, 167 f., 171–172, 178; Fox, *The Super-Powers*, pp. 95–96; and F. L. Schuman, "Regionalism and Spheres of Influence," in Morgenthau, *Peace, Security and the United Nations*, p. 105.

10. Cf. Lippmann, *U.S. War Aims*, pp. 187, 193, 194, and *U.S. Foreign Policy: Shield of the Republic*, pp. 7, 9, 71 ff., 149.

11. Cf. Wolfers, "The Small Powers and the Enforcement of Peace," pp. 12 ff.; Lippmann, *U.S. Foreign Policy*, p. 73; and Fox, pp. 153–154.

12. See Schuman, p. 90, for the quoted phrase; Carr, *Nationalism and After*, pp. 54–57, 61–67, for a guarded return to general organization; and Cobban, pp. 163–165, for deliberate attempt to combine the regional pattern with global organization.

13. Cf. especially *The British Empire*, A Report on its Structure and Problems by a Study Group of Members of the Royal Institute of International Affairs (1937); Ernest Barker, *The Ideas and Ideals of the British Empire* (2nd ed., 1951); Dexter Perkins, *The Evolution of American Foreign Policy* (1948), pp. 58 ff., 117 ff., and *Hands Off: A History of the Monroe Doctrine* (1946); Duggan, *The Americas: The Search for Hemisphere Security, passim;* and Carter, *The British Commonwealth and International Security*, pp. 94–95 and *passim*.

14. Cf. Spykman, *America's Strategy in World Politics: The United States and the Balance of Power* (1942), pp. 62 ff.

15. Cf. Frank Tannenbaum, "An American Commonwealth of Nations," *Foreign Affairs* (July 1944), p. 581; W. K. Hancock, *Survey of British Commonwealth Affairs* (1937), Vol. I, pp. 67–68, 276 ff.; and Eric A. Walker, *The British Empire* (1947), p. 192 and *passim*.

16. Cf. Carter, p. 314 and *passim*, and the same author's "The Commonwealth in the United Nations," *International Organization*, (May 1950), pp. 247–260; Lionel Gelber, "The Commonwealth and the United Nations," *Regional Arrangements for Security and the United Nations*, pp. 49–64; and Evatt, "Australia's Approach to Security in the Pacific," in Panikkar, pp. 15, 17.

17. See C. C. Abbott, "Economic Penetration and Power Politics," *Harvard Business Review*, (July 1948), pp. 411 ff.; Seton-Watson, *The East European Revolution* (1951), pp. 254 ff.; Bedrich Bruegel, "Methods of Soviet Domination in Satellite States," *International Affairs* (January 1951), pp. 32–37; Adam B. Ulam, *Titoism and the Cominform* (1952); Dana Adams Schmidt, *The Anatomy of a Satellite* (1952); Crane Brinton, "The Pattern of Aggression," *Virginia Quarterly Review* (Spring 1949), pp. 172–173, and Raymond L. Garthoff, "The Concept of the Balance of Power in Soviet Policy Making," *World Politics* (October 1951), pp. 85–111.

Chapter 6. *The Pattern of Integration*

1. On the "federalizing process," see Friedrich, "Federal Constitutional Theory and Emergent Proposals," in Arthur W. MacMahon, ed., *Federalism: Mature and Emergent* (1955), pp. 514 f. See also Kunz, "Supra-national Organs," *American Journal of International Law* (October 1952), p. 697, and Briggs, "The Proposed European Political Community," *ibid.* (January 1954), pp. 114–115.

2. For the quoted phrases, see Schwarzenberger, *Power Politics* (1951), p. 98, and Friedrich, *Constitutional Government and Democracy* (rev. ed., 1950), p. 19. In addition, cf. Emerson, *State and Sovereignty in Modern Germany* (1928), pp. 259, 262-265; Elliot, *The Pragmatic Revolt in Politics*, pp. 142 ff.; John Dickinson, "A Working Theory of Sovereignty," *Political Science Quarterly* (December 1927), pp. 526 ff.; and Claude, *National Minorities*, pp. 31–32.

3. Cf. Tannenbaum, "The Balance of Power versus the Coördinate State," *Political Science Quarterly* (June 1952), pp. 173–197, and Friedrich, *Foreign Policy in the Making*, pp. 126–127, 133–135, 221.

4. The principal collective-security provisions of the North Atlantic Treaty are in Article 5, the community provisions in the Preamble and Articles 2 and 3. Cf. Appendix I in *Atlantic Alliance: NATO's Role in the Free World*, A Report by a Chatham House Study Group, Royal Institute of International Affairs (1952). See also Fox, "NATO and Coalition Diplomacy," *The Annals of the American Academy of Political and Social Science* (July 1953, "NATO and World Peace," ed. by E. M. Patterson), pp. 114–118; Alfred J. Hotz, "NATO: Myth or Reality," *ibid.*, pp. 126–133; and Dulles, "Policy for Security and Peace," pp. 353 ff.

5. The quoted phrases are from *Atlantic Alliance*, pp. 82, 84, 126–127.

6. See *Atlantic Alliance*, pp. 52–54, 65 (note 2), 121; Dulles, "Policy for Security and Peace," p. 356; and McGeorge Bundy, ed., *The Pattern of Responsibility* (1952), pp. 74–75.

7. Cf. Ambassador Warren Austin's statement in the *North Atlantic Treaty Hearings*, 81st Congress, 1st Session, 1949, pp. 92, 97; Dean Acheson's statement in Bundy, p. 68; and Dulles, "Policy for Security and Peace," p. 363.

8. See *Atlantic Alliance*, pp. 33, 100, and also for the so-called Pearson Report on the Atlantic Community; and Kaufmann, ed., *Military Policy and National Security* (1956).

9. See *Atlantic Alliance*, p. 94, and Elliott, et al., *United States Foreign Policy*, pp. 170–171, for the quoted phrases.

10. The constitutions of the United States, Switzerland, and Australia, for instance, provide for equal representation in the upper chamber irrespective of population. Canada, Germany, and more recently the various European Communities have favored proportionality modified in the direction of equality. Cf. Friedrich, "Federal Constitutional Theory and Emergent Proposals," p. 522.

11. Cf. *The British Empire*, pp. 19 ff. and 202; K. C. Wheare, *Federal Government* (1951), pp. 60–61; and H. L., "The Future of the Central African Federation," *The World Today* (December 1955), pp. 539–548.

12. Cf. Alfred Vagts, "The United States and the Balance of Power," *Journal of Politics* (November 1941), pp. 401–449, and my "The Multiple Equilibrium and the American National Interest in International Organization," *Harvard Studies in International Affairs* (February 1954), pp. 35–50.

13. The quoted phrase is from Guy Mollet, "France and the Defense of Europe," *Foreign Affairs* (April 1954), p. 368. See also M. J. Bonn, *Whither Europe—Union or Partnership?* (1952), and John Goormaghtigh, "European Integration," *International Conciliation* (February 1953), pp. 60–62.

14. Cf. Friedrich, "Federal Constitutional Theory and Emergent Proposals," pp. 528–529; Briggs, p. 121; E. van Raalte, "The Treaty Constituting the European Coal and Steel Community," *International and Comparative Law Quarterly*, Part 1, Vol. I (1952), pp. 73–85; *Etudes sur le fédéralisme*, Mouvement Européen (1952–53), Vol. II, pp. 43–44, 109 ff.; and the texts of the respective treaties.

15. See Kunz, "Treaty Establishing the European Defense Community," *American Journal of International Law* (April 1953), p. 277, for the last-quoted phrase. The text of the Tripartite Declaration made at the signing of the European Defense Treaty is in "Conventions on Relations with the Federal Republic of Germany and a Protocol to the North Atlantic Treaty," United States, 82nd Congress, 2nd Session, *Senate Documents*, Executive Q and R, June 2, 1952, pp. 253–254 (includes the text of the Treaty constituting the Euro-

pean Defense Community). For the text of an agreement between Great Britain and the proposed European Defense Community on British coöperation with the latter see *New York Times*, April 15, 1954, p. 4; and see *New York Times*, April 17, 1954, p. 2, for President Eisenhower's message pledging maintenance of American troops in Europe, consultation and integration within and between NATO and EDC, and the indefinite duration of NATO.

16. Cf. Goormaghtigh, "European Coal and Steel Community," *International Conciliation* (May 1955), pp. 343–408. The Swiss example is based on Rappard, *Collective Security in Swiss Experience 1291–1948* (1948), pp. 77–78, 143–150.

17. Eduard Beneš, "The Organization of Postwar Europe," *Foreign Affairs* (January 1942), p. 227.

18. Cf. Article 5(b) of the Trusteeship Agreement for the Territory of Tanganyika as Approved by the General Assembly on December 13, 1946, *U.N. Doc. T/Agreement/2*, June 9, 1947, reprinted in Goodrich and Hambro, *Charter of the United Nations*, pp. 635–640. For discussion of the matter see Goodrich and Hambro, p. 425.

19. Cf. the Memorandum of the Secretary General maintaining that "the Security Council is not restricted to the specific powers set forth in Chapters VI, VII, VIII, and XII of the Charter of the United Nations." The Security Council upheld this interpretation by a vote of 10 to 0. *U.N. Doc. S/P.V./91*, quoted in Kunz, "The Free Territory of Trieste," *Western Political Quarterly* (June 1948), p. 102. See also "Reparation for Injuries Suffered in the Service of the United Nations," I.C.J. Reports, 1949, Advisory Opinion, April 11, 1949, *American Journal of International Law* (July 1949), pp. 593, 595, for the quotations.

20. See Smuts, *The League of Nations*, pp. 25–26, and *passim*.

Conclusion: *And Back to the Balance of Power — With a Difference*

1. This idea is effectively worked out and illustrated by Haas, "Regionalism, Functionalism, and Universal Organization," *World Politics* (January 1956), pp. 238–263. I would question only the author's conclusion that changes in international relations will invalidate the concept of balancing. More likely, they will only change the objects and terms of barter, the pattern of balancing and compromise being of the essence of all, and notably parliamentary or quasi-parliamentary, politics.

2. Cf. Howard C. Johnson and Gerhart Niemeyer; "Collective Security: The Validity of an Ideal," *International Organization* (February 1954), p. 35.

3. Cf. Schumpeter, *Business Cycles*, Vol. I, pp. 68 ff., and Stigler, *The Theory of Price*, p. 28. The concept of equilibrium is criticized

by Easton, *The Political System*, pp. 266 ff., and Wright, *The Study of International Relations*, pp. 515 ff.

4. Cf. Richard C. Snyder et al., *Decision-Making as an Approach to the Study of International Politics*, Foreign Policy Analysis Series No. 3, Organizational Behavior Section, Princeton University (June 1954).

INDEX